DECOLONIZING EDUCATION FOR SUSTAINABLE FUTURES

Bristol Studies in Comparative and International Education

Series Editors: **Michael Crossley**, Emeritus Professor of Comparative and International Education, University of Bristol, UK, **Leon Tikly**, UNESCO Chair in Inclusive, Good Quality Education, University of Bristol, UK, **Angeline M. Barrett**, Reader in Education, University of Bristol, UK, and **Julia Paulson**, Reader in Education, Peace and Conflict, University of Bristol, UK

The series critically engages with education and international development from a comparative and interdisciplinary perspective. It emphasizes work that bridges theory, policy and practice, supporting early career researchers and the publication of studies led by researchers in and from the Global South.

Also available

Transitioning Vocational Education and Training in Africa
A Social Skills Ecosystem Perspective
By **VET AFRICA 4.0 COLLECTIVE**

Forthcoming

Education and Development in Central America and the Latin Caribbean
Global Forces and Local Responses
Edited by **D. Brent Edwards Jr.**, **Mauro C. Moschetti**, **Pauline Martin** and **Ricardo Morales-Ulloa**

Assembling Comparison
Understanding Education Policy Through Mobility and Desire
By **Steven Lewis** and **Rebecca Spratt**

Find out more at

bristoluniversitypress.co.uk/
bristol-studies-in-comparative-and-international-education

Forthcoming

Education, Crisis and Resilience
Challenges and Opportunities in Sub-Saharan Africa
Edited by **Mary Mendenhall, Gauthier Marchais, Yusuf Sayed**
and **Neil Boothby**

Higher Education in Small Islands
Challenging the Geographies of Centrality and Remoteness
Edited by **Rosie Alexander** and **Holly Henderson**

Education for Sustainable Development in an Unequal World
Biopolitics, Differentiation and Affirmative Alternatives
By **Beniamin Knutsson, Linus Bylund, Sofie Hellberg** and
Jonas Lindberg

Education, Conflict, War and Peace
From Pacification to Social Transformation
By **Mario Novelli**

Find out more at
bristoluniversitypress.co.uk/
bristol-studies-in-comparative-and-international-education

Find out more at
bristoluniversitypress.co.uk/
bristol-studies-in-comparative-and-international-education

DECOLONIZING EDUCATION FOR SUSTAINABLE FUTURES

Edited by
Yvette Hutchinson,
Artemio Arturo Cortez Ochoa,
Julia Paulson and Leon Tikly

BRISTOL
UNIVERSITY
PRESS

First published in Great Britain in 2023 by

Bristol University Press
University of Bristol
1–9 Old Park Hill
Bristol
BS2 8BB
UK
t: +44 (0)117 374 6645
e: bup-info@bristol.ac.uk

Details of international sales and distribution partners are available at bristoluniversitypress.co.uk

British Library Cataloguing in Publication Data
A catalogue record for this book is available from the British Library

ISBN 978-1-5292-2608-9 hardcover
ISBN 978-1-5292-2610-2 ePub
ISBN 978-1-5292-2611-9 ePdf

Cover design: Blu Inc
Front cover image: Tapa Cloth: Papua New Guinea
Bristol University Press use environmentally responsible print partners.
Printed and bound in Great Britain by CPI Group (UK) Ltd, Croydon, CR0 4YY

FSC
www.fsc.org
MIX
Paper | Supporting
responsible forestry
FSC® C013604

Contents

Series Editor Preface

The *Bristol Studies in Comparative and International Education* series and the Centre for Comparative and International Research in Education (CIRE) are pleased to have been involved in the initiation and development of this challenging, co-edited volume from the outset. Initial discussions began when ways of linking CIRE's long-time engagement with diverse 'ways of knowing', context-sensitive research and post-colonial theorizing, to UNESCO's 'Futures of Education' initiative, were first explored. This inspired a three-part seminar series on the theme of 'decolonizing education for sustainable futures' (Cortez Ochoa et al, 2021) a subsequent widening of the debate, the engagement of new writers, and planning for the present book. This was a creative and dialogic process in its own right, and one that, as readers will see, generated contributions from researchers, advocates, policy makers, agency personnel, activists and practitioners. This is, therefore, a cross-cutting volume that bridges the worlds of theory, policy and practice, and one that reflects a diversity of positions while generating a coherent, challenging and inspiring framework for ongoing analysis.

In doing so, the book makes a timely and stimulating multi-disciplinary contribution to contemporary decolonization, sustainability and 'education futures' discourses while, from a Comparative and International Education perspective, recognizing that:

> These are challenging times ... when global socio-political changes and tensions are prioritising the critical interrogation of the intellectual foundations of our field, the nature and rationale for international development, the foregrounding of decolonisation debates, and the implications of climate change and environmental uncertainty for more equitable education futures. (Crossley, 2021)

Here then, is a book that extends critical scholarship to multiple audiences, disrupting many epistemological and methodological assumptions, opening up debate across constituencies, focusing upon the global challenges of our times and seeking to engage with theorists and stakeholders – at all levels – involved in the formulation, implementation and critique of emergent international agendas.

The chapters that follow elaborate upon these and other related themes in ways that all involved hope will contribute to ongoing debate and to the advancement of both theoretical thinking and transformative educational policies and practices.

In many ways, this captures much of the rationale for the *Bristol Studies in Comparative and International Education* series as a whole, making this an ideal and 'positional' foundation volume for our relaunch with Bristol University Press.

Michael Crossley
Emeritus Professor of Comparative and International Education
University of Bristol

References

Cortez Ochoa, A.A., Tikly, L., Hutchinson, Y. et al (2021) Synthesis report on the Decolonising Education for Sustainable Futures (UNESCO Chair seminar series), Bristol Conversations in Education and UNESCO Chair Seminar Series, University of Bristol, DOI: https://doi.org/10.5281/zen odo.50124.

Crossley, M. (2021) Epistemological and methodological issues and frameworks in comparative and international research in education, *New Era in Education, The Journal of the World Education Fellowship*, 102(1): 5–16.

List of Figures and Table

Figures

Table

List of Abbreviations

ARSG	Anti-Racism Steering Group
BAME	Black, asian or minority ethnic
BILT	Bristol Institute for Learning and Teaching
BME	Black or minority ethnic
BRICS	Brazil, Russia, India, China, and South Africa
CHIRAPAQ	Centre for Indigenous Cultures of Peru
CIRE	Centre for Comparative and International Research in Education
CO_2	Carbon dioxide
CPD	Continuous professional development
CPFP	Critical pedagogy and feminist praxis
DBEIS	Department for Business, Energy and Industrial Society
DCG	Decolonizing the Curriculum Group
DfE	Department for Education
EdJAM	Education, Justice and Memory network
EFA	Education for All
ESD	Education for sustainable development
FFF	Fridays for Future
GCSE	Graduate Certificate of Secondary Education
GDP	Gross domestic product
GTDF	Gesturing Towards Decolonial Futures
ICFE	International Commission on the Futures of Education
IKS	Indigenous Knowledge Systems
INGOs	International non-governmental organizations
IPCC	Intergovernmental Panel on Climate Change
MAPA	Most Affected Peoples and Areas
MBA	Masters of Business Administration
NEU	National Education Union
NGOs	Non-governmental organizations
OECD	Organisation for Economic Co-operation and Development
OHCHR	The United Nations Office of the High Commissioner for Human Rights
PhD	Philosophy Doctorate

SARCHI	South African Research Chairs Initiative
SDGs	Sustainable development goals
SS4C	School Strikes for Climate
UKRI	UK Research and Innovation
UN	United Nations
UNDP	United Nations Development Programme
UNESCO	United Nations Educational, Scientific and Cultural Organization
UNICEF	United Nations Children's Fund
WCED	World Commission on Environment and Development
WEF	World Economic Forum

Notes on Contributors

Alvin Birdi is Associate Pro Vice Chancellor (Education Innovation and Enhancement) and Professor of Economics Education at the University of Bristol, UK. Alvin has been Director of the Economics Network since July 2012. As part of this role, he is also a member of the Economics Network management board and CHUDE (the Conference of Heads of University Departments of Economics). Alvin sits on the Council of the Scottish Economic Society and chairs the Education Committee of the European Economic Association. He is a member of the editorial board of the *International Review of Economics Education.*

Common Worlds Research Collective, commonworlds.net, is an interdisciplinary network of researchers concerned with our relations with the more-than-human world. On behalf of the Collective, this discussion of the future of education has been confabulated by: Affrica Taylor, University of Canberra, Australia; Iveta Silova, Arizona State University, USA; Veronica Pacini-Ketchabaw, Western University, Canada; and Mindy Blaise, Edith Cowan University, Australia.

Artemio Arturo Cortez Ochoa is Lecturer in Education and Pathway Lead of the MSc in Educational Leadership and Policy at the School of Education, University of Bristol, UK. He was a Research Associate at the REAL Centre, University of Cambridge, UK, in the Leaders in Teaching initiative – Rwanda. His research interests include quality education, teacher evaluation systems and continuous professional development in low- and middle-income contexts. His most recent publication on school principals' evaluation is part of the *International Encyclopedia of Education* (4th edn).

Terra Glowach is Senior Lecturer in ITE at the Department of Education, University of the West of England (UWE, Bristol), UK. She has several years of engagement in research and educational practice in Canada, Japan, Ethiopia, India and the UK. Her work with teachers, practitioners and academics via the Bristol Decolonising Network has ignited an interest in curriculum development, pedagogy and education, focusing on decolonial possibilities for change. Her publications include experiences from teacher-led initiatives and professional learning networks in England.

Tanisha Hicks-Beresford is Lead Teacher of Citizenship at Bristol Cathedral Choir secondary school. She is part of a larger teacher-led movement working on making education and schools more inclusive as learning spaces. She is interested in the decolonization of the curriculum, particularly in ways of people's representation and history, and how to share 'black joy/strength'. In her role as a practitioner, she has been critical of and has acted upon racist ideologies as they present in and through the school curriculum. She was a guest speaker at 'Decolonising the Curriculum in Bristol: across the subjects, from school to university'.

Yvette Hutchinson is Senior Consultant at the British Council. Based in the Schools team, she is responsible for Quality Assurance and Teacher Training. She leads on the research portfolio and organizes policy dialogues with education ministries, policy makers and senior leaders. Yvette is a panel member for the Economic and Social Research Council and Chair of UKFIET, the education and development forum.

Rafael Mitchell is Lecturer in Education at the School of Education, University of Bristol, UK. He is Co-Director of the Centre for Comparative and International Research in Education (CIRE) and a co-founder of the African Education Research Database. His research addresses schooling and school improvement, leadership and pedagogies for inclusive education in Africa. His work responds to inequalities in knowledge production in education, focusing on global policy instruments, African research and partnerships. He is Co-Investigator in the Transforming Education for Sustainable Futures (TESF) project. He has published widely in his field and undertaken commissioned research and consultancies for international organizations, including UNESCO, IIEP-UNESCO, FAWE and others.

Kevin Myers is Professor in History and Education and Director of Education, School of Education at the University of Birmingham, UK. He works on the history and sociology of education and has published extensively in social history, memory, multicultural education and race. He is a member of the editorial boards for the journals *Education Review, History of Education* and *Paedagogica Historica: International Journal for History of Education.*

David Nally is Associate Professor in Human Geography and Fellow of Jesus College, University of Cambridge, UK. He is a human geographer and a convening member of the department's Vital Geographies Research

Group. His interests include the events, ideas, material processes and everyday practices that shape the world. His publications address topics such as famines, colonial rule, food regimes and American philanthropy, but a defining theme is the expression of power in the social landscape. His titles include *Human Encumbrances*, published with the University of Notre Dame Press, and *Key Concepts in Historical Geography* (Sage Publications, 2014).

Catherine A. Odora Hoppers is Professor of Education (Gulu University, Uganda), Professor Extraordinarius at the University of South Africa, and Founder and Director of the Global Institute of Applied Governance in Science and Innovation. She is a scholar and policy specialist on international development, education, North–South questions, disarmament, peace, and human security. She is a UNESCO expert in basic education, lifelong learning, information systems and science and society. She has published research about Indigenous knowledge, knowledge systems, epistemological justice, and decolonization of education.

Julia Paulson is Professor in Education, Peace and Conflict at the University of Bristol, UK, where she is also Co-Director of the Centre for Comparative and International Research in Education. With colleagues in Cambodia, Colombia, Pakistan, Uganda and the UK, Julia leads the Education, Justice and Memory network (EdJAM), which is a £2million project exploring creative approaches to teaching and learning about violence and injustice in order to build hopeful, just and reparative futures.

Esther Priyadharshini is Associate Professor at the School of Education and Lifelong Learning, University of East Anglia, UK. She is the Co-Director for Research in the school and co-leader of the Cultural Studies in Education research group. Her research is focused on educational futures, youth/childhood, schooling and gender. Her work is located in the intersection of futures studies, youth studies and education. She is interested in how education can be reframed to better respond to the challenges of the Anthropocene and support young people in the making of more desirable futures.

Pedro Ramos-Pinto is Associate Professor in International Economic History and Fellow of Trinity Hall, University of Cambridge, UK. He is interested in understanding how contemporary inequalities are shaped by the past, bringing a more long-term view to explain how and why societies distribute resources, opportunities and capabilities. He directs a research network on the topic of *Inequality and History*. His publications include titles such as *Lisbon Rising: Urban Social Movements in the Portuguese Revolution,*

1974–1975 (Manchester University Press, 2013) and several peer-reviewed journal articles and book chapters on his areas of expertise.

Tarcila Rivera Zea is Founder and President of CHIRAPAQ, Centre for Indigenous Cultures of Peru, which promotes the assertion of cultural identity and capacity-building for Indigenous women and youth as leaders. She has received awards from UNICEF, Ford Foundation, Sacred Fire Foundation, and Peru's Ministry of Culture for her remarkable career and valued contributions to promoting and advocating Indigenous cultures and rights. She was a member of the Global Advisory Committee of the Civil Society of UN Women and an expert member of the UN Permanent Forum on Indigenous Issues (2017–2019).

Tania Saeed is Associate Professor of Sociology at the Lahore University of Management Sciences (LUMS), Pakistan. Her research focuses on Comparative and International Education, exploring questions around education and securitization, citizenship and social justice. She is the author of *Islamophobia and Securitization: Religion, Ethnicity and the Female Voice* (Palgrave Macmillan, 2016) and the co-author of *Youth and the National Narrative: Education, Terrorism and the Security State in Pakistan* (Bloomsbury, 2020). Her current research explores ideologies of exclusion within educational institutions, focusing on school curricula, textbooks and pedagogy in government, low-fee private and refugee schools in Pakistan.

Robin Shields is Professor of Education at the School of Education, University of Bristol, UK. Robin's research focuses on the globalization of education. He is particularly interested in applying new forms of quantitative data collection and analysis (such as social media datasets, social network analysis) to study global trends and processes in education. He publishes research across several substantive areas related to globalization and education, including higher education internationalization, climate change and higher education, international aid to education, technology and education, and education in conflict-affected contexts. He is co-editor of the *Comparative Education Review* and has served on the Executive Committee of the British Association for International and Comparative Education (BAICE).

Ben Spence is the School Principal of May Park Primary School in Bristol, UK. She has actively participated in various initiatives, such as the Black teachers' networks and One Bristol Curriculum. She is interested in examining primary and secondary curricula to address racism in educational settings and initiate conversations on the decolonization of the curriculum. Her view on decolonial efforts is one of plurality, where staff, parents, students and the broader community can be heard. She was a guest speaker at Bristol Conversations in Education Seminar Series on Decolonising Education for Sustainable Futures.

Arathi Sriprakash is Professor of Education at the School of Education, University of Bristol, UK. She is a sociologist of education whose work focuses on the racial politics of knowledge, particularly in the field of education and international development. She is interested in examining the politics of education reform in the Indian and Australian contexts and the global governance of childhood and the family. She is particularly interested in examining the active erasures of racism and coloniality in the field of education. She is co-author of *Learning Whiteness: Education and the Settler Colonial State* (Pluto Press, 2022) and several peer-reviewed journal articles and book chapters.

Leon Tikly is UNESCO Chair on Inclusive and Quality Education for All at the University of Bristol, UK. He currently directs the Transforming Education for Sustainable Futures (TESF) Network Plus, which includes partners in India, Rwanda, Somalia and South Africa. The aim of TESF is to better understand how education can contribute to sustainable livelihoods, communities and positive climate action. Leon is also actively involved in efforts to decolonize the curriculum at the University of Bristol.

Acknowledgements

We are grateful to the many colleagues and institutions who have accompanied us throughout the reflective and intellectually stimulating journey that we titled *Decolonizing Education for Sustainable Futures*. This edited volume originates from an online 'Bristol Conversations in Education' seminar series supported by UNESCO and the School of Education at the University of Bristol. We are grateful to colleagues, including Keith Holmes, Noah Sobe, Arathi Sriprakash and Michael Crossley, for their contributions to the series organization. The series would not have been possible without the hard work of Christine Smith, Caroline Bardrick, Carolina Valladares, Kerry Parson, Silvia Espinal, Rosemary Luz and Teresa López González. Thanks to Keston Perry for his inspiring and thought-provoking contribution to the seminar series.

We are indebted to the Bristol communities that grapple with issues of decolonization and sustainability day in and day out and who have provided insight into the implications of this book for practice and reparative possibilities. We particularly thank Lawrence Hoo, Chaz Golding, Prince Taylor and the CARGO Movement; the growing number of teachers and school leaders embracing these topics in their classrooms; and students, including the children from May Park Primary School whose experiences are shared within the book, and the many students in the School of Education at the University of Bristol who have inspired and challenged this work. To all of you, our sincerest gratitude.

We want to thank those who provided constructive feedback to improve the volume, including Keri Facer, Tamara Walker, Stephanie McNulty and Kate Moles. We are grateful to colleagues at the British Council, attendees of a panel at the Comparative and International Education Society 2021 conference, where we presented early work on the book, and reviewers of the book for their constructive feedback. It has been a pleasure to work with colleagues from Bristol University Press: thanks, especially to Philippa Grand, Stephen Wenham and Zoe Forbes.

Finally, thank you to all the contributors to this book for their excellent chapters and for making the process of putting the book together so enjoyable.

Introduction

Yvette Hutchinson, Artemio Arturo Cortez Ochoa,
Julia Paulson and Leon Tikly

I play son huasteco, *a Mexican folkloric music genre interpreted with adapted guitars and violins. Some characteristics of this music style include intricate melodic arrangements and singers' high-pitch falsetto voices. In order to achieve such a high voice, it is common among son* huasteco *musicians to tune the instruments about a semitone below the most standard 440-ish frequency.*

I was tuning my violin as we were putting the chapters of this book together and was reflecting on the two exercises. The problem is that available strings (nylon and metallic) in the region where this music is played are now typically made for European violins and guitars. Using these strings, it is unlikely that the sound huasteco *musicians produce will ever achieve the brilliance and potential for which the strings they use were made. Nor are strings that* huasteco *musicians use the ones best suited for the brilliance and potential of* huasteco *music.*

Several reflections can be drawn from this situation; the most evident is why aren't strings made for folkloric musicians, such as those from the huasteco *community? What impact will that have in the long-term on the* huasteco *sound? Is there a danger that son* huasteco *diminishes as the easily available strings redefine the traditional sound? Have other* son huasteco *musicians noticed that they play with strings not made for their instruments and requirements?*

Reflections on *son hausteco,* Artemio Arturo Cortez Ochoa

Why a book on decolonizing education for sustainable futures?

These reflections, from Artemio Arturo Cortez Ochoa, *son huasteco* violinist and one of the editors of this book, connect to many of the themes explored in these pages. They serve to illustrate, for example, some of the complexities in ensuring sustainable futures, in this case the sustainability of a form of cultural expression and the histories and ways of life it embodies. They also illustrate the nature of what Maldonado-Torres (2007), Ndlovu-Gatsheni (2013; 2015) and many contributors to this book describe as 'coloniality', the enduring presences of colonial extraction and oppression in the post-colonial present. Cortez Ochoa's reflections capture themes that are explored throughout this book: the predominance of Western approaches, including in ways that we may not be immediately aware of (the strings on a *huasteco* violin, the 'standard' 440 frequency), alternatives to these approaches, and the potential for new strings, a plurality of pitches, and the reparative educational processes that might make these possible.

The need to envision and realize more sustainable futures for people and the planet has become increasingly urgent in recent years, as evidenced by the limited progress the world has made in achieving the 17 sustainable development goals (SDGs) adopted by United Nations member states in 2015 and which are intended as an holistic framework for realizing sustainable futures by 2030 (UN, 2015). While limited progress has been made in some of the SDGs, including absolute poverty reduction, maternal and child health, access to electricity, and gender equality, these gains are not enough to achieve the goals by 2030. A recent report indicates that progress has either stalled or even reversed in other vital areas, including reducing inequality, lowering carbon emissions, and tackling hunger (UN, 2015). The Covid-19 pandemic has further set back efforts to achieve the goals. The quest for more sustainable futures is given impetus by the increasing threat posed by climate change. As the Intergovernmental Panel on Climate Change (IPCC, 2022) has persuasively argued, unless more drastic action is taken to reduce greenhouse gases in the atmosphere, it is now increasingly unlikely that we will remain below the 1.5-degree (C) increase in global temperatures from pre-industrial levels, with potentially devastating implications for human beings and for the biosphere. As Robin Shields notes in his contribution to this volume, we are in the midst of a climate emergency.

Education is often deeply implicated in debates about sustainable futures. The idea of sustainable futures lies at the heart of UNESCO's Futures of Education initiative. The initiative aims to reimagine how knowledge and learning can shape the future of humanity and the planet by equipping learners with diverse ways of being and knowing. Providing future generations with a plurality of ways of understanding the natural and social

2

worlds is a crucial starting point for tackling the 'wicked' problems posed by unsustainable development. As Leon Tikly argues in his opening chapter, the problems of unsustainable development are rooted in the unrelenting quest for economic growth, which lies at the heart of Western capitalist models of development and of 'modernity' (what it is to be 'modern') that have predominated since colonial times. The global pursuit of growth through industrialization policies along with patterns of mass consumption, particularly in the global North, have contributed, among other things, to the pollution of land, rivers and seas, deforestation and desertification, damage to ecosystems, biodiversity loss and climate change. The effects of climate change have often been felt most acutely by people of colour living in the global South in the form of flooding, drought and other natural disasters.

Colonialism also often involved the undermining and, in some cases, destruction of Indigenous knowledge systems, values, religions and languages and their replacement with a Western frame of thinking and system of beliefs. Colonial violence sought to destroy Indigenous sovereignty and, in many parts of the world, settler colonialism maintains these systems of violent erasure and refuses to acknowledge sovereignty that has never been ceded (see, for example, Moreton-Robinson, 2015; Coulthard, 2014). It is, important not to homogenize Indigenous thought and to recognize tremendous diversity in Indigenous knowledge systems over time and geographical context. We must also recognize the multiple and ongoing struggles of Indigenous peoples to live (and learn) in Indigenous sovereignty (for example, Bishop, 2020; McCarty and Lee, 2014) and the importance for settlers and other groups to learn to live on stolen lands and in acknowledgement of that sovereignty (for example, Bruyneel, 2021; Carlson-Manathara, 2021; Kwaymullina, 2020). It is also important to recognize the contested and indeed fallible nature of both Western and Indigenous knowledge systems. Nonetheless, as the Common World Collective and Catherine A. Odora Hoppers argue in their respective contributions to this volume, at a general level, and in contrast to Western individualism, Indigenous cultures often encompass more collectivist ways of conceiving the relationships between human beings. Furthermore, and in contrast to the objectivist way of perceiving nature as something outside human existence that can be objectified and exploited, many Indigenous cultures are based on a more holistic view of human beings as integral to the natural world. As these authors go on to argue, these insights, along with the recovery of more harmonious ways of coexisting with nature are hugely relevant in coping with natural disasters linked to climate change and in the quest for more sustainable futures.

As many have argued, education played a crucial role in processes of cultural dispossession under colonialism, processes that Boaventura de Sousa Santos (2017) refers to as *epistemicide*. That is to acknowledge that the spread of Western education under colonialism was intended not only to produce the skills required to service the colonial economy but also to impart the values, dispositions and attitudes required to create politically docile and economically useful colonial subjects. All aspects of colonial education, from its elitist nature to the organization of the school day, the Eurocentric nature of the curriculum, the emphasis on Christianity and on European languages as media of instruction, sought to inculcate Western thinking and values. Today, curricula in many parts of the post-colonial world continue to reflect these Eurocentric roots, often with scant attention paid to local and Indigenous knowledge systems and languages and with limited relevance for local contexts and the day-to-day realities faced by communities. This is made clear in Tarcila Rivera Zea's contribution, which includes reflections on her own experience with formal education as a Quechua Indigenous woman in Peru. Furthermore, during the colonial period, universities were sites for the propagation of scientific racism that legitimized and normalized white supremacy under colonialism. As others have argued, the idea of 'race' and the normalization of racial hierarchies continue to cast a long shadow in Western development discourse (Wilson, 2012; Sriprakash et al, 2019).

As Leon Tikly and Tania Saeed point out in their respective chapters, the Eurocentric nature of curricula has been challenged by anti-colonial activists. Protests, including those led by Black Lives Matter, Rhodes Must Fall, Indigenous and other anti-colonial, anti-racist social movements, have called for education to be decolonized. Rather than offer a single definition, we acknowledge the emergent and context-specific nature of decolonizing as a discourse. That is to say that debates about what decolonizing education means take on different forms and emphases across different historical and geographical settings. Nonetheless, in the context of this book and at a general level, 'decolonization' (both in terms of knowledge production and as pedagogy or curricular practice) is seen as an epistemic intervention linked to wider inequalities and power relationships. Decolonization in education is about more than simply diversification, and it is not supplementary to the existing Eurocentric curriculum (see Ahmed, 2019. Decolonization, instead, asks us to think about the unspoken assumptions that we currently practice with respect to the question of knowledge: What is admitted as 'legitimate knowledge'? Who is given the privilege of 'expertise'? What positions and contexts do we view as being 'objective', 'disinterested' or 'universal'? At its heart, decolonial theory asks us to consider how our extant intellectual practices remain rooted in the coloniality of power (Ndlovu-Gatsheni, 2013) and, more specifically, one particular epistemic project (that derived from the European Enlightenment) among others, and one whose force has been to subjugate, oppress and expropriate large swathes of the world. From there, it asks us to 'decentre' colonial epistemology such that it becomes merely one epistemic tradition among many that we platform in our teaching and learning.

Central to our understanding is the idea that decolonizing education must also be a reparative process, that is, one that acknowledges and seeks reparation in relation to the injustices of the past. It also entails realizing what others have described as a planetary humanism: a view of human nature and social reality that is based on a positive recognition of diverse racial and cultural identities and how these intersect with class and gender-based identities (Gilroy, 2006; Mbembe and Posel, 2005). Such an inclusive vision has often been at the forefront of anti-racist and anti-colonial movements and is reflected in, for example, the speeches of visionary leaders such as Nelson Mandela, Malcolm X, Steve Biko, Angela Davies and Martin Luther King. Keston Perry (2020a; 2020b), who shared his ideas in the seminar series that shaped this book, explicitly connects a reparatory global redistributive justice to sustainable futures with his attention to climate reparations. Here Perry shows how a reparative approach can explicitly connect the two strands of this book – sustainable futures and decolonization – with its orientation towards justice in reckoning with the past and imagining better futures.

In Part III of the book, we develop the argument that repair, reparations and reparative processes are key to connecting the agendas of sustainable futures and decolonization. Many future-making activities, including many focused on sustainability, actively ignore the past or treat it as distant and settled (Bendor et al, 2021). This risks casting current inequalities as future inevitabilities, ignoring or eliding historical processes of violence, dispossession and oppression and their contemporary afterlives and the injustices generated by both (Nordstrom, 2004) and not seeing the resistances, alternatives and contingencies present in the past, as well as here in the present and possible in the future (Tuck and Yang, 2016; Sriprakash et al, 2022).

Recently, the 'boom' and 'buzz' around decolonization has led to critiques about the 'decolonial bandwagon' and the co-optation of decolonization discourse for initiatives that do little to disrupt coloniality and enduring racial hierarchies in education (Moosavi, 2020). Decolonial theory, it is argued, has been co-opted and corrupted, reappropriated in performative ways that are far from transformative and can even reinscribe existing power dynamics (Táíwò, 2022). In many ways, these critiques highlight a version of decolonization that is vulnerable to similar failings as those future-making activities that ignore past and present injustices. An insistence upon repair and reparations, which Part III of the book develops, requires historical engagement and demands action to reckon with, redress the harms of, and prevent recurrence of forms of violence and oppression that have generated deep injustices in the opportunities that groups and individuals have to flourish (Bhambra, 2022). We hope our exploration of 'reparative futures' positions this as one that honours and seeks to build from the longer tradition of liberatory and transformative approaches to decolonization, rather than as one jumping on the bandwagon.

The *Futures of Education* report as a context for the book

As mentioned, a key point of reference for this book is provided by the work of UNESCO's Futures of Education commission, which aims to reimagine how knowledge and learning can shape the future of humanity and the planet by equipping learners with diverse ways of being and knowing.[1] Chaired by Sahle-Work Zewde, President, Federal Democratic Republic of Ethiopia, the commission included leading experts in education from around the globe and used a wide-ranging consultative process spanning two years. Non-governmental organizations (NGOs) and civil society organizations, governmental entities, academic institutions and research organizations, private sector, youth and student organizations and networks, as well as UNESCO national commissions, contributed to the global conversation on the futures of education between 2019 and 2021 through focus group discussions, thematic reports, webinars and other activities. The report that emerged from this process provides an important point of reference for the book. Several of the contributions to this book were originally developed as background papers for the commission and fed into the drafting process for the main report. Many of the papers were also presented as part of an online seminar series convened by the UNESCO Chair on Inclusive and Quality Education for All at the University of Bristol (Cortez Ochoa et al, 2021). The seminar series was held in 2020 during a period where many parts of the world were under Covid-19 lockdown. Three sessions were held, loosely corresponding to the three parts of this book. In total, they were attended by over 800 people from 79 countries whose lively presence and contributions demonstrated the importance of connecting sustainable futures and decolonial agendas. The report from the series (Cortez Ochoa et al, 2021) also fed into the wider consultation process organized by the commission.

In important respects, many of the key themes of UNESCO's report outlined here resonate with ideas expressed in the chapters of this book. In other regards, however, the chapters also challenge and extend some of these key insights. The report makes a compelling case for a new social contract in education 'grounded in human rights and based on principles of non-discrimination, social justice, respect for life, human dignity and cultural diversity. It must encompass an ethic of care, reciprocity, and solidarity. It must strengthen education as a public endeavour and a common good' (ICFE, 2021: 1). The report argues the need for a transformation of education in which pedagogy should be organized around the principles of cooperation, collaboration and solidarity. It also posits that curricula should emphasize ecological, intercultural and interdisciplinary learning that supports students to access and produce knowledge while also developing their capacity to critique and apply it. The report argues that transformation also requires support for teachers' professional agency and ensuring that schools are protective and inclusive spaces. The report celebrates the transformative potential of digital technologies, and these are seen as enhancing rather than replacing the work of teachers. The report also reiterates UNESCO's commitment to the idea of lifelong quality education. An enhanced role for universities and the co-creation of knowledge between universities and the communities they serve are seen as essential for progressing the research and innovation required for sustainable futures. Many of these themes set out in the report are echoed in the chapters of this book.

Importantly for our purposes, the report also emphasizes the need to recognize a plurality of possible educational futures. For the authors of the report, this is linked to the idea of a new social contract that must be based on the inclusion of diverse voices and interests concerning the aims and purposes of education. The report calls for a deepening of democratic representation in the governance of education at the global and national scales to include the voices of those historically marginalized from processes of educational governance. The contributions to this volume seek to add value to the report through foregrounding the agency and voice of young people who are already making the crucial connection between sustainable futures and decolonization, as is clearly demonstrated in Ben Spence's chapter where she shares work produced by pupils at the Bristol primary school that she leads. In this regard, and from the perspective of this book, the UNESCO report's focus on deepening democratic participation while welcome, does not go far enough. Rather, it raises a further series of questions and challenges that we seek to address in this book.

These include questions about the relationship between sustainable futures and the predominance of Western ways of conceiving the future. In this respect, we ask: In what ways are agendas for decolonizing education and sustainable futures connected? What are the tensions? What does decolonizing education for sustainable futures involve? How should it be conceived and enacted? A key feature of our seminar series, and one of the reasons it was so well attended, was its focus not just on theorizing and conceptualizing the connections between decolonialization and sustainable futures, but also its exploration of ongoing practices to connect the two. Attention to how decolonization can be and is being enacted in different settings, from schools to universities to NGOs such as the British Council, helps us to answer this question and to appreciate tensions as well as opportunities, while also raising further questions. In this regard, we ask what the roles and responsibilities are of educational organizations/institutions, individuals and civil society stakeholders in decolonizing education. Finally, as a group of authors, we are committed to the reparative possibilities of education as a starting point for realizing transformative change. In this regard, we ask: What forms of repair and reconstruction are required for sustainable futures of education? What are the possibilities for 'reparative' justice in and through education, given education's enduring complicity with coloniality and environmental injustice?

Aims and structure of the book

The overarching aim of this edited volume is to generate critical discussion concerning the relationship between the role of education in supporting more sustainable futures on the one hand and demands to decolonize education on the other. In doing so, we hope the book and its wider 'handprint' – to quote Robin Shields' afterword – can contribute to ongoing global debates about the futures of education. Therefore, the book is intended for multiple audiences, including policy makers, practitioners, teachers, students and researchers in education, and other constituencies that have an interest in the subject matter, including those working in NGOs and community-based organizations. The specific objectives of the book are threefold. The contributions to the first part of the book seek to deepen understanding of the relationship between the idea of sustainable futures and struggles to decolonize education. In his opening chapter, Leon Tikly sets out some conceptual starting points for considering this relationship. He argues that global discourses around the sustainable development goals (SDGs) involve competing notions of sustainable futures that are offered in response to the organic crisis of contemporary capitalism. He offers a critique of the dominant conception of sustainable futures in global discourses favoured by the World Bank and other global financial institutions and based on the idea of inclusive growth, arguing that, given the history of unsustainable development, the very notion of inclusive growth represents a contradiction in terms. He goes on to other visions of sustainable futures apparent in global discourses, including human–rights–based approaches championed by UNESCO and a range of international NGOs, and approaches inspired by the capability theory of Sen and Nussbaum. While providing useful starting points for considering a normative basis from which more sustainable futures might be conceived, the anthropocentric bias of these perspectives has increasingly been called into question by those working within a more environmentally oriented approach. Against this backdrop, Tikly then outlines how decolonizing narratives provide an essential basis for conceiving sustainable futures through decentering the Eurocentric bias of existing approaches.

The second chapter is authored by the Common Worlds Research Collective, an interdisciplinary network of researchers concerned with our relations with the more-than-human world. Members work across the fields of childhood studies, early childhood education, children's and more-than-human geographies, environmental education, feminist new materialisms, and Indigenous and environmental humanities. The chapter makes a compelling case for education to be reimagined and reconfigured around the future survival of the planet and in the face of the multiple existential threats we have brought upon ourselves. To this end, they authors offer seven visionary declarations of what education could look like in 2050 and beyond. These declarations proceed from three premises. First, human and planetary sustainability is one and the same thing. Second, any attempts to achieve sustainable futures that continue to separate humans from the rest of the world are delusional and futile. And third, education needs to play a pivotal role in radically reconfiguring our place and agency within this interdependent world. This requires a complete paradigm shift: from learning about the world in order to act upon it to learning to become with the world around us. Our future survival, they argue, depends on our capacity to make this shift.

In her contribution to the first part (Chapter 3), leading scholar and activist in the area of sustainable futures, Catherine A. Odora Hoppers turns attention to the epistemic challenges involved in seeking to decolonize sustainable futures. She starts by recognizing that, as a people, we know that no community is complete without the 'other' and that without the otherness of the other, the self is incomplete and even vulnerable. What is true of society is true of knowledge. No knowledge is complete in itself, and, unless we are able to embrace plurality with hospitality, reciprocity and generosity, no 'commons' of knowledge is possible. From this, she argues that we need an 'education' that is enlarged beyond the Western practice of schools and subjects and that is deepened to fill the empty spaces in our inclusive imaginary, which should be occupied with diverse knowledges. These knowledges include traditional knowledge, Indigenous knowledge and civilizational knowledges from all parts of the world. This, in turn, demands a new governance model at the local–global interface focusing on issues of sustainability and fostering an increased consciousness of a human mission in a complex world.

The second part of the book builds on the first by seeking to shed more light on the possibilities and real challenges involved in decolonizing education. Tania Saeed's chapter (4) looks specifically at the role of students whose activism draws on the interrelated injustices facing humanity and the planet. Recognizing the courage of students to take on the 'biggest challenges of the Anthropocene epoch', Saeed identifies these social movements for change as movements for environmental and climate, civic and racial justice. She then suggests possibilities for realizing justice within critical pedagogy and feminist praxis (CPFP); an approach that is intersectional and that generates learning inside and outside the classroom. CPFP offers students access to the curriculum through expanding and crossing intellectual and physical borders, a pedagogy that Saeed argues brings awareness to the student of where power is located and how it is experienced by different groups. Saeed's investigation of student movements to decentre the human in relation to land and to decentre the dominant voices of institutional formation, proposes a future for education that moves beyond disciplinary boundaries and towards civic responsibilities 'within and beyond the nation state'.

In Chapter 5, Yvette Hutchinson, a Senior Consultant at the British Council, looks at the interplay between grassroots activism and corporate policy for decolonization. A cultural relations organization with offices in over 100 countries, the British Council has a long history of working in education. It could be argued that, to some extent, this 'cultural engagement', has been part of the colonial project or, uncritical and left unexamined, the legacy of the UK's colonial past. Exploring the notion of a 'liminal' position for minoritized employees, Hutchinson identifies this liminality as a category that placed those employees on the outside of decision-making for policy and with no clear route to make suggestions for programming to explore issues of race, equality and justice. Through interviews and a review of corporate documents, Hutchinson illustrates how Black and Brown grassroots activists, from this liminal position created a series of decolonization webinars across the global network and were able to realize the 'audacious ask' of including decolonization as part of the corporation's anti-racism strategy.

In the following chapter, Alvin Birdi, Associate Pro Vice Chancellor for Education Innovation and Enhancement at Bristol University, also looks at practical initiatives to decolonize the curriculum within a long-established institution. Birdi asks questions about the ways in which we understand and define decolonization, and offers different interpretations of 'curriculum'. Recognizing the nuanced understanding of these terms, Birdi acknowledges that decolonization initiatives will sit within a domain that is between those different interpretations. Like other authors in this book, Birdi accepts that decolonizing for the future must begin by acknowledging the legacy, impact and ongoing manifestations of an institution's colonial past. Looking at decolonization as it is practised at different levels at Bristol University, Birdi cautions that tweaks to the curriculum and an uncritical application of 'plurality' can be tokenistic gestures that evade the serious and radical business of decolonization. The blend of local practices and institutional leadership, Birdi suggests, is a way forward that must be enhanced by a pedagogy that gives students agency.

Chapter 7 opens by reflecting on the National Curriculum for schools in England. Outlining the strictures of the curriculum and current political climate, Rafael Mitchell argues that it is through teacher agency and intentional acts that are counter to the prevailing and dominant views that decolonization can take place. Mitchell introduces the work of two Bristol-based secondary teachers, Terra Glowach and Tanisha Hicks-Beresford, who use a CPD (continuous professional development) event to share their decolonial practice. Both teachers look critically at the curriculum; Glowach from the perspective of the learner who benefits from community engagement, and Hicks-Beresford posits a heuristic method for teacher self-reflection that practically applies high expectations, equity and diversity. Mitchell concludes that the teachers illustrate in one case the use of agency to open up spaces for decolonizing initiatives and, in the other, to deploy Givens' (2021) 'fugitive pedagogy' to covertly begin change as an individual within a school setting.

In the last chapter in this part, Ben Spence, Principal of May Park Primary School in Bristol introduces the work of her pupils on decolonization and justice. Responding to the poem 'If', by the Bristol-based poet and activist Lawrence Hoo, the pupils write about their learning expectations. They recognize equity and ecology as inseparable elements of the curriculum; they write candidly about their need for schooling that helps them to realize the sustainable futures they deserve. Ben Spence curates their work and reflects on the initiative to think about decolonizing the curriculum for the primary sector. She concludes that decolonial practice must be embedded in the curriculum and commit to equity that lasts beyond the initial galvanizing fervour of social justice movements.

Finally, the third part of the book deals with the potential for education to become a site for processes of reparation of past injustices, which must take place as a condition for achieving sustainable futures. Chapter 9 opens this argument powerfully by reprinting, in English and Spanish, the contribution that Quechua women's rights activist Tarcila Rivera Zea made to the seminar series from which this volume grew. Rivera Zea's contribution began with a Quechua greeting and then proceeded in Spanish. The English translation included here is the work of Mirna Carolina Valladares Celis and Artemio Arturo Cortez Ochoa, with thanks to Silvia Espinal Meza. Rivera Zea explains the historical and ongoing exclusion and dehumanization of Indigenous peoples, including via education and as knowledge producers, reflecting on her personal experiences of discrimination within education. She then shares how she joined other Quechua women to found the Indigenous rights organization CHIRAPAQ (Centre for Indigenous Cultures of Peru), whose work began with 'looking inwards' in order to heal and recover the dignity that so many institutions had tried to deny. Rivera Zea argues that from this 'looking towards ourselves' came a series of educational proposals for reparation and sustainable peace, grounded in recognizing the dignity of each human and their contributions, conducting dialogue respectfully across differences, democratizing opportunities and repairing relations with nature. Education, argues Rivera Zea, 'must be dignifying and strengthen our souls, emotions and visions to coexist with mother nature.'

Subsequent chapters expand upon the demand for repair, defining the idea of 'reparative futures' and offering various proposals for or examples of practice that might contribute towards them. They highlight the openness, complexity and creativity involved in building reparative futures and the demands for action towards justice that accompany the concept. As Arathi Sriprakash, David Nally, Kevin Myers and Pedro Ramos-Pinto argue in Chapter 10, many efforts towards sustainable futures, like much work in education and international development, proceeds without attention to past injustices, their afterlives in the present or their prospects for enduring into the future. The chapter focuses on histories of racial and colonial domination and develop the concept of 'reparative futures' as an invitation for future-making activities that challenge rather than reproduce these systems and their unjust material, epistemic and affective impacts of people's lives. Sriprakash and colleagues explore the idea of 'historical thinking' in education as a means by which such reparative futures might be built, proposing processes of dialogue and exchange that start from an explicitly anti-racist position of fundamental human equality. Rich in theorizing the case for reparative futures and in illuminating its possible constructions via historical thinking and dialogic pedagogy in education, the chapter provides the argument and core concepts upon which subsequent chapters build, namely that acknowledging and repairing past injustices is a necessary prerequisite to both decolonizing and sustainable future building and as such is a demand and an obligation that can put these two areas of practice and theory-building together.

In Chapter 11, Esther Priyadharshini explores the reparative possibilities opened by decolonizing the ways in which academic knowledge is produced and reproduced through citation practices. Outlining the colonial and patriarchal undertones of dominant practices that reproduce knowledge hierarchies and exclude or silence scholarship along gendered, raced and geographic lines, Priyadharshini explores alternative models of citation. The practices that Priyadharshini identifies are reparative in that they support epistemic justice and in that they open possibilities for engaging with and acknowledging other forms of knowledge, including the more than human – an acknowledgement that is necessary for responding to the Anthropocene and imagining sustainable futures. Priyadharshini's chapter is rich with examples of citation that, as she demonstrates, are rooted in care and offer possibilities for more respectful and dialogic acknowledgement of those we learn with and from. These reparative citational practices can enable knowledge sharing in more creative and accessible ways, but they also ask bigger questions about indebtedness, sustainability, and justice in knowledge generation.

Chapter 12 explores the idea of reparative pedagogies. Other chapters have established the need for reparation in education, including in material, epistemic and symbolic forms. Pedagogy – teaching and learning relationships and practices – is a daily way in which reparative approaches in education can be enacted (or denied). Julia Paulson, draws on examples primarily from the work of the Education, Justice and Memory network (EdJAM), to describe features of reparative pedagogies, outlining that they are dignifying, truth-telling, multiple, enable responsibility and are creative. Paulson shows that reparative pedagogies are often interventions in education spaces and systems that are still steeped in unjust relationships and ways of narrating the past or that often take place outside classrooms and formal schooling, seeing these spaces as 'beyond repair'. The idea of reparative pedagogies, therefore, is connected to and a way of enacting 'reparative futures' – necessarily open and interconnected but requiring the redress of past and present injustices that can be imagined both within and beyond the current configurations of schooling.

The book closes with Robin Shields' costing of the journey of the book. Taking up the invitations of praxis and accountability developed across the book, the afterword seeks to identity how the book might contribute towards sustainability, but how its own creation could be unsustainable. Shields explores the methodological possibilities for calculating the carbon footprint involved in producing this book – describing the ways in which we have worked virtually and physically and the emissions generated as a result. The afterword highlights the complexities in arriving at or offsetting the footprint of a book project, including exploration of some of the exclusionary assumptions that underpin this accounting process. It argues that footprint calculations should be in dialogue with 'handprints' – the ways in which activities – in this case bringing together this book – might prevent future harms and have positive sustainability outcomes. This handprint is equally difficult to calculate and dependent on the future actions not just of the authors but of the readers. Shields argues that a significant handprint is the best way to repair the ecological costs of the journey and we hope that this book may contribute towards ensuring commitments to decolonization and repair as teachers, students, policy makers, leaders, civil society organizations and others take forward the responsibility of building sustainable futures.

A note on authorship

Given the focus of the current book on decolonizing sustainable futures, and in light of some of the recent criticisms about decolonization, it is important to be reflexive and transparent about the authorship of the current book. The chapters bring together a range of voices, including learners, teachers, Indigenous activists, educational researchers, policy makers and practitioners working in a range of NGOs and community-based settings. In this respect, authorship reflects, at least to some extent, the wider consultation process undertaken by UNESCO for the Futures of Education initiative. Although we are a diverse group of authors, our book coheres around a common understanding of the tremendous potential of education to contribute towards sustainable futures based on principles of epistemic, social and environmental justice but also the realization that, if it is to do so, then education itself needs to be fundamentally transformed. Nonetheless, there are also absences and omissions both of possible perspectives, geographic locations, sites of practice and identity groups. In this regard, we hope the book is an opening; contributing to further discussion and exploration of the ideas it hopes to connect.

The editorial team is comprised of: a Senior Consultant at the British Council, Yvette Hutchinson; a Lecturer in Education, Leadership and Policy at the University of Bristol, Artemio Cortez; a Professor in Education, Peace and Conflict at the University of Bristol, Julia Paulson; and an UNESCO Chair on Inclusive and Quality Education for All at the University of Bristol, Leon Tikly. As editors, we represent diverse backgrounds. Three of the team are from racialized minority backgrounds and two are women. Nonetheless, we are all based in the United Kingdom, working at elite institutions whose own histories are implicated with the expansion of the British Empire and benefiting from its accumulation of wealth. The University of Bristol, despite its efforts to decolonize, which Alvin Birdi explores in his contribution, still displays its logo consisting of the crests of prominent university benefactors who profited directly or indirectly from the transatlantic slave trade.

When we shared plans for the book at the Comparative and International Education Society (CIES) conference in 2022, attendees asked about the composition and location of our editorial team. This is a valid question and one we have reflected on, first, as we convened the lockdown seminar series and then as we moved forward with this book. We have consciously focused on Bristol within the book, exploring ongoing initiatives and praxis of decolonization in the city that made global headlines in 2020 when the statue of Edward Colston (who made his fortune through trade in enslaved people and whose crest is one that appears in the university's logo) was toppled during Black Lives Matter protests. It has been important for us to put our city (for Leon, Julia and Artemio) into global conversation, particularly because of what we and other educators can learn from the decolonial and sustainable future making, activism and education that is being theorized and developed elsewhere. We have tried to see our roles as convenors and facilitators of dialogue, discussion and debate; hoping, first with the seminar series and now with this book, to connect and amplify experiences and colleagues whose work here in the city and internationally we are honoured to be in contact with and learn from. We have had to question our own privilege and positioning of knowledge in this project. The degree to which we have been able to manage this task and engage with our commitments to decolonization in ways that avoid tokenism, appropriation and the diminishment of the challenges at hand will be for readers to judge.

Note

[1] Since its founding 75 years ago, UNESCO has commissioned several global reports to rethink the role of education at key moments of societal transformation. These began with the Faure Commission's 1972 report 'Learning to Be: The World of Education Today and Tomorrow', and continued with the Delors commission's report in 1996, 'Learning: The Treasure Within'.

References

Bendor, R., Eriksson, E. and Pargman, D. (2021) Looking backward to the future: On past-facing approaches to futuring, *Futures,* 125(102666).

Bhambra, G.K. (2022) For a reparatory social science, *Global Social Challenges Journal,* 1(1): 8–20.

Bishop, M. (2020) Indigenous education sovereignty: Another way of 'doing' education, *Critical Studies in Education,* 63(1): 131–146.

Bruyneel, K. (2021) *Settler Memory: The Disavowal of Indigeneity and the Politics of Race in the United States,* Chapel Hill: University of North Carolina Press.

Carlson-Manathara, E. with Rowe, G. (2021) *Living in Indigenous Sovereignty,* Halifax: Fernwood Publishing.

Cortez Ochoa, A.A., Tikly, L., Hutchinson, Y. et al (2021) Synthesis report on the Decolonising Education for Sustainable Futures (UNESCO Chair seminar series), Bristol Conversations in Education and UNESCO Chair Seminar Series, University of Bristol, DOI: https://doi.org/10.5281/zen odo.50124.

Coulthard, G.S. (2014) *Red Skin, White Masks: Rejecting the Colonial Politics of Recognition,* Minneapolis: University of Minnesota Press.

Gilroy, P. (2006) A new cosmopolitanism, *Interventions: International Journal of Postcolonial Studies,* 7(3): 287–292.

Givens, J.R. (2021) *Fugitive Pedagogy,* Harvard University Press.

ICFE (2021) *Reimagining our Futures Together: A New Social Contract for Education,* Paris: UNESCO.

IPCC (2022) *Climate Change 2022: Impacts, Adaptation and Vulnerability.* IPCC. Climate Change 2022: Impacts, Adaptation and Vulnerability | Climate Change 2022: Impacts, Adaptation and Vulnerability (ipcc.ch).

Kwaymullina, A. (2020) *Living on Stolen Land,* Broome: Magabala Books.

Maldonado-Torres, N. (2007) On coloniality of being: Contributions to the development of a concept, *Cultural Studies,* 21(2): 240–270.

Mbembe, A. and Posel, D. (2005) A critical humanism, *Interventions: International Journal of Postcolonial Studies,* 7(3): 283–286.

McCarty, T. and Lee, T. (2014) Critical culturally sustaining/revitalizing pedagogy and Indigenous education sovereignty, *Harvard Educational Review,* 84(1): 101–124.

Moosavi, L. (2020) The decolonial bandwagon and the dangers of intellectual decolonization, *International Review of Sociology,* 30(2): 332–354.

Moreton-Robinson, A. (2015) *The White Possessive: Property, Power and Indigenous Sovereignty*, Minneapolis: University of Minnesota Press.

Ndlovu-Gatsheni, S. (2013) *Coloniality of Power in Postcolonial Africa*, Senegal: CODESRIA.

Ndlovu-Gatsheni, S. (2015) Decoloniality as the future of Africa, *History Compass* 13(10): 485–496.

Nordstrom, C. (2004) *Shadows of War: Violence, power and international profiteering in the 21st century*, Berkeley: University of California Press.

Perry, K. (2020a) The new 'bond-age', climate crisis and the case for climate reparations: Unpicking old/new colonialities of finance for development within the SDGs, *SSRN Electronic Journal*, DOI: 10.2139/ssrn.3739103.

Perry, K. (2020b) For politics, people, or the planet? The political economy of fossil fuel reform, energy dependence and climate policy in Haiti, *Energy Research & Social Science*, 63: 101397.

Sousa Santos, Boaventura de (2017) *Epistemologies of the South: Justice against epistemicide*, Abingdon: Routledge.

Sriprakash, A., Rudolph, S. and Gerrard, J. (2022) *Learning Whiteness: Education and the settler colonial state*, London: Pluto Press.

Sriprakash, A., Tikly, L. and Walker, S. (2019) The erasures of racism in education and international development: Re-reading the 'global learning crisis', Compare, DOI: 10.1080/03057925.2018.1559040.

Táíwò, O. (2022) *Again Decolonization: Taking African agency seriously*, London: Hurst.

Tuck, E. and Yang, K.W. (2016). What justice wants, *Critical Ethnic Studies*, 2(2): 1–15.

UN (2015) Transforming our World: The 2030 agenda for sustainable development.

Wilson, K. (2012) *Race, Racism and Development: Interrogating history, discourse and practice*, London: Zed Books.

PART I

Connecting Decolonial and Sustainable Futures in Education

1

Decolonizing Education for Sustainable Futures: Some Conceptual Starting Points

Leon Tikly

Introduction

As the recent report of the International Commission on the Futures of Education argues (see ICFE, 2021, pp 7–8), anticipating education futures has profound implications for the present:

> Anticipating futures is something we do all the time as humans. Ideas about the future play an important role in educational thinking, policy, and practice. They shape everything from students' and families' everyday decision-making to the grand plans for educational change developed in ministries of education. ... All exploration of possible and alternative futures raises profound questions of ethics, equity, and justice – what futures are desirable and for whom? And since education is not merely impacted by external factors but plays a key role in unlocking potential futures in all corners of the globe, it is natural if not obligatory that reimagining our futures together involves a new social contract for education.

As this quote suggests, narratives about the future can play an important role in shaping education policy and practice and education has a role in shaping futures for people and for the planet through its contribution to sustainable development (see also Amsler and Facer, 2017; Facer, 2013 and 2021). Narratives about sustainable futures and sustainable development are, however, highly contested. The first aim of this chapter is to contribute towards conceptual understanding of how we may conceive of sustainable futures in and for education. As such, the chapter will introduce some of the ideas developed further by other contributions to this book. The chapter begins by setting out how different discourses around sustainable futures and sustainable development can be conceived in terms of struggles for hegemony between competing interests within the global polity and civil society and in the context of the current organic crisis of global capitalism. The second part of the chapter provides a review of contemporary narratives of sustainable futures that are evident in the literature.

Within contemporary debates about sustainable development, including the sustainable development goals (SDGs), it is possible to identify four key narratives concerning sustainable futures, each with different implications for education. Although each narrative has shifted over time and can be seen to reflect sometimes contradictory viewpoints, each coheres around some central themes (see Tikly, 2020). Although the narratives identified are not explicitly about the future, each has important implications for how the future might be conceived, including the future of education. Exponents of the dominant, growth-led narrative, for example, advocate for prosperous futures based on the idea of 'inclusive green growth'. This provides continuity to orthodox, Western, modernist views of progress and development but is contested by environmentalist narratives that point to the unviability of growth-led models in however 'inclusive' or 'green' a form. Environmentalists propose alternative visions of sustainable futures in which economic and social development is harmonious with the aims of environmental protection. Rights-based narratives, along with those inspired by the capability approach of Sen and Nussbaum, also provide alternative views of sustainable futures based on the realization of human rights and capabilities for existing and future generations. It is argued in this chapter, and in keeping with environmentalist narratives, that the dominant, growth-led model is deeply flawed and is a root cause of unsustainable development. It is also argued, however, that, while rights-based and capability-inspired narratives provide important insights for conceiving sustainable futures, they remain, like dominant, growth-led narratives, often largely situated within Western modernist thinking.

It is this grounding in the Western *episteme* (ground-base of knowledge) that recent scholarship on decolonizing development has sought to disrupt. To date, however, these discussions have not focused specifically on the extent to which the idea of sustainable futures can be viewed through a decolonial lens. The aim of this chapter is to do precisely that: to critically consider existing narratives about sustainable futures from a decolonial perspective. As the other contributions to this volume make clear, the silencing – or (in de Sousa Santos' terms) 'epistemicide' –committed under the name of European colonialism on Indigenous and other non-Western ways of knowing the natural and social worlds has also severely constrained the possibilities for a plurality of possible sustainable futures to emerge as envisaged by the ICFE. Education has been centrally implicated in these processes of erasure (see, for example, Sriprakash et al, 2019), but, as is suggested by various contributions to this book, also has the potential to contribute to new ecologies of knowledge that can transcend the limitations of Western monoculture and equip learners with the understanding required to imagine and realize a plurality of possible sustainable futures. Here, it is suggested, there is a growing synergy between environmentalist and decolonizing narratives and it is at this interface that many of the contributions to the current volume lie.

The meaning of sustainable futures

The idea of sustainable futures is becoming increasingly prevalent in debates about development as evidenced by the inclusion of this term in the report by the ICFE. This reflects not only the increasing influence of futures-thinking as a way of framing the present but also as a response to the perceived limitations of dominant, Western, modernist views of 'development' itself. It is important to be clear, however, about what we understand by the idea of 'sustainable futures', and how this idea relates to contemporary debates about the meaning of sustainable development. There are many ways of understanding the future and many orientations towards futures-thinking (Bell, 2003; Facer, 2021; Bryant and Knight, 2019).

At a conceptual level, the understanding of sustainable futures developed here may be described as Gramscian in inspiration but draws on more recent scholarship on complexity theory as it has been applied to an understanding of the interplay between social (economic, political and cultural) systems (Walby, 2009 and 2015) and between social and environmental systems (Wells, 2013; Urry, 2016; Tikly, 2020). A starting point is to situate the idea of sustainable futures within an understanding of what Gramsci (1992) describes as the organic crisis of capitalism. The term 'organic crisis' denotes the complex interplay between economic, political, cultural and environmental systems in generating crisis. Rather than being rooted in one system (such as the economic system), organic crises in this view are seen as multi-causal and multidirectional, the consequence of what Prigogine (1997) describes as the 'cascading interdependence' between systems. Education as an example of a social system, is implicated in these processes of cascading interdependence, albeit in contradictory ways. On the one hand, education has contributed to the current crisis through its complicity in supporting unsustainable development. On the other, education can potentially play a role in resolving the crisis through contributing to the realization of more sustainable futures.

The current organic crisis of global capitalism is manifested at an economic level by responses to the 2008 financial crash, often in the form of austerity measures that have been exacerbated by the impact of the Covid-19 pandemic. At a political level, it is manifested in the crisis in world order, including the increasing challenge to the dominance of the USA and its Western allies posed by the rise of the BRICS economies and a resurgence in religious fundamentalisms and ethno-nationalisms. It is also increasingly manifested as a risk to the future legitimacy of the capitalist system itself posed by the existential threat of climate change (Harris, 2021). Urry (2016), drawing on Williams (1977), argues that part of the crisis at least as it is experienced in the Northern hemisphere has involved changes in the 'structure of feeling' from the optimism of the 1990s to a growing catastrophism linked to the increasingly visible manifestations of climate change and biosphere collapse. It is also manifested in what has been described elsewhere as the post-colonial condition (Tikly, 2020) in which formerly colonized countries continue to occupy a marginal position in relation to processes of economic, political and cultural globalization, and where there is growing inequality within and between formerly colonized and colonizing countries and populations and in which countries in the global South are more likely to be at the sharp end of the effects of climate change.

In the context of the current chapter, narratives about the future can be seen as emerging from and integral to, struggles for hegemony (intellectual and moral leadership) between competing interests within the global economy, polity and civil society over the nature, causes and solutions to crisis. They might be dystopian in nature, in which case they can serve as a call to arms for different interest groups. Many environmentalist narratives, for example, can be seen in these terms. Conversely, they may be utopian in nature (Levitas, 2013) and may serve to mobilize conflicting interests around alternative visions of what 'ought to be'. Many political projects are characterized in this way. As with narratives about the past, ways of thinking about the future, whether dystopian or utopian, can play an ideological role in legitimizing dominant interests in their pursuit of specific political projects and accumulation strategies. In relation to the discussion here, hegemonic projects, in seeking to offer 'solutions' to crisis, must also engage with changes to the 'structure of feeling' inherent in the crisis (see also Sharma and Tygstrup, 2015; Ahmed, 2015) and must engage with increasing demands on the part of the formerly colonized to recognize the legacies of colonialism and slavery and for reparative justice.

Narratives about the future can also be understood in Foucault's (1975) terms as instances of discourse. That is, they are fundamentally acts of power that can delimit what can and can't legitimately be said about the future, by whom and with what authority. Discourses are constitutive of versions of reality as well as of group and individual identities. Hegemonic discourses, however, are also challenged and contested by the emergence of alternative, counter-hegemonic narratives about the future linked to struggles within the global polity and civil society against dominant interests. Importantly, different hegemonic and counter-hegemonic projects may also emphasize alternative orientations towards the future and ways of anticipating the future with implications for education policy – a point that will be returned to later. Also of relevance here is Williams' (1977) understanding of how hegemony is structured in times of crisis and change. In William's terms, 'dominant' global discourse on sustainable futures need to be understood in relation to 'emergent' counter-hegemonic discourses as part of the same totality. Both dominant and emergent discourses often draw on 'residual' elements of past eras of thinking, creating continuities as well as discontinuities between past and present struggles for hegemony and visions of the future. This point is further illustrated later on.

Understood in this way, versions of sustainable futures can be seen as integral to hegemonic and counter-hegemonic views of sustainable development that are proposed as solutions to crisis. As suggested, it is possible to identify four narratives that each relate a vision of sustainable futures to priorities for sustainable development and education. These have been discussed in depth elsewhere (Tikly et al, 2020). Added to this, for the purposes of this chapter is a fifth 'decolonizing narrative' that, it is argued, provides an indispensable point of reference for considering the other narratives. Each narrative is summarized in Table 1.1. Rather than see each narrative as hermetically sealed off from the others, it is more useful to think about them relationally, with fluid boundaries between them. This is to acknowledge that the idea of sustainable development is itself something of a 'meta-fix' (Lélé, 1991) in that it weaves together different understandings of sustainable development, often linked to different economic and political interests and world views under one umbrella. In this regard, key policy texts such as the SDGs or indeed the UNESCO Futures of Education document may contain elements of each narrative, positioned in sometimes contradictory ways. Individuals and groups may also straddle more than one narrative, again with potentially contradictory implications. Thus, in the following sections it will be argued that a way of conceiving of education for sustainable futures that is relevant for many of the contributions to the present book might usefully bring into conversation several of the approaches described. Furthermore, it is suggested that tensions between the narratives may be seen as generative.

In providing a critical evaluation of the various approaches, a useful starting point is provided by the concept of 'just transitions', which is a way of conceiving how and in whose interests transitions to sustainable futures might be realized. Swilling (2020, p 7) defines a just transition as:

> a process of increasingly radical incremental changes that accumulate over time in the actually emergent transformed world envisaged by

Table 1.1: Five narratives of sustainable futures

Narratives of sustainable futures	Growth-led narratives	Rights-led narratives	Capability and social justice narratives	Environmental narratives	Decolonizing narratives
Vision of the future	A prosperous, inclusive and green future	Based on the realization of human rights	Based on the flourishing of human beings and the natural world	Based on synergy between human beings and the natural world	A pluriverse of possible futures liberated from Western modernity
Priorities for sustainable development	Promote inclusive, green growth	Promote human rights for all	Promote the capabilities of human beings, other species and natural systems	De-growth, post-growth, post-extractivism, Indigenous perspectives	Decolonizing development, post-development
Key advocates	World Bank, OECD, WEF, regional development banks	United Nations agencies, INGOs	Sen, Nussbaum, Schlossberg Human Development report	Latouch, Blewitt, Raworth, Amsler, Facer, Andreotti	Mignolo, De Sousa Santos, Escobar
Priorities for education	Provide human capital with 21st-century, green skills	Inclusive, lifelong learning for all	Develop valued capabilities and functionings	Environmental education, education for sustainable development	Decolonizing the curriculum and research, democratizing education

the SDGs and sustainability. The outcome is a state of well-being founded on greater environmental sustainability and social justice (including the eradication of poverty). These changes arise from a vast multiplicity of struggles, each with their own context-specific temporal and spatial dimensions.

This definition resonates with the view of social, epistemic and environmental justice developed here. It is fundamentally concerned with linking together the struggles of historically marginalized groups, including those of workers and peasants against capitalist exploitation and women and girls against patriarchy, as well as the struggles of Indigenous peoples and peoples of colour against the effects of coloniality and imperialism. The idea also draws attention, however, to the structural and discursive barriers to transition that are also elaborated on in the following sections.

Growth-led narratives

A key point of reference in contemporary discourses about sustainable development and the sustainable development goals is the notion of 'inclusive growth', which has been popularized through sometimes contradictory discourses emanating from key multilateral organizations including the World Bank (2012) the OECD (2014), the UN Development Programme (2017) and regional organizations including the African Development Bank (2014). Although there are differences in emphasis in the way that inclusive growth is defined, at the most basic level it is premised on a vision of the future in which broad-based growth across sectors is made more 'inclusive' largely through the creation of job opportunities arising from the removal of regulatory constraints and by creating a climate conducive to investment. In this narrative, inclusive growth is also conceived as 'green' growth in the sense that growth is assumed to be compatible with environmental protection through processes of adaptation and the use of green technologies.

The idea that sustainable development needs to be led by the imperative of achieving economic growth has a long history in development thinking and goes back to the dawn of the so-called 'development era' itself in the period immediately following the Second World War. A major influence on early thinking about 'development' was modernization theory originally proposed by Rostow (1960). It is based on the idea of development comprising discrete stages from the traditional to the high-consumption society. This narrative itself drew on ideas about the nature of modernity and progress going back to Durkheim and Weber. The stages are summarized in Figure 1.1.

Education is deeply implicated in the project of modernization and in achieving economic growth through its role in providing the skills,

Figure 1.1: The Rostow model of development

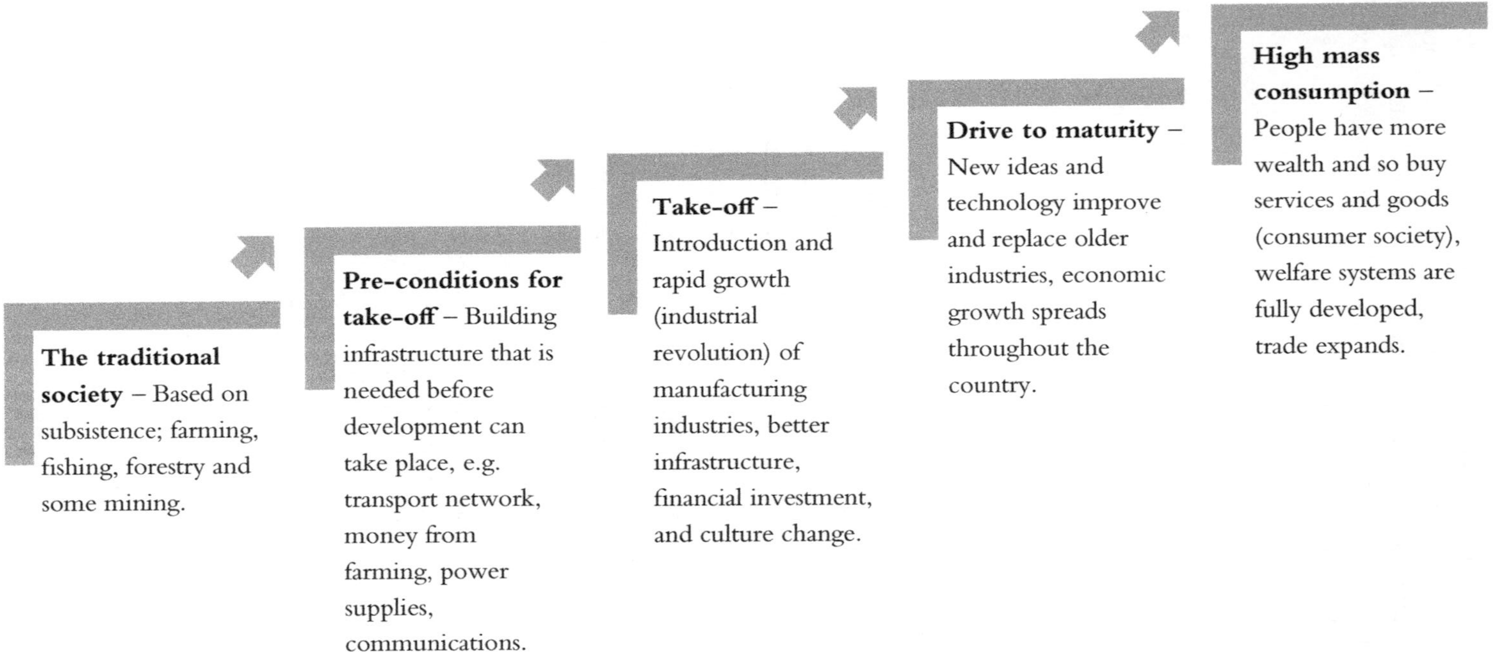

The traditional society – Based on subsistence; farming, fishing, forestry and some mining.

Pre-conditions for take-off – Building infrastructure that is needed before development can take place, e.g. transport network, money from farming, power supplies, communications.

Take-off – Introduction and rapid growth (industrial revolution) of manufacturing industries, better infrastructure, financial investment, and culture change.

Drive to maturity – New ideas and technology improve and replace older industries, economic growth spreads throughout the country.

High mass consumption – People have more wealth and so buy services and goods (consumer society), welfare systems are fully developed, trade expands.

Source: adapted from Rostow (1960)

attitudes and dispositions required to produce 'modern' citizens. Human capital theory has been particularly influential through positing a role for education in providing the human capital required to support growth. Traces of modernization theory are evident in the SDGs in the view of prosperity based on technological, social and economic 'progress' (UN, 2015). Much educational thinking continues to be informed by the idea of education providing human capital with the skills necessary to drive technological development and growth. Most recently, this has been reflected in the idea of 21st-century skills proposed by the World Economic Forum (2015) and in the idea of green skills advocated by the World Bank (2012).

Western, growth-led narratives about development have long been a subject of critique. During the 1960s and 1970s, anti-colonial intellectuals such as Nkrumah (1966), Nyerere (1967) and Rodney (1973), along with exponents of the dependency school (for example, Frank, 1970), critiqued Western models of capitalist development for eliding the role of the global capitalist system in perpetuating relationships of neo-colonialism. Rather than demonstrating a linear process of development, it was argued, capitalist development is better characterized by periods of sustained crisis and growing inequalities within and between countries at the centre and periphery of the global economy.

Marxist-inspired critiques of the fundamentally crisis-driven, unequal and contradictory nature of the Western capitalist model have been further developed in the context of the shift towards neoliberalism in the global economy since the 1980s and the impact of structural adjustment and austerity policies on exacerbating poverty and inequality (see, for example, Amin, 1997 and 2003; Harvey, 2003 and 2011; Walby, 2009 and 2015). Some Marxist critiques, notably in South Africa (such as Legassick and Hemson, 1976; Wolpe, 1988) and in the United States (Robinson, 1984, for example), pointed towards the fundamentally racist nature of the capitalist system in perpetuating racial hierarchies, while feminists have focused their critiques on the patriarchal nature of Western development models that has reproduced gendered inequalities (for example, Saunders, 2004; Federici, 2004 and 2011;). As will be discussed, the Western basis of modernization, and indeed much Western-led development theorizing, has also been subject to sustained critique over many years by scholars writing within post-development (Escobar, 1995 and 2004;), post-colonial (Said, 1978; Sardar, 1999) and decolonial frameworks (Wilson, 2012).

Within the environmentally oriented literature, there has been a sustained critique of growth-led narratives. One important line focuses on the idea that growth is a driver of sustainable development. For example, for advocates of the ideas of 'degrowth' (Latouche, 2007 and 2010;), 'prosperity without growth' (Jackson, 2016) or 'post-growth' (Blewitt and Cunningham, 2014; Blewitt, 2018), the very idea of 'growth' is antithetical to the idea of a sustainable environment given the limit to natural resources and the damage that growth under capitalism has historically wrought on natural systems. The emphasis on the use of 'adaptive measures' (an implicit idea in the concept of inclusive growth) has been criticized in the environmental literature as being based on the assumption that climate change and environmental degradation can be dealt with primarily through processes of technological innovation. Rather, for many environmentalists, these solutions are insufficient for tackling the root causes of climate change, which lie in patterns of production and consumption as they have developed under petroleum-driven capitalism and particularly in the global North. Some environmentalists, however, have increasingly focused their critique on the underlying view of Western modernity itself. Here there is a clear synergy emerging between environmentalist and decolonizing narratives, a synergy that many of the contributions to this book seek to build on and to develop further.

The emphasis on economic growth also often leads to a narrow, instrumental set of priorities regarding the kinds of skills and competencies that education needs to develop, (Tikly, 2004; Vally and Motala, 2014). As will be explored, rights- and capability-based narratives offer alternative, more expansive conceptions of the skills, competencies and capabilities that are necessary for human flourishing. The idea of 'green skills' has also been critiqued for assuming that an emphasis on the role of education in producing green skills outside a more thorough-going effort to make processes of production more sustainable leads to an idealized view of the role of education in greening the economy that actually serves to legitimize the status quo (Death, 2014 and 2016; McGrath et al, 2020; McGrath, 2020).

Environmentally-oriented narratives

Since the 1990s, much of the environmentalist literature has been written with reference to visions of a dystopian future linked to climate change and biosphere collapse (see Urry, 2016 for a recent summary of this literature). Kate Raworth's work, however, offers a recent example of the possibilities for environmentally sustainable futures (Raworth, 2017). It has also been developed in the context of the adoption of the UN's agenda 2030 (UN, 2015) and refers to the 17 SDGs. At the heart of the understanding is a view of the purpose of economic development as meeting social needs on the one hand, and operating within ecological boundaries on the other. The model thus provides a way of conceiving of the relationship between the environmental and social dimensions of the SDGs. These ideas are encapsulated in Figure 1.2. For Raworth, the aim of economic policy is to achieve a dynamic equilibrium in the 'sweet spot' between the social foundation and the environmental ceiling of economic activity (hence the term 'doughnut economics' which Raworth applies to her model).

The model suggests that, rather than focusing on the relationship between education and economic growth and the contradictory implications that

Figure 1.2: The model of doughnut economics for sustainable development

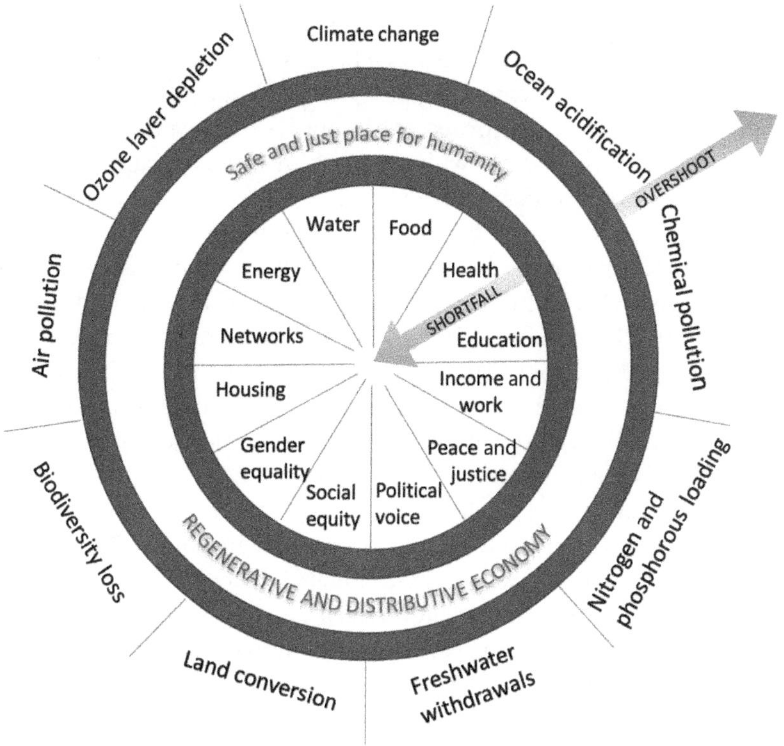

Source: adapted from Raworth (2017)

flow from this, it is preferable to consider the relationship between education and sustainable futures based on regenerative and distributive economies. In addition, unlike human capital theory, which posits a linear relationship between the production of human capital and economic growth, the model suggests a multidirectional relationship between education and the economic domain, mediated by the effects of other areas of social development, which is more in keeping with the view of complex systems outlined earlier. Raworth's model is useful in that it can be seen to address many of the flaws with linear, growth-led models of economic development such as that proposed by Rostow. Nonetheless, the model is less strong at dealing with what Stein et al (2019) describe as the modern/colonial global imaginary underlying much development thinking including the SDGs. This includes engaging with the Eurocentric bias in the way that development is conceived and the unequal power relations between former colonized and colonizing populations that Western capitalist models have sustained, albeit in new forms.

As we have seen, environmentally oriented approaches have also been implicated in contemporary debates about green skills. The notion of green skills has been criticized for being a part of the 'greenwashing' of growth-led narratives of sustainable futures. An alternative notion of green skills seeks to explore what types of skills, work and industries need to develop if the climate crisis is to be overcome, and how such transformations can be achieved (McGrath et al, 2019; Rosenberg et al, 2020). Importantly, this literature is not just focused on the formal sector but has rural and informal sector dimensions, and also engages with systemic dynamics of transformations to sustainability (Lotz-Sisitka and Ramsarup, 2019).

Environmentally oriented approaches, however, are most often associated with forms of environmental education that have a long history in global discourses going back to the Stockholm conference and Tbilisi declaration of the 1970s (Tikly, 2020). Environmental education is fundamentally concerned with developing understanding of the natural environment and of the integrity of ecosystems and the role of human beings in managing natural systems. Whereas environmental education approaches often strongly overlap with sustainable development approaches in the curriculum and in policy, the latter have tended to place a greater emphasis on the human development (economic and social) aspects of sustainability (Wals and Kieft, 2010), in some contexts, where environmental discourses are closely related to conservation rather than environmental justice discourses. Importantly, however, from a decolonizing perspective, there are long-standing traditions in the global South that have considered environmental education as interacting with biophysical, social, political and economic relations (see, for example, NGO Forum, 1992; O'Donoghue and McNaught, 1991; Lotz-Sisitka, 2004; REEP, 2012; Leff, 1999). More recently, some of this scholarship has taken an explicitly decolonial turn, a point that will be elaborated on in the following sections.

Rights-based narratives

Rights-based narratives posit a vision of sustainable futures in which the universal human rights of existing and future generations are realized. In contrast to growth-led narratives, advocates of a rights-based approach see development as multifaceted, involving a spectrum of economic, political and cultural dimensions and linked to the realization of peace, human security and environmental sustainability. Human rights are seen as fundamental, indivisible and integral to the development process (Piron with O'Neill, 2005; UNDP, 1998). The idea of universal, inalienable human rights has had an important influence on the evolution of the idea of sustainable development in the period following the Second World War and in the context of the formation of the United Nations. The *Proclamation of the Universal Declaration of Human Rights* and subsequent legally binding covenants and conventions have sought to create a framework intended to guarantee a dignified life for all human beings regardless of race, culture or gender. The mandates for both UNESCO and UNICEF arise from their roles in advancing human rights in education and other spheres. The Bruntland report *Our Common Future* (WCED, 1987) was a key milestone in the emergence of the idea of sustainable development. It drew on a conception of the role of development in meeting basic needs, which are themselves rooted in the idea of human rights (the right to food, shelter, health, education and so on). More recently, the five principles underpinning the SDGs – people, planet, prosperity, peace and partnership – are also derived from the idea of inalienable human rights (UN, 2015).

The human rights approach to education is interested in the role of education in securing rights *to* education, rights *in* education and rights *through* education (Subrahmanian, 2002; Unterhalter, 2007). In this sense, human rights discourses have often been advocated by UN agencies, international non-governmental organizations (NGOs) and civil society organizations at the international, national and local level (Mundy and Murphy, 2001). Rights-based approaches have also underpinned the development of the Education for All (EFA) movement. The principles governing EFA have remained consistent over the past quarter of a century as encapsulated in the various targets set out in key declarations and frameworks, including the Jomtien declaration, the Dakar framework for action and more recently the Muscat agreement and the 2015 Incheon declaration and framework for action (IDFA) (Tikly, 2017). They also form the basis for the education goal (goal 4) of the SDGs, which advocates for inclusive, good-quality and lifelong learning for all.

The concept of 'life skills' developed through the EFA movement can be seen as a counter-narrative to that of 21st-century skills and has been used in different but overlapping ways by various international organizations working within a rights-based framework. Within the EFA movement, life skills was a catch-all term for 'skills for sustainable livelihoods', which has historically formed part of UNESCO's wider education for sustainable development (ESD) discourse (Maclean and Wilson, 2011). Closely linked to the idea of life skills is that of lifelong learning, which is seen as essential for developing relevant life skills in rapidly changing societies and economies across the life span. The idea of lifelong learning has a long pedigree in the post-colonial world. It was used by Nyerere, for example, to encapsulate his view of education in relation to self-reliance (Nyerere, 1967). The global influence on the evolution of rights-based approaches in education, as in other spheres, is interesting to note in the context of decolonizing discourses (discussed later).

While providing an alternative, liberal, egalitarian view of development to that posited by modernization theory and neoliberalism, the idea of universal human rights has, however, also been subject to criticism. Human rights frameworks have been described as an example of a universalizing Western discourse and have, as such operated as a source of hypocrisy and contradiction. For some critics, for example, many Western democracies supposedly founded on human rights principles have been implicated in colonialism, racism and slavery and have sometimes turned a blind eye to the most gross violations of human rights, including genocide. It is also argued that the emphasis on individual rights, including individual property rights, provides a source of tension with the idea of collective rights (de Sousa Santos, 1999). Policies drawing inspiration or making reference to human rights have also sometimes been criticized for being too homogenizing and top-down in their application, often removed from Indigenous and local discourses about ethics with which they are seldom brought into conversation. In this respect, a criticism of the basic needs approach that underpinned the Bruntland report is that the document does not make explicit how basic needs are defined in different contexts and who decides what constitutes basic needs.

Despite the shortcomings of a rights-based approach, some of the educational ideas associated with it, including life skills and lifelong learning, appear to resonate more closely with the realities of the development challenges facing many parts of the low-income, post-colonial world than does the list of 21st-century skills. However, the idea of life skills has also been subject to similar critiques as the idea of 21st-century skills in that it presents a top-down, 'one size fits all' approach to skills development. Here, advocates of the capability approach (CA) argue that it provides a way of reconceptualizing skills and competencies in relation to the capabilities and functionings that communities, governments and other stakeholders have reason to value.

Capability and social justice narratives

An alternative but related starting point for considering the ethical basis for sustainable development comes from the capability approach of Sen and Nussbaum. Sen's work has been influential to thinking within the UN about how human development can be conceptualized and measured. He provides a critique of the idea of growth as measured in gross domestic product (GDP), seeing it rather as a means for achieving the true purpose of development, which lies in the fulfilment of human wellbeing and freedom. For Sen, instead of development being measured by the extent to which economies can fulfil basic needs (as in the Bruntland formulation), development needs to be assessed in relation to the capabilities (opportunity freedoms)[1] that individuals have to convert resources into valued functionings (beings and doings) that they have reason to value and that will contribute to well-being, freedom and human flourishing. In the context of the shift to sustainable development (SD) as the dominant development paradigm,

Sen (2013) has argued for an expansion of this idea of capabilities to take account of the capabilities of future generations and how this necessitates a concern with environmental protection as inseparable and integral to the realization of human capabilities now and in the future. The idea, inherent in the capability approach, that what count as valued functionings are in some important respects relative and dependent on context, also draws attention to the importance of informed public dialogue as a basis for decision-making. In keeping with decolonizing narratives, the capability approach opens up the possibility for a plurality of futures, albeit rooted in universalized liberal principles.

Scholarship within the field of education and training using the capability approach has blossomed over the past 20 years. It has been used to provide an alternative rationale beyond the instrumentalism of human capital theory and the limitations of rights-based approaches to think about the goals and purpose of education and training. As such, it has contributed to contemporary debates about the quality of education (Tikly and Barrett, 2013) including in schools (Lotz-Sisitka et al, 2017), technical and vocational education and training (TVET) settings Powell and McGrath, 2019; De Jaeghere, 2017) to higher education (Walker, 2006) as well as informal settings (McGrath et al, 2020). It has also been used to address different kinds of disadvantage and as a means of advocating for gender justice (Unterhalter et al, 2005; Unterhalter, 2007); the rights of speakers of minority and Indigenous languages (Tikly, 2016); and understanding the aspirations of working-class learners (Hart, 2015).

In educational terms, the capability approach draws attention to the importance not only of providing basic resources necessary to facilitate access to a good-quality education, such as classrooms, textbooks and qualified teachers, but also opportunities that are available to different groups of learners to convert these into valued outcomes. As is argued later, this is significant because, in highly unequal education systems, many individuals and groups, including the socio-economically disadvantaged, girls, speakers of minority languages, Indigenous groups, and children with disabilities, who may be subject to further forms of discrimination, often experience limited educational opportunities compared with their more advantaged peers. It is also significant because a concern with increasing opportunities in the face of multiple, intersecting inequalities entails moving beyond the idea of basic entitlements to education (as sometimes implied in a rights-based approach) and a recognition that some individuals and groups may require different levels and kinds of resource to achieve similar outcomes. In relation to decolonial thought, the idea of targeting resources to correct historically rooted injustices is also consistent with ideas of reparative justice.

There are, however, potential shortcomings of the capability approach that are important to acknowledge. For example, Sen's is an anthropocentric view of capability – a view of capability as applying only to human beings. Nussbaum has begun to articulate a view of other species having capabilities linked to their inherent dignity (Nussbaum, 2006). Extending this view, Schlosberg (2007, p 142) argues the importance of understanding species as parts of wider ecosystems and that systems themselves have capabilities and functionings and might be considered 'agents for the work they do in providing the various capacities for their parts to function – i.e., purifying water, contributing oxygen, providing nutrition, sustaining temperature.' This implies that the idea of capabilities can be applied to natural systems and to other species. As other contributors to this volume argue, recognizing the integrity and the right to flourish of other species and ecosystems is in keeping with many Indigenous knowledge systems in Africa and elsewhere that have posited a more organic, symbiotic and custodial relationship between human beings and the natural world (Maware and Mubaye, 2016).

In addition, like rights-based approaches, the approach is sometimes characterized as being ontologically individualistic; as being concerned with the realization of individual capabilities. As Sen (2011) has argued, however, while it is still useful methodologically to measure capabilities at an individual level, it is both possible and necessary to conceive of capabilities as applying as much to groups as to individuals. Taking account of these differences requires a recognition of the wider structural and discursive barriers that limit the agency freedom of some individuals and groups either to access and convert educational and other resources into valued functionings or to have their voices heard and/or interests represented in public debates about what constitute valued capabilities and functionings.[2]

For example, DeJaeghere (2020) sets out a relational view of capability that sees the development of agency freedoms in relation to post-colonial and feminist forms of analysis that draws attention to the continuing effects of colonialism and patriarchy on the capabilities of formerly colonized populations and people of colour and of girls and women respectively. Other scholars have sought to theorize capabilities in relation to other complementary theories of justice. Unterhalter and DeJaeghere for example, consider the capabilities of girls and women in relation to an analysis of patriarchy in education and of gender justice (Unterhalter, 2007; DeJaeghere, 2020). In a recent study, Walker (2019) draws on Fricker's ideas of epistemic justice to consider how the voices of different marginalized and racialized groups are recognized and validated in educational settings and in public discourse more widely. Several theorists have sought to link the capability approach and theories of global justice, drawing on Nancy Fraser's understanding of distributive, recognitional and participatory justice,[3] which provides a multi-dimensional way of conceiving the opportunities and barriers facing some groups in realizing valued functionings and constraining the abilities of other species and natural systems to flourish (for example,

Schlosberg, 2004 and 2007; Tikly and Barrett, 2013). Linking the capability approach to consideration of issues of justice, power and inequalities in the world provides a possible point of rapprochement with decolonizing narratives, including those that draw attention to the continuing powerful effects of coloniality in shaping outcomes for different groups.

Decolonizing narratives

Decolonizing narratives bring together a range of perspectives that have in common a critique of the Western-centric nature of development and of development discourse since colonial times. Some of the critiques of growth-led, human-rights and capability-inspired narratives have been noted in earlier sections. Given this emphasis on critique of Western modernity, decolonizing narratives do not offer an explicit vision of sustainable futures and indeed can be seen as antithetical to such a project unless it involves a radical decentring of Western conceptions of development and of sustainability itself. It is, however, possible to infer from these narratives a dystopian and a utopian vision of the future. The former is based on the continued cultural hegemony of the West and the 'epistemicide' (de Sousa Santos, 2012) of non-Western and Indigenous cultures and languages. The latter involves an emergent utopian vision in which a pluriverse of possible futures for humanity and for the planet are counterposed to the continued imposition of a Western monoculture. Both of these aspects of a future vision will be explored in this section. It will be argued that both are significant for conceiving of sustainable futures in education.

As with other narratives discussed, it is important to recognize that decolonial thought builds on and re-articulates in new ways previous eras of thought. Anti-colonial activists from Gandhi to Nyerere to Rodrigues and Biko have provided a trenchant critique of the valorization since colonial times of Western forms of knowledge and the systematic undermining of Indigenous knowledge systems, languages and cultural values. The pan-African movement, for example, with its roots in anti-colonial struggle has emphasized the need to reassert, alongside demands for economic and political independence, African cultures (whether in Africa or in the wider diaspora) onto the global stage; a theme that has been taken up more recently by exponents of the idea of an African Renaissance (Tikly, 2003). The negritude movement in the 1930s, under the influence of thinkers such as Aimé Césaire and Leopold Senghor, drew attention to the racializing effects of Western colonial discourse and sought to challenge this through the projection of positive conceptions of Black identities.

Drawing on insights from psychoanalysis, phenomenology and Marxism, the Martiniquan psychoanalyst and revolutionary Frantz Fanon, drew attention to the damaging effects on the Black psyche arising from the internalization of racialized identities transmitted through Western language and culture (Fanon, 1961 and 1986). Fanon's work was in turn influential on the thinking of Steve Biko (1978) and other leaders of the Black Consciousness movement in South Africa. Anti-colonial activists, including, for example, the Kenyan writer and dramatist Ngũgĩ wa Thiong'o (1986) and the South African former political prisoner, Neville Alexander (1999) have also highlighted the need to reinstate Indigenous languages as key in supporting Indigenously led development. In the Indian context, contemporary demands to decolonize the curriculum build on an anti-caste struggle that predates the anti-colonial struggle (Batra, 2020).

More recently, post-colonial thought has provided a lens through which scholars have challenged the cultural hegemony of the West. Drawing on post-structuralist as well as Marxist ideas and providing continuity on the work of earlier anti-colonial intellectuals, post-colonial scholarship has drawn attention to the role of Western knowledge in perpetuating the dominance of the West through the non-Western 'other' as an aspect of the post-colonial condition (Said, 1978; Spivak, 1988; Bhabha, 1984 and 1996). It also draws attention to the contingent and contested nature of post-colonial identities with clear echoes of Fanon's thought (Hall, 1996). Some of this literature also draws on Southern philosophies such as *buen vivir* and *ukama*, which point to a relatedness, 'that is not restricted to human relations but extends to the natural environment, the past, the present and the future' (Murove 2009, p 28).

Closely aligned with post-colonial scholarship are the ideas of post-development thinkers such as Escobar (1995 and 2004), Rist (1997) and Wilson (2012). Escobar and Rist have provided critiques of the powerful role of Western development discourse in re-creating the 'Third World' in the image of the West and in the interests of the West. Nustad (1996) has argued that the field of development has primarily been the purview of technocrats and a technocratized discourse that marginalizes other perspectives on human lives and living practices. Wilson's work draws attention to the racialized nature of much contemporary development discourse, which, she argues, provides continuity on Western constructions of the non-European 'other' going back to colonial times.[4] According to Stein et al (2019), these elements comprise what they refer to as the modern/colonial global imaginary. They go on to argue that contemporary global agendas including the UN SDGs, while advocating greater voice for marginalized groups in the development process, do little to disrupt this global imaginary.

Demands to decolonize education have, however, been given fresh impetus in recent years by student protests at the University of Cape Town in 2015. Although initially targeted at the continued presence of a statue in memory of the imperialist Cecil Rhodes, the protests soon escalated into a wider critique of the Eurocentric nature of the curriculum. The *#RhodesMustFall* protests spawned similar campaigns at universities in South Africa, the UK, the US and elsewhere under the theme of #WhyismyCurriculumWhite? The protests ran parallel to a sister campaign #FeesMustFall.[5] Debates about decolonizing the university have been given further impetus through the Black Lives Matter protests that started in 2016 in the US and have spread to other countries in the global North, most recently in the context of the police killing of George Floyd. In India, they have resonated with demands to introduce Dalit studies as a response to the silencing of issues to do with caste in the existing curriculum (Rege, 2007). The construction of national imaginaries in the diverse societies of South Asia has the potential to provide new discourses to educational reform; going beyond the abstract goals set by disconnected international experts and the institutional processes they represent (Batra, 2019).

Demands to decolonize education have also been informed by the work of scholars such as de Sousa Santos (2007; 2012; 2017), Mbembe and Posel (2005); Mbembe (2016), Dei and Kempf (2006); Dei, (2017) Maldonado-Torres (2007), Ndlovu-Gatsheni (2013; 2015), Comoroff and Comoroff (2011), Connell (2007; 2012; 2014) and others. In seeking to decentre Eurocentric thought, decolonizing narratives provide useful pointers for how Western hegemony has worked in and through education. Much decolonial thinking has focused on a critique of the assumption at the heart of Western knowledge and Western science, in particular, that it represents a universalizing truth. For these authors, despite its claims to objectivity, Western science since the European enlightenment has been linked to European colonialism and the development of global markets. They also link the dominance of Western knowledge to the marketization of education and the commodification of knowledge, which they argue detracts from the role of the university in promoting critical, independent thought (de Sousa Santos, 2017; Mbembe, 2016).

Decolonizing perspectives draw attention to the extent to which systems of mass education and institutions such as schools and universities around the globe also reflect a Western monoculture in terms of their basic organization and governance. With their roots in the expansion of European colonialism, education systems have often remained top-down, authoritarian and bureaucratic in nature.[6] The very nature of educational institutions, from the organization of the curriculum to the temporality imposed by the structure of the school day, reflects their performative and disciplinary role in instilling Western modernist dispositions in non-Western populations. These critiques of the epistemic basis of post-colonial education systems are a necessary corrective to the emphasis in the other narratives of sustainable education futures in which the emphasis is on increasing access to the existing (Western-centric) curriculum and forms of education and training.

Decolonizing narratives demand a radical questioning of these assumptions and begin to sketch out alternative visions. For de Sousa Santos (2017), for example, decolonizing the curriculum entails bringing the disciplines as enshrined in the university curriculum into conversation through forms of knowledge production with grassroots movements and with Indigenous knowledge to create new 'ecologies of knowledge'. For de Sousa Santos, the aim is to develop a 'pluriversity' based on a recognition of multiple ways of 'knowing' the world that can benefit social and environmental justice. For Mbembe (2016), a key goal must be to challenge the very basis of Western humanism itself, which he claims lies in the separation of subject from object, nature from culture and human beings from other species. Rather, 'a new understanding of ontology, epistemology, ethics and politics has to be achieved. It can only be achieved by overcoming anthropocentrism and humanism, the split between nature and culture' (p 42). For both de Sousa Santos and Mbembe, this involves a more fundamental shift in the way that the role of the university is perceived. For de Sousa Santos, it involves protecting the idea of the university as a public good. For Mbembe and Dei, it means developing diasporic intellectual networks that can transform the curriculum to reflect the experiences of Africans in Africa and in the diaspora. It also means engaging with and challenging new configurations of racism and in particular 'to explore the emerging nexus between biology, genes, technologies and their articulations with new forms of human destitution' (Mbembe, 2016, p 44).

For Connell, decolonization is linked to the recovery of Southern theory; a renewed focus on the scholarly works of non-Western scholars. In her book *Southern Theory* (2007), she draws attention to the depth and breadth of non-Western scholarship that she claims has been subsumed by the hegemony of Western knowledge. As de Sousa Santos (2007) reminds us, however, this is not an appeal to naïve relativism in which all forms of knowledge, Western and non-Western, are considered equally valid in all contexts. Rather, the aim is to enable learners to critically evaluate the relevance of different kinds of knowledge (Western, Indigenous and so on) for solving different kinds of problems and, concomitantly, to recognize the fallibility of all knowledge systems. It is important to develop understanding among learners of the historicity of different knowledge systems and how they have evolved in relation to specific geographical and socio-historical contexts and interests as well as in relation to other knowledge systems. Thus, it is important to develop understanding of, for example, the enormous debt (often unacknowledged) owed by modern science to other cultures and civilizations on which some of its major insights, innovations and methods have been built (Tikly, 2020).[7] As many of the other contributions to this volume make clear, efforts to decentre the Eurocentric bias in the curriculum is a necessary first step if education is to play a role in realizing more just futures. Others stress the role that education can play in realizing reparative futures through addressing past injustices and in developing future literacies based on principles of reparative justice (see also Facer and Sriprakash, 2021).

As noted earlier in the chapter, there has been an increasing rapprochement between decolonizing and environmentalist narratives concerning sustainable futures in education and it is at this intersection that many of the contributions to the current volume lie. A good example is the work of the Gesturing Towards Decolonial Futures (GTDF) collective, which brings together scholars, artists, students and Indigenous knowledge keepers. The collective seeks to work at the interface of questions related to historical, systemic and ongoing violence and questions related to the unsustainability of our current habits of being that is based on exponential growth, overconsumption and the extraction of fossil fuels (see Stein, 2019 and 2020). The pedagogical approach used in the collective's work is based on a non-Western form of psychoanalysis grounded in translations of insights and practices of Indigenous communities from Canada and South and Central America. Part of the work of the GTDF collective is to map out ethical pathways for forming relationships and collaborations with Indigenous communities based on trust, respect, consent and accountability, rather than extraction and appropriation (Jimmy et al, 2020; Whyte, 2020).

As is discussed in several of the contributions to this volume (see the chapters by the Common World Collective, Odora Hoppers and Rivera Zea), the spiritual relationship and custodial role of human beings in relation to the natural environment has been an aspect of Indigenous knowledge systems long pre-dating colonial encounters, and environments are integral to the materiality of livelihoods in these contexts. By contrast, the modern (Western) practices of bifurcating and producing dualist abstractions of nature and culture are less embedded in the lives and being of communities.

Decolonizing the curriculum involves engaging with the processes by which knowledge is validated and selected for inclusion in the curriculum. These are not neutral, but often highly politicized, processes. Rather than remaining the domain of experts, the politics of curriculum production needs to be made transparent and democratized though opening up to wider public scrutiny and debate questions of what should be taught as well as related questions about pedagogy and assessment. Ultimately, however, transforming the Western, and indeed patriarchal and classist, nature of the curriculum requires engaging with the politics of knowledge production itself. The disciplines as we know them today have emerged over many centuries and in the context of the development of capitalism, colonialism and patriarchy. Decentring the Eurocentric, capitalist and patriarchal bias of the curriculum is intimately linked to debates about widening participation to historically marginalized groups and the need to reorient research towards the interests of the historically marginalized and dispossessed. There is also a need to revolutionize the way that research is funded and processes of publication that currently favour English-speaking academics based in Northern universities. These are areas in which higher education institutions, funding bodies and publishing houses can demonstrate a material commitment to reparative justice.

In this respect, as Maldonado-Torres (2007) and 2015) argue, decolonizing the curriculum is part of a wider project of 'decoloniality' that implies 'the dismantling of relations of power and conceptions of knowledge that foment the reproduction of racial, gender, and geo-political hierarchies that came into being or found new and more powerful forms of expression in the modern/colonial world' (Ndlovu-Gatsheni, 2015, p 117). For decolonial scholars such as Eve and Tuck, this requires moving beyond a concern with simply diversifying the curriculum and appreciating how sustainable education futures must play a role in wider processes of transformation and counter-hegemonic struggles for reparative justice. Several of the contributions to this volume, including those by Saeed and by Sriprakash et al, link struggles to decolonize education to wider struggles for social, environmental and epistemic justice.

Conclusion: decolonizing sustainable futures

The first half of the chapter argued that dominant, growth-led visions of sustainable futures are contradictory and ultimately unviable. It suggested that environmentalist, rights-based and capability-inspired narratives offer useful insights on which visions of sustainable futures might be built. It also suggested, however, that these narratives were flawed, largely due to their failure to take account of their Western-centric bias. Here it has been argued that decolonial narratives have a crucial correcting role to play in how we conceive of sustainable educational futures through exposing and decentring this bias and providing a basis for more inclusive visions of the future and that such efforts to decolonize education are a prerequisite for realizing just transitions towards sustainable futures. Here, however, decolonial scholarship also points to the pervasive and ubiquitous effects of the colonial matrix of power. In this respect, such changes are not in the short-term interests of the powerful and there are considerable dangers that either justice or transition, or both, will be resisted or subverted. In this regard, it is crucial to link struggles for sustainable education futures to wider counter-hegemonic struggles for social, environmental, epistemic and reparative justice.

Notes

[1] In Nussbaum's (2011) terms, the idea of capability equates to having the basic capacity (access to resource and skill/aptitude) plus the opportunity to turn these into valued functionings.

2   Here Robeyns (2017) argues that the core concepts of the capability approach need to be considered alongside other theoretical approaches that allow for a consideration of these wider structural inequalities.

3   Fraser draws attention to three dimensions of social justice. The first, redistribution, relates to access to different kinds of material resources or to services such as education and health. The second, recognition, means first identifying and then acknowledging the claims of historically marginalized groups. Participatory justice includes the rights of individuals and groups to have their voices heard in debates about social justice and injustice and to actively participate in decision-making.

4   For example, Wilson draws attention to the role of racialized constructions of non-Western sexualities in discussions about overpopulation and the spread of HIV/AIDS.

5   While the *Rhodes Must Fall* and *Why is My Curriculum White?* protests focused on issues of representation in the curriculum, the *Fees Must Fall* protests rather took aim at another issue perceived by students as preventing the access of disadvantaged learners to higher education, namely the imposition of tuition fees. Critical accounts of these student protests have been provided elsewhere (such as Jansen, J. (2018) *As By Fire: The end of the South African university*, Cape Town: Tafelberg).

6   Ironically these characteristics have proved very hard to shift, despite efforts by Western development agencies to introduce more decentralized models of governance in keeping with the trajectory of educational reforms in many Western societies (Tikly, 2020).

7   In the case of Western science, for example, the development of fields as diverse as astronomy, navigation, medicine and algebra are hugely indebted to African and Asian scholarship that pre-dates the emergence of the modern disciplines since the European enlightenment.

References

African Development Bank (2014) Inclusive Growth: An imperative for African agriculture, Tunis-Belvedere: AfDB Group.

Ahmed, S. (2015) *Cultural Politics of Emotion*, Abingdon: Routledge.

Alexander, N. (1999) An African renaissance without African languages?, *Social Dynamics*, 25(1): 1–12.

Amin, S. (1997) *Capitalism in the Age of Globalisation*, London: Zed Books.

Amin, S. (2003) *Obsolescent Capitalism*, London: Zed Books.

Amsler, S. and Facer, K. (2017) Contesting anticipatory regimes in education: Exploring alternative educational orientations to the future, *Futures*, 94: 6–14.

Batra, P. (2019) Comparative education in South Asia: Contribution, contestation, and possibilities, in: C. Wolhuter and A.W. Wiseman (eds) *Comparative and International Education: Survey of an infinite field (International Perspectives on Education and Society)*, Bingley: Emerald Publishing, pp 183–211.

Batra, P. (2020) Echoes of 'coloniality' in the episteme of Indian educational reforms, *On Education*, 3(7).

Bell, W. (2003) *Foundations of Futures Studies: Volume 1: History, Purposes, and Knowledge*, Abingdon: Routledge.

Bhabha, H. (1984) Of Mimicry and Man: The ambivalence of colonial discourse, *October*, 28: 125–133.

Bhabha, H. (1996) The Other question: Difference, discrimination, and the discourse of colonialism, in: H. Baker, M. Diawara and R. Lindeborg (eds) *Black British Cultural Studies: A reader*, London: University of Chicago Press, pp 87–91.

Biko, S. (1978) *I Write What I Like*, London: Bowerdean Press.

Blewitt, J. (2018) *Understanding Sustainable Development*, London: Routledge.

Blewitt, J. and Cunningham, R. (2014) *The Post-Growth Project: How the end of economic growth could bring a fairer and happier society*, London: London Publishing Partnership.

Bryant, R. and Knight, D. (2019) *The Anthropology of the Future*, Cambridge: Cambridge University Press.

Comoroff, J. and Comoroff, J. (2011) *Theory from the South: Or, how Euro-America is evolving towards Africa*, Boulder CO: Paradigm.

Connell, R. (2007) *Southern Theory: The global dynamics of knowledge in social science*, London: Allen and Unwin.

Connell, R. (2012) Just education, *Journal of Education Policy*, 27(5): 681–683.

Connell, R. (2014) Using Southern theory: Decolonizing social thought in theory, research and application, *Planning Theory*, 13(5): 210–223.

Death, C. (2014) Environmental movements, climate change, and consumption in South Africa, *Journal of Southern African Studies*, 40(6): 1215–1234.

Death, C. (2016) Green states in Africa: Beyond the usual suspects, *Environmental Politics*, 25(1): 116–135.

Dei, G. (2017) *Reframing Blackness and Black Solidarities Through Anti-colonial and Decolonial Prisms*, Cham: Springer International.

Dei, G. and Kempf, A. (2006) *Anti-colonialism and Education: The politics of resistance*, Rotterdam: Sense Publishers.

DeJaeghere, J. (2017) *Educating Entrepreneurial Citizens: Neoliberalism and youth livelihoods in Tanzania*, London: Routledge.

DeJaeghere, J. (2020) Reconceptualizing educational capabilities: A relational capability theory for redressing inequalities, *Journal of Human Development and Capabilities*, 21(1): 17–35.

de Sousa Santos, B. (1999) Towards a Multicultural Conception of Human Rights, *Spaces of Culture: City–Nation–World*.

de Sousa Santos, B. (2007) Beyond abyssal thinking: From global lines to ecologies of knowledge, *REVIEW*, XXX(1): 45–89.

de Sousa Santos, B. (2012) Public sphere and epistemologies of the South, *Africa Development*, 37(1): 43–67.

de Sousa Santos, B. (2017) *Decolonising the University: The challenge of deep cognitive justice*, Newcastle Upon Tyne: Cambridge Scholars Publishing.

Escobar. A. (1995) *Encountering Development: The making and unmaking of the third world*, Princeton: Princeton University Press.

Escobar, A. (2004) Development, violence and the new imperial order, *Development*, 47(1): 15–21.

Facer, K. (2013) The problem of the future and the possibilities of the present in education research, *International Journal of Educational Research*, 61: 135–143.

Facer, K. (2021) Futures in education: Towards an ethical practice, Paper commissioned for the UNESCO Futures of Education report, available at: unesdoc.unesco.org/ark:/48223/pf0000375792.locale=en [accessed 6 February 2023].

Facer, K. and Sriprakash, A. (2021) Provincialising futures literacy: A caution against codification, *Futures*, 133.

Fanon, F. (1961) *The Wretched of the Earth*, London: Penguin.

Fanon, F. (1986) *Black Skins White Masks*, London: Pluto Press.

Federici, S. (2004) Women, land-struggles and globalization: An international perspective, *Journal of Asian and African Studies*, 39(1–2): 47–62.

Federici, S. (2011) Women, land struggles, and the reconstruction of the commons, *WorkingUSA*, 14(1): 41–56.

Foucault, M. (1975) *Discipline and Punish: The birth of the prison*, London: Penguin.

Frank, A. (1970) *Latin America: Underdevelopment or Revolution*, New York: Monthly Review Press.

Gramsci, A. (1992) *Prison Notebooks Volume 1* (translated by J.A. Buttigieg and A. Callari), New York: Columbia University Press.

Hall, S. (1996) New ethnicities, in: D. Morley and K. Chen (eds) *Stuart Hall: Critical dialogues in cultural studies*, London: Routledge, pp 442–451.

Harris, J. (2021) Global capitalism and the battle for hegemony, *Science & Society*, 85(3): 332–359.

Hart, C. (2015) *Aspirations, Education and Social Justice*, London: Bloomsbury.

Harvey, D. (2003) *The New Imperialism*, Oxford: Oxford University Press.

Harvey, D. (2011) *The Enigma of Capital and the Crises of Capitalism.* London: Profile Books.

ICFE (2021) *Reimagining our Futures Together: A new social contract for education*, Paris: UNESCO.

Jackson, T. (2016) *Prosperity Without Growth*, London: Routledge.

Jimmy, E., Andreotti, V. and Stein, S. (2020) *Towards Braiding*, Gesturing Towards Decolonial Futures Collective.

Latouche, S. (2007) *Le Pari,* Paris: Fayard.

Latouche, S. (2010) *Farewell to Growth,* London: Wiley.

Leff, H. (1999) Educação ambiental e desenvolvimento sustentável. [Environmental education and sustainable development], in: M. Reigota and D. De Paulo (eds) *Verde cotidiano: Meio ambiente em questão,* Rio de Janeiro: De Paulo Ed, pp 111–130.

Legassick, M. and Hemson, D. (1976) *Foreign Investment and the Introduction of Racial Capitalism in South Africa,* London: Anti-Apartheid Movement.

Lélé, S. M. (1991) Sustainable development: A critical review, *World Development*, 19(6): 607–621.

Levitas, R. (2013) *Utopia as Method: The imaginary reconstitution of society*, Basingstoke: Palgrave Macmillan.

Lotz-Sisitka, H. (2004) Positioning Southern African environmental education in a changing context, Environmental Education Research, 10: 291–295.

Lotz-Sisitka, H. and Ramsarup, P. (2019) Green skills research: Implications for systems, policy, work and learning, in: E. Rosenberg, P. Ramsarup and H. Lotz-Sisitka (eds) *Green Skills Research in South Africa: Models, cases and methods*, London: Routledge.

Lotz-Sisitka, H., Shumba, O., Lupele, J. et al (2017) Schooling for Sustainable Development in Africa, Switzerland: Springer.

Maclean, R. and Wilson, D. (2011) International Handbook of Education for the Changing World of Work: Bridging academic and vocational learning, Netherlands: Springer.

Maldonado-Torres, N. (2007) On coloniality of being: Contributions to the development of a concept, *Cultural Studies*, 21(2–2): 240–270.

Maware, M. and Mubaye, T. (2016) African Philosophy and Thought Systems: A search for a culture and philosophy of belonging. Mankon: Langaa RPCIG.

Mbembe, A. (2016) Decolonizing the University: New directions, *Arts and Humanities in Higher Education,* 15(1): 29–45.

Mbembe, A. and Posel, D. (2005) A critical humanism, *Interventions*, 7(3): 283–286.

McGrath, S. (2020) Skills for Sustainable Livelihoods, Bristol: TESF.

McGrath, S., Powell, L., Alla-Mensah, J. et al (2020) New VET theories for new times: The critical capabilities approach to vocational education and training and its potential for theorising a transformed and transformational VET, Journal of Vocational Education and Training, e-pub ahead of print June 2020, DOI: 10.1080/13636820.2020.1786440.

McGrath, S., Ramsarup, P., Zeelen, J. et al (2019) Vocational education and training for African development, Journal of Vocational Education and Training, DOI: doi.org/10.1080/13636820.2019. 1679969.

Mundy, K. and Murphy, L. (2001) Transnational advocacy, global civil society? Emerging evidence from the field of education, *Comparative Education Review,* 45(1): 85–126.

Murove, M. F. (2009) An African environmental ethic based on the concepts of ukama and ubuntu, in: M. F. Murove (ed.) *African Ethics: An anthology for comparative and applied ethics*, Pietermaritzburg: University of Kwazulu-Natal Press, pp 154–186.

Ndlovu-Gatsheni, S. (2013) *Coloniality of Power in Postcolonial Africa,* Senegal: CODESRIA.

Ndlovu-Gatsheni, S. (2015) Decoloniality as the future of Africa, *History Compass,* 13(10): 485–496.

NGO Forum, (1992) The People's Earth Declaration: A proactive agenda for the future, Rio de Janeiro: NGO Forum.

Nkrumah, K. (1966) *Neo-colonialism: The last stage of imperialism*, London: Thomas Nelson and Sons.

Nussbaum, M. (2006) The moral status of animals, *Review of The Chronicle of Higher Education*, 52(22): B6-B8.

Nussbaum, M. (2011) *Creating Capabilities*, London: Harvard University Press.

Nustad, K. (1996) The politics of 'development': Power and changing discourses in South Africa, *Cambridge Anthropology*, 19(1): 57–72.

Nyerere, J. (1967) Education for Self-Reliance, Dar Es Salaam: Ministry of Information and Tourism.

O'Donoghue, R. and McNaught, C. (1991) Environmental education: The development of a curriculum through 'grass-roots' reconstructive action, *International Journal of Science Education,* 13(4): 391–404.

OECD (2014) Report on the OECD Framework for Inclusive Growth, available at: oecd.org/mcm/IG_MCM_ENG.pdf [accessed 6 February 2023].

Piron, L-H. with O'Neill, T. (2005) *Integrating Human Rights into Development: A synthesis of donor approaches and experiences*, London: ODI.

Powell, L. and McGrath, S. (2019) *Skills for Human Development: Transforming vocational education and training*, London: Routledge.

Prigogine, I. (1997) *The End of Certainty: Time, chaos, and the new laws of nature,* London: Free Press.

Raworth, K. (2017) *Doughnut Economics: Seven ways to think like a 21st Century economist*, London: RH Business Books.

REEP, S. (2012) Learning for a sustainable future: Fifteen years of Swedish-SADC co-operation in environment and sustainability education, Stockholm: SIDA.

Rege, S. (2007) Dalit studies as pedagogical practice: Claiming more than just a 'little place' in the academia, *Review of Development and Change,* 12(1): 1–33.

Rist, G. (1997) *The History of Development: from Western origins to global faith*, London: Zed Books.

Robeyns, I. (2017) *Wellbeing, Freedom and Social Justice*, Cambridge: Open Book Publishers.

Robinson, C. (1984) *Black Marxism: The making of the Black radical tradition*, London: Penguin.

Rodney, W. (1973) *How Europe Underdeveloped Africa*, London: Bogle-L'Ouverture Publications.

Rosenberg, E., Ramsarup, P. and Lotz-Sisitka, H. (2020) *Green Skills Research in South Africa*, Abingdon: Routledge.

Rostow, W. (1960) *The Stages of Economic Growth*, Cambridge: Cambridge University Press.

Said, E. (1978) *Orientalism*, New York: Pantheon Books.

Sardar, Z. (1999) Development and the locations of eurocentricism, in: R. Munck and D. O'Hearn (eds) *Critical Development Theory*, London: Zed Books, pp 44–62.

Saunders, K. (2004) Feminist Post-Development Thought: Rethinking modernity, post-colonialism and representation, New Delhi: Zubaan.

Schlosberg, D. (2004) Reconceiving environmental justice: Global movements and political theories, *Review of Environmental Politics*, 13(3): 517–540.

Schlosberg, D. (2007) Defining Environmental Justice: Theories, Movements and Nature, Oxford: Oxford University Press.

Sen, A. (2011) The Idea of Justice, Cambridge, MA: Harvard University Press.

Sen, A. (2013) The ends and means of sustainability, *Review of Journal of Human Development and Capabilities*, 14(1): 6-20.

Sharma, D. and Tygstrup, F. (2015) Structures of Feeling, Berlin: De Gruyter.

Spivak, G.C. (1988) Can the subaltern speak?, in: C. Nelson and L. Grossberg (eds) *Marxism and the Interpretation of Culture*, London: MacMillan, pp 24–28.

Sriprakash, A., Tikly, L., and Walker, S. (2019) The erasures of racism in education and international development: re-reading the 'global learning crisis', *Compare*, DOI: 10.1080/03057925.2018.1559040.

Stein, S. (2019) The ethical and ecological limits of sustainability: A decolonial approach to climate change in higher education, *Australian Journal of Environmental Education*, 35(3): 198–212.

Stein, S. (2020) Gesturing towards decolonial futures, *Nordic Journal of Comparative and International Education*, 4(1): 43–65.

Stein, S., Andreotti V. and Suša, R. (2019) 'Beyond 2015', within the modern/colonial global imaginary? Global development and higher education, *Critical Studies in Education*, 60(3): 281–301.

Subrahmanian, R. (2002) Engendering education: Prospects for a rights-based approach to female education deprivation in India, in: M. Molyneux and S. Razavi (eds) *Gender Justice, Development, and Rights*, Oxford: Oxford University Press, pp 204–237.

Swilling M (2020) *The Age of Sustainability*, Abingdon: Routledge.

Tikly, L. (2003) The African Renaissance, NEPAD and skills formation: An identification of key policy tensions, *International Journal of Educational Development*, 23: 543–564.

Tikly, L. (2004) Education and the new imperialism, *Comparative Education*, 40(2): 173–198.

Tikly, L. (2016) Language-in-education policy in low-income, postcolonial contexts: towards a social justice approach, *Comparative Education*, 52(3): 408–425.

Tikly, L. (2017) The future of Education for All as a global regime of educational governance, *Comparative Education Review*, 61(1): 22–57.

Tikly, L. (2020) *Education for Sustainable Development in the Postcolonial World: Towards a transformative agenda for Africa*, Abingdon: Routledge.

Tikly, L. and Barrett, A. (2013) Education Quality and Social Justice in the Global South: Challenges for policy, practice and research, Abingdon: Routledge.

Tikly, L., Duporge, V., Herring, E. et al (2020) Transforming Education for Sustainable Futures, Bristol, TESF Foundations paper, DOI: https://doi.org/10.5281/zenodo.4279935.

UN (2015) Transforming Our World: The 2030 agenda for sustainable development, available at: sdgs.un.org/2030agenda [accessed 6 February 2023].

UNDP (1998) *Integrating Human Rights with Sustainable Human Development: A UNDP policy document*, New York: UNDP.

UNDP (2017) UNDP's Strategy for Inclusive and Sustainable Growth, available at: undp.org/publications/undps-strategy-inclusive-and-sustainable-growth [accessed 6 February 3023].

Unterhalter, E. (2007) *Gender, Schooling and Global Social Justice*, London: Routledge.

Unterhalter, E., Challender, C., and Rajagopalan, R. (2005) Measuring gender equality in education, in: S. Aikman and E. Unterhalter (eds) *Beyond Access: Transforming policy and practice for gender equality in education*, Oxford: Oxfam GB, pp 60–79.

Urry, J. (2016) *What is the Future?*, Cambridge: Polity Press.

Vally, S. and Motala, E. (2014) *Education, Economy & Society*, Unisa Press.

Walby, S. (2009) *Globalization and Inequalities: complexity and contested modernity*, London: Sage.

Walby, S. (2015) *Crisis*, Cambridge: Polity Press.

Walker, M. (2006) *Higher Education Pedagogies: A capabilities approach*, Maidenhead: Open University Press.

Walker, M. (2019) Why epistemic justice matters in and for education, *Asia Pacific Educ. Rev*, 20: 161–170.

Wals, A.E.J. and Kieft, G. (2010) Education for Sustainable Development: Research overview, Sida, https://edepot.wur.nl/161396.

wa Thiong'o, N. (1986) *Decolonising the Mind: The politics of language in African literature*, Woodbridge: James Currey.

WCED (1987) *Our Common Future*, Oxford: Oxford University Press.

Wells, J. (2013) *Complexity and Sustainability*, London: Routledge.

Whyte, K. (2020) Too late for Indigenous climate justice: Ecological and relational tipping points, *Wiley Interdisciplinary Reviews: Climate Change*, 11(1): 1.

Williams, R. (1977) *Marxism and Literature*, Oxford: Oxford University Press.

Wilson, K. (2012) *Race, Racism and Development: Interrogating history, discourse and practice*, London: Zed Books.

Wolpe, H. (1988) *Race, Class and the Apartheid State*, Paris: UNESCO.

World Bank (2012) *Inclusive Green Growth*, World Bank Publications.

World Economic Forum (2015) The New Vision for Education: Unlocking the potential of technology, available at: widgets.weforum.org/nve-2015/index.html [accessed 7 February 2023].

2

Learning to Become With the World: Education for Future Survival

Common Worlds Research Collective[1]

> If our species does not survive the ecological crisis, it will probably be due to our failure to imagine and work out new ways to live with the earth ... We will go onwards in a different mode of humanity, or not at all
>
> Val Plumwood, 'A review of Deborah Bird Rose's "Reports from a Wild Country: Ethics for Decolonisation"', 2007

Introduction: education for future survival

We live in a critical moment of epochal transition from the Holocene into the Anthropocene ('the Age of Man'), in which human forces have fundamentally altered the planet's geo/biospheric systems, triggering a cascade of ecological crises and threatening the future of life on Earth as we have known it, including that of our own species (Crutzen, 2002; Steffen et al, 2007). As our carbon emissions continue to overheat the planet, we face a climatic trajectory of intensifying floods, droughts and fires (IPCC, 2018). As we continue to clear forests, destroy habitats, and diminish biodiversity, we precipitate mass displacements and extinctions and create the conditions for ongoing, devastating, zoonotic pandemics (Grandcolas and Justine, 2020). Without the will to redress the root causes of the Anthropocene, we are now suffering the tragic consequences. Like Plumwood (2007), we believe that first and foremost this is indicative of our failure to imagine alternative ways of living with the Earth.

Education is directly implicated in the crises of the Anthropocene and our failure to imagine alternatives. Despite efforts to promote education as key to achieving sustainable lives, schools and higher education systems continue to prioritize workforce supply for economic growth over environmental sustainability. The Cartesian dualisms that structure our curricula and pedagogies are instrumental in perpetuating the delusion that we are somehow separate from the world around us and can act upon it with impunity (Taylor and Pacini-Ketchabaw, 2018). The fact that the world has the highest number of 'educated' people in its history and yet is the nearest to ecological breakdown is a stark reminder that 'more of the same kind of education will only compound our problems' (Orr, 2011, p 238; see also Komatsu et al, 2020; Rappleye and Komatsu, 2020; Silova, 2020). In the face of the multiple existential threats that we have brought upon ourselves, business as usual is no longer an option. It is time to step up to the challenge and fundamentally reconfigure the role of education and schooling in order to radically reimagine and relearn our place and agency in the world.

To this end, we offer seven visionary declarations of what education could look like in 2050 and beyond. These declarations are based on three premises. First, that human and planetary sustainability are one and the same thing. We are an inseparable part of the ecosystems we have perilously destabilized and which now threaten life on Earth as we have known it. Second, that any attempts to achieve sustainable futures by continuing to separate humans from the rest of the world are delusional and futile, even if the intentions are well meaning. And third, that education must play a pivotal role in radically reconfiguring the ways we think about our place and agency within this interdependent world and, therefore, the ways we act. This requires a complete paradigm shift, from learning about the world in order to act upon it to learning to become with the world around us. Our future survival depends on our capacity to make this shift.

Visionary declarations for education by 2050

1. By 2050, we have critically reassessed and reconfigured the relationship between education and humanism. We now retain the best aspect of education's previous humanist mission – to promote justice – but extend it beyond an exclusively human or social framework.

Education's new remit is to promote ecological justice by teaching the arts of living respectfully and responsibly on a damaged planet (Tsing et al, 2017) and learning how to survive well together (Haraway, 2016). Along with this ecological reframing of justice, we have radically reassessed education's humanist knowledge traditions.

Now wary of human-centric modes of thinking and acting, we actively resist the premise of human exceptionalism and refuse the perilous proposition of human dominion on Earth.

As the 21st century unfolded, it became increasingly clear that capitalist extraction, production and consumption, so closely associated with human 'progress and development', were not only unsustainable but had fundamentally destabilized Earth's geo-biospheric systems. Faith in education's key role to ensure 'sustainable development' (UNESCO, 2019) waned, and it became impossible to deny that humanist education had been co-opted by a myopic obsession with perpetual economic growth in the guise of human advancement. Humanist-inspired projects aimed at achieving social justice, equality and sustainability had been hijacked by economic development and productivity agendas.

When the UN's (2015) sustainable development goals (SDGs) failed to be met by 2030, we were forced to admit that its foundational humanist epistemologies were incapable of addressing the cascading ecological crises threatening the future of life on Earth. Even more confronting, we had to acknowledge that by reiterating and perpetuating delusional, human-centric and exceptionalist preoccupations, education had become part of the problem, not the solution (Silova et al, 2018; Komatsu et al, 2020). By 2050, we have finally discarded the Cartesian dualisms that structured the unswerving humanist belief that our supreme rationality and the exclusivity of our intentional agency sets us apart from, and above, the rest of the living world (Plumwood, 1993). We have also debunked the associated belief that humans can endlessly act upon the rest of the world with impunity – either to exploit its resources or to 'improve' upon it at will. In short, we have undone the Euro-Western human-centric stranglehold on education.

To consolidate a more-than-human notion of justice and meet education's new charter of learning how to survive well together (Haraway, 2016), we have sought out ecologically attuned alternatives that acknowledge the collective agency and interdependence of all earthly beings, entities and forces. We have taken on board the critiques of humanism's lacunae disseminated by Western scholars in response to the Anthropocene (Gibson et al, 2015; Haraway, 2016; Stengers, 2017; Latour, 2018), and abandoned the totalizing Euro-Western epistemologies that propped up the 'one-world' framework (Carney et al, 2012; Law, 2015) that was driving neoliberal globalization for much of the late 20th and early 21st centuries.

In looking 'beyond the Western horizon' (Silova et al, 2020), we have increasingly engaged with the 'pluriversal' frameworks (Mignolo, 2011; Escobar, 2018; Kothari et al, 2019) associated with the 'epistemologies of the South' (Connell, 2007; Santos, 2014) and other non-Western thought traditions that presuppose that there are infinite human and more-than-human worlds within worlds, all of which are animate and radically interdependent. We have also acknowledged that there is much to be learned from land-based Indigenous relational ontologies, not the least because Indigenous ways of knowing and being in reciprocal relationship with the land and all its creatures provide an ancient blueprint for sustainable living (Rose, 1992 and 2011a; Turner, 2010; LeGrange, 2018; Tallbear, 2019).

Through learning and teaching the principles of pluriversality – including the multiplicity of ways of knowing and being, the wisdom of Indigenous ontologies, and the animacy of worlds beyond the human – we have expanded our notion of justice. As a result, the practice of education is now infinitely more inclusive.

2. By 2050, we have fully acknowledged that humans are embedded within ecosystems and that we are ecological, not just social, beings. We have dissolved the boundaries between 'natural' and 'social' sciences, and all curricula and pedagogies are now firmly grounded in an ecological consciousness.

It took us a while to break with the delusion that we live and learn in autonomous human societies, which are somehow outside the 'natural' ecological communities that we 'study'. It was hard to fully understand ourselves as ecological insiders. At first it was more of a halfway or partial recognition. In the early part of the 21st century, some were starting to heed the scientists' warning that our dangerous levels of carbon emissions were triggering planetary-scaled ecosystems' collapse that would ultimately threaten us (Ripple et al, 2020). But we still had an enduring faith in human ingenuity to 'fix' or at least 'manage' these problems – as if we still had a foot outside these ecosystems. This was evidenced by decade-long debates that pivoted around whether we should prioritize human adaptation to or mitigation of disturbed and degraded environments. The reiteration of notions such as ecosystems 'servicing' human well-being (Millennium Ecosystem Assessment, 2005) exemplified how emerging understandings that healthy ecologies are essential for sustaining human life initially fell short of conveying that we are inseparable constituents of these same ecologies. It took some time to stop splitting ourselves off and to let go of the double delusion that ecosystems exist to serve and sustain us, and that we can 'manage' them to this end.

The continuing disciplinary divide between the social and the natural sciences remained a lingering obstacle to the recognition of our ecological being (Matthews, 1991) and to a fully integrated approach to unfolding ecological catastrophes. Despite the UN's (2015) insistence that the three pillars of SDGs – economic, cultural and environmental – were all 'interconnected', 'indivisible' and 'balanced', they were still differentiated along disciplinary lines. Following the adoption of SDGs in 2015, the goals associated with increasing economic growth and achieving social equity were consistently prioritized over the environmental ones. Notably, as education was predominantly aligned with the social sciences, most educators focused on the human development goals, believing they were critical for redressing social inequities concentrated in the global South and among pockets of Indigenous and other marginalized peoples living in the global North. Environmental goals were primarily addressed through science and technology curricula, promoting techno-fixes and managerial stewardship as the ultimate solution.

But history revealed these to be false divisions and choices. By 2030, it was clear that the historical pattern of exploitation of colonized lands and peoples by the overdeveloped global North was even more entrenched. Social inequity gaps had widened and environmental goals were far from met. Moreover, those in the global South who had the smallest ecological footprint and were the least responsible for precipitating the accelerating ecological crises were tragically the most adversely affected by them. Failure to meet the 2030 SDGs prompted a critical reassessment of the implicit dualisms that continued to thwart the achievement of not just interconnected but inextricably enmeshed human and environmental goals.

With the ultimate, harsh realization that human fates are inextricably bound up with those of all other beings, elements and forces on this living Earth, we finally came to accept that living and learning is a facet of ecological being (Taylor, 2020). Having dissolved the disciplinary boundaries between the 'natural' and the 'human' sciences, we now practice education with an overarching ecological consciousness.

3. By 2050, we have stopped using education as a vehicle for promulgating human exceptionalism. We are teaching that agency is relational, collectively distributed and more-than-human.

Now that we have broken with the anthropocentric preoccupations of modern schooling, we no longer promote human exceptionalism and its baseline Cartesian logics of exclusive human rationality and intentional agency. In hindsight, we can see that it was these delusional logics that justified the hierarchical and exploitative 'man–over–nature' relations that resulted in the Anthropocene. We also recognize that modern education systematically perpetrated human exceptionalism, by positioning teachers and students as the agentic all-knowing subjects and the world 'out there' as the inert matter to be studied and known about. Because educators, like everyone else, were once well schooled in these human exceptionalist logics, it is still hard for us to accept that the world is not simply ours to study and act upon at will (Stengers, 2017). It is hard to escape the self-fulfilling logics of human exceptionalism – to resist the heroic impulse to fix the ecological crises we have caused, by coming up with smarter, bigger and better 'humans-to-the rescue' solutions (Taylor, 2019).

It has been helpful to remind ourselves that, despite its systematic uptake within mainstream education, human exceptionalism and (neo)liberal individualism have never been universally embraced. They are anathema to Indigenous and African cosmologies and sacred and ancient land knowledges (Rose, 1992 and 2011a; Martin and Mirraboopa, 2003; LeGrange, 2012 and 2018; Tallbear, 2015; Styres, 2019), antithetical to a multiplicity of local knowledge systems and eco-activist movements in the South Americas (Viveiros de Castro, 2004; Mignolo, 2011; Escobar, 2018), and inconsistent with Asian philosophical traditions (Zhao, 2009; Abe, 2014; Sevilla, 2015; Komatsu and Rappleye, 2020).

The Cartesian bedrock of human exceptionalism has also had powerful internal critics. Ever since the late 20th century, a swathe of Western philosophers and theorists, who came to be associated with the post-humanities, were starting to dispute hierarchies of being, with humans at the apex. They were replacing these hierarchies with flattened ontologies akin to 'assemblages' or 'networks' of multiple human and non-human actors with distributed agency (Deleuze and Guattari, 1987; Latour, 1993, 2004, 2005). They took on the nature/culture 'great divide' (Latour, 1993) and blurred the categorical boundaries between humans, animals and machines, giving us the hybrid notion of 'cyborgs' and 'naturecultures' (Haraway, 1985 and 1988). They exposed how the structuring dualisms that assert humans' 'mastery of nature' amount to no more than a disavowed dependency upon a subordinated other, whose agency is denied (Plumwood, 1993 and 2002; Merchant, 1996). They stressed the symbiogenesis of all life (Haraway, 2008a and 2008b) and the lively and agentic interactions between all kinds of matter (Barad, 2007 and 2008; Alaimo and Hekman, 2009; Bennett, 2010). In short, they argued that agency is not something that is 'held' and 'exercised' exclusively by humans but emerges as an effect of constellating human and non-human relations and forces.

By the early 21st century, a deepening understanding of agency as collective, more-than-human, and relational made inroads into the academic research in the field of education (Bowers, 1995; Waghid and Smeyers, 2012; Waghid, 2014; Snaza and Weaver, 2015; Taylor and Hughes, 2016; LeGrange, 2018; Zhao, 2018; Petrovic and Mitchell, 2018; Ringrose et al, 2018; Tuhiwai Smith et al, 2019; Takayama, 2020). However, these more-than-human reconceptualizations of agency were much slower to gain traction in education policy and the everyday practice of schooling. It was not until the effects of the Anthropocene really started to bite in the mid-2020s that we had to acknowledge that we needed to tap into the Earth's transformative powers because we could not do it alone. To this end, we began the enormous task of radically reconfiguring our curricula and pedagogies in accordance with more-than-human, collective and relational notions of agency. Instead of relying on human ingenuity and technology as the ultimate 'fix' for environmental problems, we are now learning how to take our place as one of many actors, makers and shapers of life on Earth.

4. By 2050, we have discarded education's human development/ al frameworks. Instead of championing individualism, we now foster collective dispositions and convivial, reparative, human and more-than-human relations.

With the benefit of hindsight, we can see now that the human development/ al frameworks that dominated education throughout the 20th and early 21st centuries were part of the much bigger imperialist project to 'modernize the world' in line with teleological Western notions of progress and development. We can clearly see that normative Western notions of 'advancement' were used as universalized standards against which the deficit notion of 'developing' individuals/cultures/nations was measured (Kothari et al, 2019).

Within education, developmental logics were originally fostered through the child-study movement of the late 19th and early 20th centuries that called for widespread scientific observation of children. Developmental psychology became the dominant discourse and produced a universalized understanding of 'the child' and a normative set of child development stages. Within this totalizing discourse, 'the individual child' was seen as moving through these stages, separate and abstracted from the world.

By the late 20th century, child-centred learning had become a revered concept of developmentalism, and it persisted well into the early 21st century. Early years and primary curricula began with the needs and interests of the child and responded to their unique characteristics. Pedagogies reinforced and supported the individual child learner in becoming autonomous, self-regulating, rational and agentic. As an ideology, child- or learner-centred pedagogy was seductive because it drew upon seemingly 'progressive' Western values, such as democracy and individual freedom (Cannella, 1997; Komatsu et al, 2021). For decades, it was routinely promoted by international development agencies as a universal 'best practice', which displaced and sometimes eliminated alternative education practices in various contexts.

As the effects of the Anthropocene started to hit home in the 2020s, it became obvious that education was not preparing young learners for the precarious ecological futures they face, and that something radically different to the outdated individualistic 20th-century human developmental frameworks was needed. Education for sustainable development had also been discredited by this stage, as it was obvious that all 'development' agendas had been thoroughly appropriated by carboniferous capitalist economic interests and concerns.

It was students themselves who pointed this out. From 2018 onwards, a growing school student movement brought millions across the world to the streets, proclaiming unending economic growth and development as an ecological catastrophe, and demanding that governments and national leaders take urgent action on climate change. They could see that education had to fundamentally change in order to be part of the solution, not part of the problem. They called for a radically different kind of education for their future survival. Educators started listening and mobilized in support (Calling Educators to Action on Climate Crisis, 2020).

At the students' insistence, we have now permanently delinked education from the twin logics of infinite economic growth and human development and re-sutured it to the logics of ecological survival. In recognition that human and more-than-human fates and futures are indistinguishable in the Anthropocene (Taylor and Pacini-Ketchabaw, 2018), we have reconfigured education around the principles of interdependence and interconnectedness that make everyone and everything a part of the Earth's ecological community.

The individualistic culture of the self is now a thing of the past. Collective dispositions are the order of the day (Taylor, 2013). Our educational practices are now characterized by an openness to the 'other' – whether other humans, species, land, ancestors, or cyborgs and machines. These open relations constitute a convivial and reparative stance that 'welcomes surprise, entertains hope, makes connections, tolerates coexistence, and offers care for the new' (Gibson-Graham, 2006, p 8).

5. By 2050, we have recognized that we live and learn in a world. Our pedagogies no longer position the world 'out-there' as the object we are learning about. Learning to become with the world is a situated practice and a more-than-human pedagogical collaboration.

The new charter of teaching and learning the arts of living responsibly and respectfully on a damaged Earth has required us to challenge education's most fundamental binary – the subject/object divide. Throughout the 20th century and into the early 21st century, this remained unchallenged. It was taken for granted that the business of education was to teach its (rational) human subjects about the world (out there). The world had always been the object of study, and humans had always been the knowing subjects, learning about this exteriorized world. In the new charter, it is simply not possible for educators to continue to draw upon and reproduce this subject/object divide. We now proceed with an ecological consciousness that firmly repositions all humans as ecological insiders, always already embedded within ecosystems.

Some of the earliest pedagogical initiatives to move beyond the established practice of learning about the world, from a distance, came from the field of early childhood education. Educators from the Common Worlds Research Collective (2020) took advantage of the fact that pre-school-aged children, who are not yet fully enculturated into the subject/object divides of modern Western education and its humanist premises, are less likely to separate themselves from the rest of the world. By focusing on the unfolding pedagogical relations between young children and more-than-human others in their common worlds, these educators started to experiment with possibilities for collaborative and collective more-than-human learning with the world (Pacini-Ketchabaw et al, 2016; Blaise et al, 2017; Taylor and Pacini-Ketchabaw, 2018; Taylor, 2019).

Subsequently, educators in a wide range of sectors (comparative education, artificial intelligence, higher education and others) also grappled with the task of reframing learning beyond the subject/object divide. By focusing on worldly relations and encounters as inherently pedagogical, acknowledging that it is not only humans that teach and learn, and by mobilizing human curiosity to learn from what is already going on in the world, we have finally managed to make the shift from only ever learning *about* the world to learning *with* it.

This also means we have adopted 'situated' pedagogical practices, which refuse 'the promise of transcendence' that is embedded in only ever learning about (Haraway, 1988). Through our situated pedagogies we insist on 'staying with the trouble' of learning with our real damaged Earth and all of our cohabitants (Haraway, 2016). We now speak from and think with partial worldly perspectives, embodied visions, and with an awareness of the non-innocence of our positions (Haraway, 1988). Learning with the world is allowing us to live well with(in) the contradictions and dangers we face, and to respond to our troubling and violent inheritances, such as anthropogenic mass displacements and extinctions of many kinds. Educators and students alike are now aware that we all act from somewhere. We know we are accountable to those who are with us and to the places we cohabit.

Perhaps most importantly, we have not lost hope. The proposition of situated pedagogies has become an insistence on learning to make 'a better account of the world' (Haraway, 1988). We have come a long way from the 'one-world' world view (Law, 2015) that presumptuously advanced a universalized Western notion of 'education for all', towards responsibly promoting situated learning as a means to co-construct worlds that are more liveable for all. We are enthusiastically undertaking the collective task of learning with those in our common worlds, as a mode of remaking these worlds together.

6. By 2050, we have re-tasked education with a cosmopolitical remit. This has moved it far beyond the universalist and anthropocentric claims of humanist, humanitarian, and human rights perspectives.

Educators now fully embrace the principles of cosmopolitics and acknowledge pluriversality, or the coexistence of many different worlds. We no longer adhere to the widely accepted humanist 'UNESCO lingua franca', dating back to the establishment of the United Nations in 1945 but also including its most recent iteration of the 'new humanism'. This humanitarian charter not only failed to achieve world peace, but also revealed that the 'humanistic definition of an emancipated human' was simply insufficient to define all inhabitants of the planet (Latour, 2004, p 457). Instead of speaking of a single world revealed through many perspectives, cosmopolitical educational approaches acknowledge both the multiplicity of interconnected worlds and our entanglements in multi-species ecologies that include different knowledges, practices and technologies. In the term cosmopolitical, cosmos 'refers to the unknown constituted by these multiple, divergent worlds, and to the articulations of which they could eventually be capable, as opposed to the temptation of a peace intended to be final, ecumenical' (Stengers, 2005, p 995).

Drawing on the principles of cosmopolitics enabled us to adopt a much broader definition of what it means 'to belong' – one that embraces everyone and everything both living and non-living – and therefore encompasses more-than-human worlds. It gave us the opportunity to learn and practice 'articulations' among multiple, divergent worlds. This not only interrupted the principle of universality, but enabled us to get on with the task of collectively assembling common worlds through networks of human and more-than-human actors (Latour, 2005). Noticing, learning with, and paying care(ful) attention became key for cosmopolitical modes of education, because common worlds do not pre-exist their articulations but need to be 'slowly composed' in the presence of others, both human and more than human (Latour, 2004, p 457). We now see the practice of cosmopolitical education as integral to the processes of 'becoming worldly', 'worlding with', or 'becoming with' (Haraway, 2003, 2004, 2008b).

Even though our new kind of education is deeply relational, it does not rely on an innocent notion of relationality. Instead, it attends to the ethics and politics of living with radically uneven and incommensurable difference, recognizing our allies in 'transgressed boundaries' and 'potent and taboo fusions' across gender, race, class, species, machines and matter (Haraway, 1985, p 52). Such learning requires a type of transversal thinking that takes 'issue with human exceptionalism while being accountable for the role we play in the differential constitution and differential positioning of the human among other creatures' (Barad, 2007, p 136). As we learned from and with our fusions with animals, matter and machines over several decades, we simultaneously unlearned how to 'be Man, the embodiment of Western logos' (Haraway, 1985, p 52). This transformed the education space to become a critical part of 'a pluriverse in the making' (Stengers, 2011, p 61), where everyone and everything can now contribute to the process of articulating or making the pluriverse.

By 2050, the practice of cosmopolitics has permeated education, culture and politics to such an extent that United Nations members are no longer satisfied to be 'just humans ... as the only acceptable member of the

Club' (Latour, 2004, p 257). In a General Assembly in September 2050, several sessions were dedicated to a thorough review of the limitations of UN's logics of human-centeredness and the urgency of philosophical and organizational changes necessary to overcome the UN's parochial allegiance to cosmopolitanism. Following intense deliberations, it was unanimously decided to replace 'Nations' with 'Naturescultures', signaling a full embrace of the principles of cosmopolitics as a practice – and an art – of living and dying as well as is possible together on a damaged planet.

7. By 2050, the goal of education for future survival has led us to prioritize an ethics of collective recuperation on this damaged Earth.

We have now completely reimagined and reconfigured education around the future survival of our planet. We have resituated the practice of education in common worlds because we no longer differentiate between the social and the environmental, and no longer frame pedagogy as an exclusively human activity. Motivated by a commitment to seeking intergenerational and multi-species justice on this damaged Earth (Taylor and Pacini-Ketchabaw, 2018), we have shifted the goal of education from a humanitarian charter to one of ecological justice. Consistent with all of these shifts, we have adopted a completely new mode of ethics that is collective, more-than-human and recuperative. Our new visions and ethics render the old notions of education for sustainable development (ESD) completely redundant.

By the early 2020s, it was widely acknowledged that ESD strategies had failed. The collapse of the Paris Agreement on carbon emission reductions, persistent, student-led global uprisings for climate action, and the ICS official declaration of the Anthropocene (Subramanian, 2019) made it untenable to keep denying the obvious – that any form of carboniferous economic development thwarts the attainment of environmental sustainability targets. We could see that even education programmes that promoted sustainability without coupling it with development still rehearsed the nature/culture divide. Those based around the principle of environmental stewardship still separated humans from the environment as its 'caretakers' and 'protectors' (Taylor, 2017). Similarly, it was clear that the presumption that we could ultimately 'save' the planet through educating a green generation and using human ingenuity to find technological solutions was also based on the delusion of human exceptionalism. Such programmes and visions did not meet the key challenge of the times – to attain and sustain a firmly grounded ecological imagination, one in which we reposition ourselves fully within the environment, and stay there (Gibson et al, 2015).

By letting go of the grandiose fantasies of humans saving the environment, we have now been able to focus on the much more modest goal of collaboratively attending to the mutual flourishing of all – human and more than human – and on recuperating our damaged common worlds together, even if only partial recuperation is possible. We have finally learned the lesson that to achieve ecological justice we must attend to our relations with others, in all their specificities (Rose, 2011b; van Dooren, 2019). By recognizing the value of our relations with Earth-others in the quest for ecological justice, we are now taking an ethical stance that deviates radically from the assumed moral high ground of human mastery and control. This ethical stance has had a profound influence on the UN. Embracing its new name and cosmopolitical principles, it now attends to the ongoing-ness of worldly relations and grapples with the question: What kinds of worlds might we recuperate together in the midst of destruction? It has become clear that the answer to this can only be enacted through the process of commoning: of humans becoming with Earth-others, as we all recompose worlds together (Haraway, 2016).

Conclusion: learning to become *with* the world

In our visionary declarations, we have speculated that, by 2050, education will be radically reconfigured around survival in the Anthropocene. We have focused upon future survival because we contend that the unravelling of anthropogenic ecological catastrophes is rapidly debunking blind-faith in the grand narrative of human progress and development, and will make it increasingly untenable for education to maintain this dangerous fiction in any guise. This includes the guise of education for sustainable development, in which humans learn to better manage the environment as a precious resource for economic growth and prosperity. It also includes the guise of education fostering human ingenuity to develop new techno-fixes in order to solve the environmental catastrophes we have created and so save the planet.

As we understand it, the Anthropocene not only portends threats to the survival of humanity, it also confirms the inextricable enmeshment of human and natural histories, fates and futures. For both of these reasons, we take Anthropocene as an urgent wake-up call (Gibson et al, 2015). It calls us to expose education's foundational human progress and development discourses as dangerous mastery mythologies based upon the delusion of human hyper-separation and exceptionalism (Plumwood, 1993). The Anthropocene's call to educators is the same as that of the students' pleas for urgent climate action. If they are to have a future, business as usual is no longer an option.

This is why our speculative visions for future survival declare the need for a fundamental break with humanist education (new or not). This is why we call for an interrelated series of shifts: from promoting humanism to exercising an ecological consciousness; from working for social justice to working for ecological justice; from understanding humans as social beings to understanding humans as ecological beings; from upholding exclusive human agency to recognizing agentic more-than-human relations; from encouraging individual development to fostering collective dispositions; from understanding teaching and learning as an exclusively human activity to approaching worldly relations as inherently pedagogical; from teaching students (as subjects) about the world (as object) to learning with others in our common worlds; from assuming universal positions and standards to considering pluriversal perspectives; from promoting human cosmopolitanism to understanding more-than-human cosmopolitics; from fostering human environmental stewardship to participating in more-than-human collective recuperative ethics; from learning how to better manage, control or save the world to learning how to become with the world.

We are convinced that the most profound challenge to making these shifts is extracting education from the Cartesian divides that structure its established humanist knowledge traditions and pedagogies. These divides – for example, mind/body, nature/culture, subject/object – ensure that we only ever learn about the world from a safe and privileged, transcendent distance. They reinforce that an exteriorized world is 'out there', separate from us and passively waiting to be 'discovered' and 'managed' by us. In other words, the divides disassociate us from our sense of ecological being and belonging – they block the ecological consciousness that we need to have.

If we are to go on, we concur that it is time for humanity to relinquish lofty self-delusions and come back 'down to Earth' (Latour, 2018). It is time to resituate ourselves as terrestrial beings firmly and fully on the grounds of our cosmopolitical common worlds, with the full ecological consciousness that we are one of many of this Earth's interdependent beings, entities and forces. It is only on these more-than-human common grounds that we can open up to what education might mean beyond the human-centric conceits and myopia that took us into this mess in the first place. It is only on these common grounds, together with all of the Earth-bound, that we can learn the collaborative, collective, mutually recuperative lessons we urgently need for future survival on this planet. We cannot do it alone. It is time for learning to become with the world in which we are already inextricably entangled and embedded and to which we will be always mortally indebted.

Note

[1]   The Common Worlds Research Collective, commonworlds.net, is an interdisciplinary network of researchers concerned with our relations with the more-than-human world. On behalf of the Collective, this discussion of the future of education has been confabulated by: Affrica Taylor, University of Canberra, Australia; Iveta Silova, Arizona State University, USA; Veronica Pacini-Ketchabaw, Western University, Canada; Mindy Blaise, Edith Cowan University, Australia.

Disclaimer

This paper was commissioned by UNESCO as a contribution to *Reimagining Our Futures Together: A new social contract for education* (UNESCO, 2021).

References

Abe, H. (2014) From symbiosis (Kyosei) to the ontology of 'Arising Both from Oneself and from Another' (Gusho), in J.B. Callicott and J. McRae (eds) *Environmental Philosophy in Asian Traditions of Thought*, New York: SUNY Press, pp 315–336.

Alaimo, S. and Hekman, S. (eds) (2009) *Material Feminisms*, Bloomington and Indianapolis: Indiana University Press.

Barad, K. (2007) *Meeting the Universe Halfway: Quantum physics and the entanglement of matter and meaning*, Durham: Duke University Press.

Barad, K. (2008) Posthumanist performativity: Toward an understanding of how matter comes to matter, in S. Alaimo and S. Hekman (eds) *Material Feminisms*, Bloomington and Indianapolis: Indiana University Press, pp 120–154.

Bennett, J. (2010) *Vibrant Matter: A political ecology of things*, Durham: Duke University Press.

Blaise, M., Hamm, C. and Iorio, J. (2017) Modest witness(ing) and lively stories: Paying attention to matters of concern in early childhood, *Pedagogy, Culture, and Society*, 25(1): 31–42, DOI: 10.1080/14681366.2016.1208265.

Bowers, C.A. (1995) *Educating for an Ecologically Sustainable Culture: Rethinking moral education, creativity, intelligence, and other moral orthodoxies*, New York: SUNY Press.

Calling Educators to Action on Climate Crisis (2020), educators-for-climate-action.com [accessed 23 January 2023].

Cannella, G.S. (1997) *Deconstructing Early Childhood Education: Social justice and revolution*, New York: Peter Lang.

Carney, S., Rappleye, J. and Silova, I. (2012) Between faith and science: World culture theory and comparative education, *Comparative Education Review*, 56(3):366–393.

Common Worlds Research Collective (2020), commonworlds.net [accessed 19 July 2020].

Connell, R. (2007) *Southern Theory*, Sydney: Allen and Unwin.

Crutzen, P. (2002) Geology of mankind, *Nature*, 415(23).

Deleuze, G. and Guattari, F. (1987) *A Thousand Plateaus: Capitalism and schizophrenia*, London: Continuum.

Escobar, A. (2018) *Designs for the Pluriverse: Radical interdependence, autonomy, and the making of worlds*, Durham and London: Duke University Press.

Gibson, K., Rose, D.B. and Fincher, R. (eds) (2015) *Manifesto for Living in the Anthropocene*, New York: Punctum Books.

Gibson-Graham, J.-K. (2006) *A Post-Capitalist Politics*, Minneapolis: University of Minnesota Press.

Grandcolas, P. and Justine, J.-L. (2020) Covid-19 or the pandemic of mistreated biodiversity?, The Conversation, available at: theconversation. com/covid-19-or-the-pandemic-of-mistreated-biodiversity-136447 [accessed 19 July 2020].

Haraway, D. (1985) A cyborg manifesto, *Socialist Review*, 80(65): 108.

Haraway, D. (1988) Situated knowledges: The science question in feminism and the privilege of partial perspectives, *Feminist Studies*, 14(3): 575–599.

Haraway, D. (2003) *The Companion Species Manifesto: Dogs, people, and significant otherness*, Chicago: Prickly Paradigm Press.

Haraway, D. (2004) *The Haraway Reader*, London and New York: Routledge.

Haraway, D. (2008a) Otherworldly conversations, terran topics, local terms, in S.Alaimo, and S. Hekman (eds) *Material Feminisms*, Bloomington and Indianapolis: Indiana University Press: 157–187.

Haraway, D. (2008b) *When Species Meet*, Minneapolis: University of Minnesota Press.

Haraway, D. (2016) *Staying with the Trouble: Making Kin in the Chthulucene*, Durham: Duke University Press.

IPCC (Intergovernmental Panel on Climate Change) (2018) Global Warming of 1.5°C, available at: ipcc.ch/sr15 [accessed 19 July 2020].

Komatsu, H. and Rappleye, J. (2020) Reimagining modern education: Contributions from modern Japanese philosophy and practice, *ECNU Review of Education*, 3(1): 20–45.

Komatsu, H., Rappleye, J. and Silova, I. (2020) Will education post-2015 move us toward environmental sustainability?, in A. Wulff (ed) *Grading Goal Four*, Leiden: Brill Sense, pp 297–321.

Komatsu, H., Silova, I. and Rappleye, J. (2021) Student-centered learning and sustainability: Solution or problem?, *Comparative Education Review*, 65(1).

Kothari, A. et al (2019) *Pluriverse: A post-development dictionary*, New York: Columbia University Press.

Latour, B. (1993) *We Have Never Been Modern*, Cambridge: Harvard University Press.

Latour, B. (2004) *The Politics of Nature: How to bring the sciences into democracy*, Cambridge, MA: Harvard University Press.

Latour, B. (2005) *Reassembling the Social: Introduction to actor network theory*, Oxford: Oxford University Press.

Latour, B. (2018) *Down to Earth: Politics in the New Climatic Regime*, New York: New York Polity Press.

Law, J. (2015) What's wrong with a one-world world?, *Distinktion: Scandinavian Journal of Social Theory*, 16(1): 126–139.

LeGrange, L. (2012) Ubuntu, ukama and the healing of nature, self and society, *Educational Philosophy and Theory*, 44: 56–57.

LeGrange, L. (2018) The notion of Ubuntu and the (post)humanist condition, in J.E. Petrovic and R.M. Mitchell (eds) *Indigenous philosophies of education around the world*, New York: Routledge, pp 40–60.

Martin, K. and Mirraboopa, B. (2003) Ways of knowing, being and doing: A theoretical framework and methods for Indigenous and indigenist re-search, *Journal of Australian Studies*, 27(76): 203–214.

Matthews, F. (1991) *The Ecological Self*, London and New York: Routledge.

Merchant, C. (1996) *Earthcare: Women and the environment*, New York: Routledge.

Mignolo, W. (2011) *The Darker Side of Western Modernity: Global futures, decolonial options*, Durham: Duke University Press.

Millennium Ecosystem Assessment (2005) Ecosystems and Human Well-Being: Synthesis, available at: millenniumassessment.org/documents/document.356.aspx.pdf [accessed 22 January 2023].

Orr, D. (2011) *Hope is an Imperative: The essential David Orr*, Washington, DC: Island Press.

Pacini-Ketchabaw, V., Taylor, A. and Blaise, M. (2016) De-centring the human in multispecies ethnographies, in C. Taylor, and C. Hughes (eds) *Posthuman Research Practices in Education*, Basingstoke: Palgrave MacMillan, pp 149–167.

Petrovic, J. and Mitchell, R. (eds) (2018) *Indigenous Philosophies of Education Around the World*, New York: Routledge.

Plumwood, V. (1993) *Feminism and Mastery of Nature*, London and New York: Routledge.

Plumwood, V. (2002) *Environmental Culture: The ecological crisis of reason*, London and New York: Routledge.

Plumwood, V. (2007) A review of Deborah Bird Rose's 'Reports from a Wild Country: Ethics for Decolonisation', available at: australianhumanitiesreview.org/2007/08/01/a-review-of-deborah-bird-roses-reports-from-a-wild-country-ethics-for-decolonisation [accessed 22 January 2023].

Rappleye, J. and Komatsu, H. (2020) Towards (comparative) educational research for a finite future, *Comparative Education*, 56(2): 190–217.

Ringrose, J., Warfield, K. and Zarabadi, S. (eds) (2018) *Feminist Posthumanisms, New Materialisms and Education*, London and New York: Routledge.

Ripple, W.J. et al (2020) World scientists' warning of a climate emergency, *BioScience*, 70(1): 8–12.

Rose, D.B. (1992) *Dingo Makes Us Human: Life and Land in an Australian Aboriginal culture*, Cambridge: Cambridge University Press.

Rose, D.B. (2011a) *Country of the Heart: An Indigenous Australian homeland*, Canberra: Aboriginal Studies Press.

Rose, D.B. (2011b) *Wild Dog Dreaming: Love and Extinction*. Charlottesville: University of Virginia Press.

Santos, B. (2014) *Epistemologies of the South: Justice against epistemicide*, Boulder: Paradigm.

Sevilla, A. (2015) Education and empty relationality: Thoughts on education and Kyoto School of Philosophy, *Journal of Philosophy of Education*, 50(4): 639–654.

Silova, I. (2020) Anticipating other worlds, animating our selves: An invitation to comparative education, *ECNU Review of Education*, 3(1): 138–159.

Silova, I., Komatsu, H. and Rappleye, J. (2018) Facing the climate change catastrophe: Education as solution or cause?, Worlds of Education, blog available at: norrag.org/facing-the-climate-change-catastrophe-education-as-solution-or-cause-by-iveta-silova-hikaru-komatsu-and-jeremy-rappleye [accessed 19 June 2022].

Silova, I., Rappleye, J. and Auld, E. (2020) Beyond the Western horizon: Rethinking education, values, and policy transfer, in G. Fan and P.S. Popkewitz (eds) *International Handbook of Education Policy Studies*, Zurich: Springer, pp 3–29.

Snaza, N. and Weaver, J.A. (eds) (2015) *Posthumanism and Educational Research*, New York: Routledge.

Steffen, W., Crutzen, P. and McNeill, J.R. (2007) The Anthropocene: Are humans now overwhelming the great forces of nature?, *AMBIO: A Journal of the Human Environment*, 36(8): 614–621.

Stengers, I. (2005) The cosmopolitical proposal, in B. Latour and P. Weibel (eds) *Making Things Public: Atmospheres of democracy*, Cambridge, MA: MIT Press, pp 994–1004.

Stengers, I. (2011) Comparison as a matter of concern, *Common Knowledge*, 17: 48–63.

Stengers, I. (2017) *Another Science is Possible: A manifesto for slow science*, New York: Polity Press.

Styres, S. (2019) Literacies of Land: Decolonizing narratives, storying, and literature, in L.T. Smith, E. Tuck and Y.K. Wayne (eds) *Indigenous and Decolonizing Studies in Education: Mapping the long view*, New York: Routledge, pp 24–37.

Subramanian, M. (2019) Anthropocene now: Influential panel votes to recognise Earth's new epoch, Nature, available at: nature.com/articles/d41586-019-01641-5 [accessed 19 July 2020].

Takayama, K. (2020) Engaging with the more-than-human and decolonial turns in the land of Shinto cosmologies: 'Negative' comparative education in practice, *ECNU Review of Edication*, 3(1): 46–65.

Tallbear, K. (2015) Theorizing queer inhumanisms: An Indigenous reflection on working beyond the human/not human, *GLQ: A Journal and Lesbian and Gay Studies*, 21(2–3): 230–235.

Tallbear, K. (2019) Caretaking relations not American dreaming, *Kalfou: A Journal of Comparative and Relational Ethnic Studies*, 6(1), DOI: https://doi.org/10.15367/kf.v6i1.

Taylor, A. (2013) *Reconfiguring the Natures of Childhood*, London and New York: Routledge.

Taylor, A. (2017) Beyond stewardship: Common world pedagogies for the Anthropocene, *Environmental Education Research*, 23(10): 1448–61.

Taylor, A. (2019) Countering the conceits of the Anthropocene: Scaling down and researching with minor players, *Discourse: Cultural Politics of Education*, 41(special issue): 340–358.

Taylor, A. (2020) Downstream river dialogues: An educational journey towards a planetary-scaled ecological imagination, *ECNU Review of Education*, 3(1): 107–137.

Taylor, C. and Hughes, C. (eds) (2016) *Posthuman Research Practices in Education*, Basingstoke: Palgrave MacMillan.

Taylor, A. and Pacini-Ketchabaw, V. (2018) *The Common Worlds of Children and Animals: Relational Ethics for Entangled Lives*, New York: Routledge.

Tsing, A.L. et al (eds) (2017) *Arts of Living on a Damaged Planet: Ghosts and Monsters of the Anthropocene*, Minneapolis: University of Minnesota Press.

Tuhiwai Smith, L., Tuck, E. and Wayne, Y.K. (eds) (2019) *Indigenous and Decolonizing Studies in Education: Mapping the long view*, New York: Routledge.

Turner, M.K. (2010) *Iwenhe Tyerrtye: What it means to be an Aboriginal person*, Alice Springs: IAD Press.

UN (2015) Sustainable Development Goals, available at: un.org/sustainable development/sustainable-development-goals [accessed 20 June 2020].

UNESCO (2019) UN Decade of ESD, available at: en.unesco.org/themes/education-sustainable-development/what-is-esd/un-decade-of-esd [accessed 20 June 2020].

van Dooren, T. (2019) *The Wake of Crows: Living and dying in shared worlds*, New York: Columbia University Press.

Viveiros de Castro, E. (2004) Exchanging perspectives: The transformation of objects into subjects in Amerindian ontologies, *Common Knowledge*, 10(3): 463–484.

Waghid, Y. (2014) *African Philosophy of Education Reconsidered: On being human*, New York: Routledge.

Waghid, Y. and Smeyers, P. (2012) Reconsidering Ubuntu: On the educational potential of a particular ethic of care, *Educational Philosophy and Theory*, 44(2): 6–20.

Zhao, G. (2009) Two notions of transcendence: Confucian Man and the modern subject, *Journal of Chinese Philosophy*, 36(3): 391–407.

Zhao, W. (2018) Historicizing tianrenheyi as correlative cosmology for rethinking education in modern China and beyond, *Educational Philosophy and Theory*, 51: 1106–1116.

3

Knowledge Production, Access and Governance: A Song from the South

Catherine A. Odora Hoppers

Introduction: the past and present

David Orr, in his poignant 1991 piece focusing not on problems in education, but on the problem *of* education, stated this (p 1):

> If today is a typical day on planet Earth, we will lose 116 square miles of rainforest, or about an acre a second. We will lose another 72 square miles to encroaching deserts, as a result of human mismanagement and overpopulation. We will lose 40 to 100 species, and no one knows whether the number is 40 or 100. Today the human population will increase by 250,000. And today we will add 2,700 tons of chlorofluorocarbons to the atmosphere and 15 million tons of carbon. Tonight the Earth will be a little hotter, its waters more acidic, and the fabric of life more threadbare. The truth is that many things on which your future health and prosperity depend are in dire jeopardy: climate stability, the resilience and productivity of natural systems, the beauty of the natural world, and biological diversity. It is worth noting that this is not the work of ignorant people. It is, rather, largely the result of work by people with BAs, BSs, LLBs, MBAs, and PhDs.

Elie Wiesel added to this in a speech to the Global Forum, Moscow in 1990, that the designers and perpetrators of the Holocaust were the heirs of Kant and Goethe. In most respects, the Germans were the best educated people on Earth, he said, but their education did not serve as an adequate barrier to barbarity. What was wrong with their education? In Wiesel's words: 'It emphasized theories instead of values, concepts rather than human beings, abstraction rather than consciousness, answers instead of questions, ideology and efficiency rather than conscience' (Wiesel, 1990, p. 99).

From a genealogical point of view, Orr has argued that historically, Francis Bacon's proposed union between knowledge and power foreshadows the contemporary governance alliance between government, business and knowledge that has wrought so much mischief. Second, Galileo's separation of the intellect foreshadows the dominance of the analytical mind over that part given to creativity, humour and wholeness. Third, in Descartes' epistemology, one finds the roots of the radical separation of self and object. Together, these three laid the foundations and governance for modern education; foundations now enshrined in myths we have come to accept without question. On this simplified foundation of the Western paradigm of 'seeing', rambling and towering edifices in education, law, science and economics have been built and are taught daily to children throughout the world.

Orr outlines six myths arising from these foundations that have trapped and locked in humanity without question. First, there is the myth that ignorance is a solvable problem. Ignorance is not a solvable problem but an inescapable part of the human condition. The advance of knowledge always carries with it the advance of some form of ignorance. A second myth is that with enough knowledge and technology we can manage planet Earth. It is not true! 'Managing the planet' has a nice a ring to it. It appeals to our fascination with digital readouts, computers, buttons and dials. But the complexity of Earth and its life systems can never be safely managed. What might be managed is us: human desires, economies, politics and communities.

A third myth is that knowledge is increasing and by implication human goodness. There is an information explosion going on, by which Orr means a rapid increase of data, words and paper. But this explosion should not be taken for an increase in knowledge and wisdom, which cannot so easily be measured. What can be said truthfully is that some knowledge is increasing while other kinds of knowledge are being lost. But it is not just knowledge in certain areas that we are losing, but vernacular knowledge as well, by which I mean the knowledge that people have of their places. In the words of Barry Lopez (cited in Orr, 1991, p 2):

[I am] forced to the realization that something strange, if not dangerous, is afoot. Year by year the number of people with firsthand experience in the land dwindles. Rural populations continue to shift to the cities. … In the wake of this loss of personal and local knowledge, the knowledge from which a real geography is derived, the knowledge on which a country must ultimately stand, has come something hard to define but I think sinister and unsettling.

He continues that in the confusion of data with knowledge is a deeper mistake that learning will make us better people. But learning is endless and in itself it will never make us ethical.

A fourth myth, of higher education in particular, is that we can adequately restore that which we have dismantled. In the modern curriculum, we have fragmented the world into bits and pieces called disciplines and sub-disciplines. As a result, after 12 or 16 or 20 years of education, most students graduate without any broad integrated sense of the unity of things. We routinely produce economists who lack the most rudimentary knowledge of ecology. This explains why our national accounting systems do not subtract from gross national product the costs of biotic impoverishment, soil erosion, poisons in the air or water, and resource depletion. As a result of incomplete education, we have fooled ourselves into thinking that we are much richer than we are. Fifth, there is a myth that the purpose of education is to give you the means for upward mobility and success. The fact is that the planet does not need more 'successful' people. It desperately needs more peacemakers, healers, restorers, storytellers, and lovers of every shape and form. It needs people who live well in their places. It needs people of moral courage who are willing to join the fight to make the world habitable and humane. And these needs have little to do with success as our culture has defined it.

Finally, there is a myth that our culture represents the pinnacle of human achievement: we alone are modern, technological and developed. This, of course, represents cultural arrogance of the worst sort, and a gross misreading of history and anthropology. The fact is that we live in a disintegrating culture. Orr (1991, p 2) ends by saying:

> Our culture does not nourish that which is best or noblest in the human spirit. It does not cultivate vision, imagination, or aesthetic or spiritual sensitivity. It does not encourage gentleness, generosity, caring, or compassion. Increasingly in the late 20th Century, the economic-technocratic-statist worldview has become a monstrous destroyer of what is loving and life-affirming in the human soul.

He wrote this in 1991. Thirty years later, the scenario is untenable.

Unsustainable existential illiteracy

John Ralston Saul in his book *A Fair Country: Telling truths about Canada* (2008) refers to the present state of global affairs around education as an 'unsustainable existential illiteracy' that bedevils the educated elite in its dealings with local contexts. He states poignantly that democracy, true democracy – in fact lived democracy, in particular in the West as it faces the colonies – is a terrifying thought. He takes us further into the colonial mind by bringing the issue of land and democracy. They wanted the land. The land belonged to somebody else. They took it. They despised the actual owner. They believed that they were pure and unique, and exempt from ethical principles. They wished every day that the original owner would die soon or perish faster, but they don't quite die. Then they imposed a legal system complete with lawyers and judges to defend that historical act of theft. The last thing they wanted was an actual voice of such a person to enter the chorus (Ralston Saul, 2008).

Ralston Saul documents painfully in his 2014 book *The Comeback* how the prevailing and dominating world view that surrounds us today, and which we are all compelled to respond to, is one that is: narrow in its vision, exclusive and detached in relating to the total environment, analytical and deductive it its perception and thinking, linear in its 'doing', and hierarchical and competitive it its management of the field of activity (Ralston Saul, 2014, p 239).

The analysis comes from the fact that the era of the empire, weak and strong at the same time, declared Africa and Indigenous peoples to have nothing. Its knowledge systems were irrelevant. We were unsuited for the 'modern' world. The Imperial, twisted, parochial mythologies taught us in Africa, for instance, that a handful of countries in Europe dominated all thoughts and actions and naturally set the pattern for the world. They mangled Darwin's theories of evolution into a populist, racist, political narrative of progress and race; and they used it to justify their untold violence on Africa and the 'third world', saying all the while that was a manifestation of scientific destiny. So, they intentionally headed everything; from table manners and dress codes to economic methods, political philosophy and governmental administration to notions of civilizational truth and destiny.

Educational curricula were filled at the base with these absurdities. They then went to mount attacks on Indigenous cultures and peoples and demean them by banning their languages, cultures, rituals and all things spiritual. Illegal, unethical acts followed. Myriad laws, regulations and administrative structures were created, and amended, in order to install a legal infrastructure and punishment, both social and economic (Ralston Saul, 2014, pp 1–12). It is stunningly untenable!

Our universities, which ought to take us to the same philosophical and cultural universe as our highest levels of justice, are instead furnished to deny all non-Western sensibilities (Ralston Saul, 2008, p 36). The intractable problems that have arisen from the approach of a 'business as usual' denial by institutions all over the world, and identified by Odora Hoppers and Richards (2012), include (among others) colonialism, deadly knowledge apartheid, global warming and the destruction of the biosphere, unemployment, war and ethnic violence (typically fuelled by historic humiliation and deep mass resentment). Our natural world doesn't need people who can read per se! It needs people who are caring, who have values, who possesses a conscience, and, sadly, these people have been labelled 'primitive' by the mainstream culture, the Western one; their value systems rendered obsolete.

Going a step back and taking science as an example, if the business of science is 'reality' as Albert Einstein (1949) said, notable Indigenous scholars point out that the 'reality' all children are taught in schools, is actually the reality based on the Western paradigms. It is easy to see that Western paradigmatic views of science are largely about measurement using Western mathematics. But nature is not mathematical. Mathematics is superimposed on nature like a grid, and then examined from that framework. According to Hayward (1997), the modern world relies on a narrow, distorted view of science to attempt to relate what reality is all about. It leaves out the sacredness, the livingness, the soul of the world. Leroy Little Bear (2000, p x) adds: 'It does get troublesome when some scientists tell us, often with a voice of authority, that the part they leave out is not really there.'

Einstein affirmed that science cannot create ends and, even less, instill them in human beings. Science, at most, can supply the means by which to attain certain ends. For these reasons, we should be on our guard not to overestimate science and scientific methods when it comes to human problems; and we should not assume that 'experts' are the only ones who have a right to express themselves on questions affecting the organization of society. As the apex of the institution of society, higher education must keep it eyes alert on how an exaggerated competitive attitude is inculcated into the student, who is trained to worship acquisitive success as a preparation for his future career (Einstein, 1949).

If science is a search for reality, and for knowledge at the leading edge of the humanly knowable, then there are other sciences other than the Western science of measurements:

> Native American science is incomprehensible to most Westerners because it operates from a different paradigm. Measurement is part of the Native American Science but it does not play the foundational role that it plays in Western science. Measurement is only one of many factors to be considered. In order to appreciate and come to know in the Native American science way, one has to understand the culture/ worldview/paradigm of the Native American people. For Kuhn, a paradigm is a whole way of working, thinking, communicating, and perceiving with the mind. A paradigm includes tacit infrastructures which are mostly unconscious pervading the work and thought of the community. (Little Bear, 2000, p x)

Every culture has a science. For native people, seeking life was the all-encompassing task. While there were specialists with particular knowledge of technologies and ritual, each member of a tribe in their own capacity was a scientist, an artist, a storyteller and a participant in the great web of life. Native science (based on metaphysics, philosophy, environmental science, art, architecture, healing and related technologies, agriculture and so on) may be seen as an exemplification of 'biophilia'. Biophilia is the innate instinct of all life forms to share an affiliation with each other. It is predicated on mutually reciprocal relationships or the communal sensibility, honouring the laws of restitution and restoration (Little Bear, 2000).

Clearly, a new sun must be born. And to protect that 'new sun', we must adopt moral salience in understanding the contours of the problem of non-dialogue, violence and humiliation that have been ingrained in the knowledge production field, and examine what cases exist that have given birth to something resembling a distant star. It is a task!

Governance in a new dispensation

Local knowledges, tribal knowledges, civilisational knowledges, dying knowledges all need a site, a theatre of encounter which is not patronising, not preservationist, not fundamentalist, but open and playful. Without this mix of theory and vision, the communities of knowledge one is searching for might be stillborn. The university must encompass not merely dissent and diversity, but also the question of violence relating to the Other beyond the fence or border. It is in this search for cognitive justice as a fraternal act that the future university lies. (Visvanathan, 2000, p 3604)

The governance of the future will have to seek to build a context in which the democratic imagination and conversation is constructed between knowledge systems for emerging leaders posited in a transdisciplinary way. A new approach to decision-making and governance is required in all the fields, and in particular education, that seeks to integrate questions of ethical and political analysis. By doing so, it will create a deeper meaning and promote the link between science and society in Africa and globally. In its base, the new governance model will have to, from the start, enhance community and acknowledge the need for plural viewpoints and collective and lifelong learning that recognizes the diversity of knowledge systems (Odora Hoppers, 2018).

In the state of the world so beset by colonialism and heightened imperialism and the hierarchization it has produced worldwide, a focus on global ethics and learning is needed to change the way we envision the institutions we have and, in particular, the systems of decision-making in all the fields of endeavour. It will have to be underpinned by lived ethics not compliance-driven ethics as is done variously by institutions now. The notion of ethics proposed here provides the base of a new governance model of local-global interface and goes further by enhancing the wider issues of sustainability and fostering an increased consciousness of a human mission in a complex world.

Knowledge systems need to learn from and validate one another. A just integration of knowledge systems is valuable both for the creation of fundamental knowledge – and a better self-understanding of humanity – and for addressing the big societal challenges of our times. The governance model envisaged therefore fosters lifelong learning in all the sectors and disciplines to raise the bar in the promotion of human rights and international understanding, thereby furthering the goals set by UNESCO (Odora Hoppers, 2018).

The governance of dialogue between knowledge systems would constitute an attempt to add to the democratic imagination, emphasizing the plurality of cultures and enhancing the relationship between knowledge and democracy by linking it to livelihood and citizenship. It will have to take into account the African philosophy and practice rooted in *Ubuntu*, a theory of caring and humility; but it will be global in the sense that it seeks to identify theories of 'caring' and humility that exist variously in the global setting so that the violence of exclusion that permeates the scientific field is brought up and discussed in public. By optimizing plurality and minimizing violence, one sets the frame for dialogic knowledge as a playful, yet disciplined and strategic way of creating the conversation of cultures: a great thought experiment.

Governance as it is applied today fetishizes information over knowledge as an ecology. By taking on 'applied' dimensions of governance, it will develop the epistemics of governance to be worked out in terms of a new vocabulary. Otherwise, the model of governance that is espoused all over is puritan and quite unnuanced about the suffering and exclusion it creates. Lived ethics interacts with epistemology to create a more ecological critique of governance. It links memory and innovation. We need to search for a new language beyond current economics and the governance that ensues from it by introducing a sense of locality, context and relevance (Odora Hoppers, 2018).

But in reality, what does this mean? The following discusses an example of a remote 'sun': South African Chair in Development Education (2008–2018).

> Modern science does not constitute the only form of knowledge, and closer links need to be established between this and other forms, systems and approaches to knowledge, for their mutual enrichment and benefit. A constructive intercultural debate is in order, to help find ways of better linking modern science to the broader knowledge heritage of humankind. (UNESCO, 2000, paragraph 35)

In 2007, South Africa launched its independent Research Chair Initiative, entitled the South African Research Chairs Initiative (SARCHI), as a strategically focused knowledge and human resource intervention with interrelated objectives of stimulation of strategic research across the knowledge spectrum. Among the first batch of chair holders was the Chair in Development Education hosted by the University of South Africa, headed by Catherine A. Odora Hoppers. The chair was given ten years to complete its work as an intervention in the higher education sector. The chair took the practices in the academy and exposed them from a peace perspective. It convened an Indigenous Knowledge Advisory Faculty, (Knowledge Sages) in the grassroots and brought them into the academy as experts in dialogues around the development, recognition and protection, of Indigenous Knowledge Systems (IKS), and to ensure that the Indigenous voices were heard directly from them. It brought thinkers and emeritus professors from quantum physics, law, economic, education and philosophy from all over the world to enter into a serious dialogue on what the world needs to restore humanity and what the academy needs to humanize itself. The chair had Masters and PhD students, and vice chancellors, leading thinkers, and the IKS faculty combined at the SARCHI retreats.

Interfaces conducted after the retreats were sponsored directly by the Department of Science and Technology. The interface was an interactive space where the National Research Foundation and the Department of Science and Technology mandated the university to link with other stakeholders, particularly those at the margins who are the holders of other epistemologies and producers of knowledge in other systems, and together work out protocols, terms and conditions for the integration of the different traditions of knowledge. It was a site for the nourishment of emerging leaders with transdisciplinary competence in understanding constitutive (underlying) codes that programme societal institutions and systems (including disciplines); developing a transnational outlook that is grounded in the African perspective; constructing arguments and critical reflection on identified knowledge questions; and establishing a safe and public space as a core social and national strategy.

By integrating citizenship education with academic explorations, research outcomes, and innovations, the chair brought society face to face with the work of, and insights generated through the academy, those previously known as 'experts'. The moral and pragmatic task was to develop new cognitive tools and propositions capable of deciphering the erasure cryptogram that hierarchized and excised the majority of African people from the global collective memory as a positive and substantive contributor to world civilization – hence denying them active citizenship in key areas of contemporary global currency, including knowledge and science. The chair generated powerful heuristics in terms of theory-building, methodological perspectives and practical interventions in a new ethical dispensation.

The chair was future oriented without explicitly stating so, and students were encouraged to extend the boundaries of inquiry beyond the immediate specificities of national history. The future-oriented methodology was chosen as specifically taking into account the potential dangers of the 'vortex' syndrome inherent in societies emerging out of trauma in which the power of that trauma can continually suck all analyses and visions back only to the traumatic episode, thereby blocking the possibility for generating the comparative and diachronic analyses so essential to making new or fresh propositions.

By turning a title and a status (the SARCHI chair) into an ethical space, the SARCHI chair expressed a commitment to actively take up the challenge of fostering a community of thinkers within higher education in South Africa, as well as strategic players in local communities, including holders of Indigenous knowledge. The SARCHI chair's work in the academy resulted in a metaphysical shift. The law curriculum in the University of South Africa underwent a transformation. The University of Cape Town's Executive MBA in the Graduate School of Business took the codes produced by the chair and produced remarkable reversals in the way the MBA curriculum is taught. The sector ministries in South Africa that had IKS units were brought into the picture. This enabled the development of a weave of ethics, a set of attitudes, and an ethics of the margins that are capable of producing perspectives on subsistence and survival which are not stymied by the Western obsession with hierarchization and alienation of the other, but which are civilizational in their own way. It mobilized a cohort of community of thinkers and organic intellectuals (academics, artists and citizens) around the human condition – plurality, epistemologies, intercultural dialogue, peace and violence, science and society, knowledge and democracy. The chair was a yeasting point, a generative hub for leadership building, a facilitative space for intellectual change management and intellectual interlocutor between the university's mission/goals and the implementation arenas.

The space created by the chair enabled understanding of the contexts that have shaped the conceptual history of IKS from generation to degeneration and regeneration. Issues and values of Indigeneity such as autonomy, self-determination, decolonization, restorative healing and justice formed the bedrock of the proceedings. IKS as a life force generating renewable energies for cultural, economic, ecological and intellectual as well as other forms of collective well-being and survival was the nexus in the formulation of the proposals for this interface. Building bridges to cross from IKS as a science to Western scientific paradigms and back was at the core of this endeavour in knowledge development in which IKS as a science was included (Odora Hoppers 2009 and 2018). This example shows an institutional case of building capacity for a transformed thought and practice process in bringing to bear dialogue among knowledge systems. The chair came to an end in 2018.

Recommendations for the future

First of all, we need to broaden and deepen our outlook and consider the following issues going forward.

1. The need to invest in Indigenous diplomacy

Governance of the future needs to invest in Indigenous diplomacy and the rights of peoples – seriously. Consider this: On 12 September 2007, the green lights of the voting systems in the UN General Assembly signalled a new global consensus when member states overwhelmingly endorsed the Declaration on the Rights of the Peoples (Henderson, 2008). This remarkable vote formally brought to an end the Nation States' history of oppression of Indigenous peoples: 143 countries affirmed the Human Rights Council's recommendation to extend fundamental freedoms to Indigenous peoples.

Many people educated in the grand narratives of Empire and colonialism were surprised by the UN's action, wondering how these poor, defeated, powerless peoples – the vulnerable bottom of global humanity – had found allies in the assembly, with its complex structures and protocols, and voice to assert their human rights. How did the Indigenous people of the world find the diplomatic skill to defeat colonial ideology through peaceful dialogue? Where did the young, Eurocentrically educated Indigenous people who had never experienced traditional civilizations find the desire for cultural restoration and the will to fight for it? How did the elders and the lost or assimilated generations come to join this network? How is it possible that so many diverse people came to the knowledge of how to proceed on the Declaration without leaders, advice or instruction?

The extension of human rights to Indigenous peoples is difficult to reconcile with the historical legacy of the violence and discrimination against them. A shift of consciousness is required to comprehend the transformational politics involved in that moment in the UN. It was a cognitive struggle, a challenge to existing ways of thinking about humanity. The Indigenous peoples achieved the art of the impossible in the realm of the improbable (Henderson, 2008). In that moment, it was realized by the Indigenous diplomatic networks that they could not settle colonial accounts in a way that would allow the spirit of colonialism to penetrate our consciousness, our activities, and thus our spirits. In the words of an Indigenous Elder on the Declaration: 'The text is made up of so many teardrops of the horrible times.' These sufferings oblige us to practice justice as healing, not punishment (as Western law teaches).

The governance of the future must invest in the generation of champions, and ethically minded knowledge brokers and scientists across the disciplines, who are capable of creating new discourses with the intent of making changes in the unhealthy bubble around us.

2. We need to cultivate the ethical space

Governance of the future needs to take what Ermine (2007) called the 'Ethical Space'. The ethical space denotes that tension-riddled enterprise of cultural border crossing the West had monopolized without any ambition to dialogue, or reciprocity, or respect, courtesy, valorization, or recognition of the 'other'. It is a precarious and fragile window of opportunity that exists for critical conversations about race, gender, class, freedom and community. It is a space with a moment of possibility to create substantial, sustained and ethical moral understanding between cultures.

It is a statement of recognition of the cultural jurisdictions at play in which dialogue about intentions, values and assumptions can be brought out and negotiated. The ethical space imperatives would include a two-way bridge of awareness-building and understanding in which there is no preconceived notion of the other's existence. It is a space in which values, motivation and assumptions are brought to bear, and, at last, dialogue on issues of plurality and diversity of knowledge, as well as dialogue around ownership, control and benefit of those knowledges can be undertaken (Ermine, 2007).

It is a space created in between the meeting of two sorts of entities with two sorts of intentions; an abstract, theoretical location in the thought world; a space of possibility when cultures, world views, knowledge systems and jurisdictions meet and agree to interact. It is a space between two cultures and ways of understanding, the confluence of ethos, discourses, histories and realities; the space between you and the other culture, a location of equal relations (human to human).

In an ethical space, non-Indigenous and Indigenous can come and participate, debate, discuss and create dialogue. It is not a place of unequal relations in terms of a hierarchical order, but rather a space in which both can be vulnerable ('naked', without agendas, without titles). It is a space with a level playing field on which possibilities can be articulated, and conditions for the *crossing* of the cultural borders must be created; an opportunity for dialogue between entities in a language of human possibility (Ermine, 2007).

3. The imperative to enhance the tacit constitution

The idea of the tacit constitution is borrowed from Michael Polanyi's idea of tacit knowledge (Polanyi, 1962; Visvanathan, 2019a). Polanyi, a distinguished chemist, became an equally creative philosopher in his later years. In his books, *The Republic of Science* and *The Tacit Dimension*, he captured the taken-for-granted world of science. He argued that science cannot be grasped fully through official statements and representations. A statement of method might capture an official grammar in a skeletal form, but it might say very little of the everyday dynamics of how science functions or perceives itself. Formal statements of method sometimes fail to capture the everydayness of craft, the implicit assumptions of an epistemology. The taken-for-granted becomes almost a world of silences. Its assumptions need to be magnified if science is to be fully understood.

Polanyi believed that science cannot be reduced to a formal statement of method; it needed a sense of interiorization. Interiorization is a method of identification. It needs a sense of indwelling. Mere looking at a thing does not help; one has to dwell in it. Without tacit content and context, words would be strictly meaningless. Polanyi argued that the power of language emerges from being a toolbox for tacit awareness. When we give words meaning, we rely upon them more than we can say. Critical to a constitution is what Polanyi calls a sense of indwelling, of a lived reality narrated as such. Formal constitutions hide such processes, and in that sense, as Polanyi puts it, 'we know more than we can tell.' It is in these interstices between stated and unstated that tacit knowing becomes operative. The hunch, a sense of the hidden, a relation between part and whole become important. Tacit knowing creates a different sense of the ontology of an object. A formal constitution is a skeletal structure, a design that unfolds through interpretation. It is code or grammar rather than an unfolding of language. It lacks a sense of indwelling, a lived sense of the categories of a society that belongs more to the body or the creative process of the mind. A formal constitution in that sense is a weak gestalt, and a tacit constitution thickens one's perception of a society and its constitution. It adds to the lucidity of the formal, a penumbra of understanding, belief and shadows of lived thought. The meaning of a constitution emerges when the interconnectivity between the two worlds is established (Polanyi, 1962).

One can also contend that a society is alive when its myths and categories are kept alive. In these days, when formal constitutions impoverish the categories of a society, reducing them to a rudimentary social contract and a thesaurus of official concepts that march in uniform – terms like security, nation-state, official citizenship – one needs a tacit constitution that keeps the unstated, the backstage, the implicit, the taken-for-granted alive. Categories, and the dynamics of categories, keep a society afloat and sustain its *weltanschaung*. World views are the webs that sustain a world (Visvanathan, 2019a).

Visvanathan argued that a combination of tacit and embedded knowledges would have been life-saving for the modern condition. In that sense, the idea of embeddedness sees a constitution as mediating two worlds and a plurality of time, which are in a dialogic relationship, seeking to cope with difference rather than engage in negotiation. The tacit constitution is a philosophical but everyday heuristic that a constitution must respond to if it wishes to save itself from being unnecessarily violent. Dialogue requires an understanding of incoherence. It is dialogue that links a formal and a tacit constitution together. Therefore, the new inclusive, and healing governance model needs to involve both the formal and the tacit constitution, a plural imperative that interconnects people across the world. Dialogue offers a different notion of truth, a different path to truth. Truth, says Bohm, needs the freer movement of the tacit mind. Taking part in truth is a process of understanding wholes. It is a challenge to the reductionist power of science that understands fragments, not wholes. Reductionism is dysfunctional for wholes: it understands neither interconnectivity nor interdependence. Dialogue demands a flow of meaning in the group. This shared meaning is the glue that holds societies together. Dialogue, unlike debates and discussions, is not competitive about being knowledge centred. There is no attempt to score points, and a mistake triggers a joint act of reconstruction. In that sense, a dialogue goes beyond negotiation (Odora Hoppers, 2018; Visvanathan, 2000.

4. The need to generate knowledge panchayats

The *panchayat* is a system of great importance in India in order to bring governance closer to the people (Visvanathan 2019b). Moving from information to knowledge, the knowledge panchayat is an affirmation that a citizen is not merely a passive consumer of knowledge but a critical commentator, evaluator and generator of that knowledge. A knowledge panchayat asserts a citizen's right to produce knowledge and evaluate decisions according to their preferred categories of knowledge. Knowledge panchayats, in that sense, become exercises in the comparative anthropology of knowledge. This assessment is done pluralistically, avoiding hierarchies and hegemonies of knowledge. Science is no longer read as monopolistic or hegemonic, nor are other knowledges viewed tolerantly as 'ethnoscience', the children of a lesser god of knowledge.

A knowledge panchayat in that sense becomes a mediator, an epistemic broker, a translator between different dialects of knowledge. The knowledge panchayat is a forum whose time has come. It has to be a chain of being that represents science not only as interest-group articulation but as a way of life where stakeholder rather than shareholder participation is emphasized. One has to realize that the knowledge panchayat is not merely an attempt to rescue the marginal farmer. It is equally an attempt to restore the integrity of a risk-oriented science that has been contaminated by corporate interests dedicated to profit.

Knowledge panchayats are not merely institutions for firefighting. They also need to invent the problematic of the future. This issue rises in a deep and demanding way when we confront issues of violence, peace and war. In this sense a knowledge panchayat is also a peace panchayat exploring non-violent forms of knowledge and creating new ethical start-ups where peace is no longer a prerogative of security experts and the state (Odora Hoppers, 2018; Visvanathan, 2019b).

5. Cognitive justice

None of the recommendations above would be possible without cognitive justice. Cognitive justice is defined as the right of all forms or traditions of knowledge to co-exist (Visvanathan, 2000), in public, without duress (Odora Hoppers, 2009). The need to base future institutions, governance structures, methodological work and actions on cognitive justice is imperative. Cognitive justice is a positive heuristic for dialogues of equally valid knowledges and knowledge systems.

Conclusion: what inclusive education must be for

First, all education must invest in Ubuntu and not trust domination or hierarchization. By what is included or excluded, we teach students that they are part of, or apart from, the natural world. The goal of education is not mastery of subject matter, but of one's person. Knowledge carries with it the responsibility to see that it is well used in the world. We cannot say that we know something until we understand the effects of this knowledge on real people and their communities.

Students hear about 'global responsibility' while being educated in institutions that often invest their financial weight in the most irresponsible things. The lessons being taught are those of hypocrisy and, ultimately, despair. Students learn, without anyone ever saying it, that they are helpless to overcome the frightening gap between ideals and reality. What is desperately needed are faculties and administrators who courageously provide role models of integrity, care and thoughtfulness, and institutions that are capable of embodying ideals wholly and completely in all of their operations (Orr, 1991).

The way learning occurs is as important as the content of particular courses. Process is important for learning. Courses taught as a series of lectures tend to induce passivity. Indoor classes create the illusion that learning only occurs inside four walls isolated from what students call, without apparent irony, the 'real world'. Campus architecture is crystallized pedagogy that often reinforces passivity, monologue, domination and artificiality. To conclude, emerging societies cannot make do just with mere components of a global information society. To remain human and liveable, knowledge societies will have to be societies of shared knowledge in which a solid 's' is attached at the end of the word knowledge itself. The plural here sanctions the need for accepted diversity. The emergence of new concepts and approaches to theorization, such as those outlined here that capture the lived realities and experiences of those long triaged from the arena of citizenship, could be the starting points for change and transformation of education for the future.

Disclaimer

This paper was commissioned by UNESCO as a contribution to *Reimagining Our Futures Together: A new social contract for education* (UNESCO, 2021). © UNESCO 2020. This work is available under the Creative Commons Attribution-ShareAlike 3.0 IGO license (CC-BY-SA 3.0 IGO). The author alone is responsible for the views expressed in this publication and they do not necessarily represent the views, decisions or policies of UNESCO.

References

Einstein, A. (1949) Why socialism?, Monthly Review, available at: monthlyreview.org/598einst.htm [accessed 24 January 2023].

Ermine, W. (2007) Ethical space of engagement, *Indigenous Law Journal*, 6(1): 193.

Gupta, A. (1999) Conserving Biodiversity and Rewarding Associated Knowledge and Innovation Systems: Honey Bee Perspective. Paper presented at the World Trade Forum. Bern. August 27-29th 1999.

Hayward, J.W. (1997) *Letters to Vanessa. On love, science and awareness in an enchanted world*, Boston: Shabhala Publications.

Henderson, S.Y. (2008) *Indigenous Diplomacy and the Rights of Peoples: Achieving UN recognition*, Canada: Purich Publishing.

Little Bear, L.R. (2000) Foreword, in G. Cajete, *Native Science: Natural laws of interdependence*, Santa Fe: Clear Light.

Odora Hoppers, C.A. (2009) *DST/NRF SARCHI Framework and Strategy*, Pretoria: University of South Africa.

Odora Hoppers, C.A. (2018) Global Institute for Applied Governance in Science and Innovations, framework document, Uganda.

Odora Hoppers, C.A and Richards, H. (2012) *Rethinking Thinking: Modenity's 'Other' and the transformation of the academy*, South Africa: University of South Africa.

Orr, D. (1991) What is education for?, In Context, 27: 52.

Polanyi, M. (1962) The Republic of Science: Its political and economic theory, *Minerva*, 1: 54–73.

Ralston Saul, J. (2008) *A Fair Country:* Telling truths about Canada, Toronto: Viking.

Ralston Saul, J. (2014) *The Comeback*, Toronto: Viking..

UNESCO (2000) *World Conference on Science*, Budapest.

Visvanathan, S. (2000) Democracy, plurality and the Indian university, Economic and Political Weekly, 35(40): 3597–3606.

Visvanathan, S. (2016) The Logic of Knowledge Commons, available at: https://www.academia.edu/1979669/The_Logic_of_Knowledge_Commons

Visvanathan, S. (2019a) The Tacit Constitution. Letter to Catherine A. Odora Hoppers (unpublished).

Visvanthan, S. (2019b) Knowledge Panchayats. Letter to Catherine A. Odora Hoppers (unpublished).

Wiesel, E. (1990) Global Education: An address at the global forum, Moscow.

PART II

Decolonizing Education for Sustainable Futures: From Theory to Practice

4

Reimagining Education: Student Movements and the Possibility of a Critical Pedagogy and Feminist Praxis

Tania Saeed

Introduction

In reimagining the futures of education in a context of growing global and local inequalities, it is crucial to expand the borders of our 'situated imagination' defined through the particularities of our experiences and surroundings (Yuval-Davis, 2013). Such expansion requires an uncomfortable confrontation with a troubling past, and a recognition of the changing nature of the human and non-human world and our role in its destruction or (re)construction. This reimagining is crucial at a time when the Anthropocene epoch is marred by the rise of right-wing populism in countries across the global North and South dictated by a market-driven ideology of capitalist expansion at the expense of planetary sustainability. Technological advancement and online connectivity that ought to have created a greater possibility of 'border crossing' (Giroux, 2005) have instead resulted in greater surveillance and control, with identities digitized for bureaucratic management in the name of security (Saunders, 2016).

The existence of such insular world views can be found in different parts of the world: in the UK's decision to leave the European Union at a time where greater cooperation and coordination is needed to take on the challenges of an environmental and climate emergency, and a refugee crisis; in the USA's decision to withdraw from the Paris Agreement that brought nations together to ensure a 'global response' to the climate emergency (Climate Action Tracker, 2020a); or in the increasing deforestation of the

Amazon in Brazil, which increased by more than 80 per cent in 2019, with environmental activists, Indigenous leaders and 'forest defenders' being killed by mafias (Human Rights Watch, 2020; Angelo, 2020; Climate Action Tracker, 2020b). These are just a few examples of how the physical and ideological borders of the nation-state are being reinforced to promote self-interest at the expense of civic, environmental, ecological and human rights.

Simultaneously, in the face of political self-interest that has wreaked human and ecological devastation, a reimagining of the future is already taking place through student-led campaigns and movements, with young people taking charge of their own futures. Such counter-narratives build on existing forms of resistance, from Indigenous leaders who have worked locally and globally to influence policy through the UN Declaration on the Rights of Indigenous Peoples (UNDRIP), the Indigenous Peoples Kyoto Declaration and the Manukan Declaration of the Indigenous Women's Biodiversity Network, among others (Whyte, 2016), to the Global Justice Movement, anti-war protests, Black Lives Matter, MeToo and anti-austerity protests in Europe and the US, among countless others that have erupted at different points around the world. What specifically stands out with more recent movements such as School Strikes for Climate (SS4C) and Fridays for Future (FFF) is that they are led by children taking on the responsibility for their futures in a context of adult failure. University students are challenging the basic core of education that relies on Western and Eurocentric cannons through movements for decolonizing the curriculum and Rhodes Must Fall that started in South Africa and gained transnational support.

In the first meeting of the International Commission on the Futures of Education in January 2020, a central question was posed: 'What do we want to become?' (UNESCO, 2020). The answer to this question is also right before us in the form of these counter narratives. Any discussion on the futures of education is incomplete without locating student voices and experiences as central to that discussion, especially when students have been politically active – organizing, agitating, speaking, writing – reimagining their own future. Campaigns such as SS4C, FFF, Rhodes Must Fall and decolonizing the curriculum are examples where environmental, ecological, civic and human rights are central to this reimagining. The role of education in such a context is crucial for equipping students with 'the knowledge, capacities, and opportunities to be noisy, irreverent and vibrant' (Giroux, 1992, p 8).

This chapter, through an exploration of secondary literature, draws on these student-led movements in order to reimagine an educational framework defined by a critical pedagogy and feminist praxis (CPFP). These movements are specifically selected for being led by school and university students who have gained transnational support and are taking on the biggest challenges of the Anthropocene epoch. The chapter begins by locating SS4C, FFF, Rhodes

Must Fall and decolonizing the curriculum within the wider literature on social movements and student activism, providing an overview of the movements and their implications for education and civic participation. This is followed by an exploration of CPFP that embodies an interdisciplinary approach to education and learning, where civic responsibility moves beyond the traditional social contract with the nation state to a deeper connection with humans and non-humans, developing a 'sensibility' (Tuana, 2019) towards communities that have been 'silenced' or marginalized on the basis of race, class, caste, ethnicity, gender, sexuality, religion or any form of human and non-human othering. It therefore creates the possibility of expanding physical and ideological boundaries through a 'pedagogy of difference' where students can 'cross over into diverse cultural zones' while 'rethinking' 'relations' of domination and subordination (Giroux, 1992, p 8). It also emphasizes an intergenerational, community-based model of learning where educational institutions are connected with the wider community, drawing on local or Indigenous forms of knowledge and learning, where civic participation is closely linked to the dynamics of the local community.

Social movements for change

In his work on social movements, Christopher A. Rootes argued that 'student movements are creatures of the societies in which they occur and as such they evince, in variable measure all the excellences and deformities of their circumstances' (Rootes, 1980, p 473). Social movements, particularly progressive movements led by students and youth activists are central to the 'process of democratization' (Giroux, 2018). Educational institutions can be instrumental in developing civic, human, ecological and environmental values among the younger generation, equipping them with the tools necessary for meaningful activism. Yet, neoliberal educational institutions, far from challenging the inequalities and injustices in the world, have adopted a profit-oriented, apolitical approach to education and knowledge production (Giroux, 2018 and 2005). Such institutions are unsustainable in a world with shrinking resources, increasing migration and displacement, as humans and non-human are caught up in conflict and an ecological emergency.

These student movements have not emerged randomly. Porta and Mattoni in their edited volume on social movements demonstrate the 'transnational dimension' of contemporary movements in relation to historical connections, and ideologies that have travelled across geographical boundaries. They illustrate how protests and movements since 2008 are located in a context of political and economic crisis experienced at different points across the world, with resistance taking different forms in response to local politics – they characterize these protests as 'movements of the crisis' (Porta and Mattoni, 2014, p 2)[1] These movements of the crisis can also create the possibility of hope, as illustrated by Hytten (2018, p 2), drawing on John Dewey's idea of democracy as a way of life: 'Through working with others on issues that they are passionate about, citizens ideally develop the habits of experimentalism and pluralism, as well as the habit of hope, sustained by evidence that other worlds are possible.'

Local movements and protests led by students have been challenging particular forms of injustice in local contexts where hierarchies of caste, class, ethnicity, gender, sexuality or race need to be dismantled. These protests are visible across south Asia, in the student movement against the 2019 Citizenship (Amendment) Act in India, or the Students Solidarity March in Pakistan (see Martelli and Garalytė, 2019; Jan, 2019); Hong Kong's uprising against the extradition bill (see Ku, 2020), or student protests against the neoliberal education system in France and the UK. All of these movements have cultivated global and transnational support. This Deweyan 'habit of hope' that can reimagine a more just future is being developed not only within the confines of a nation state but, given the scale of the crisis, has transnational appeal, across borders, as students challenge the status quo together.

The struggle for environmental and ecological rights and justice: School Strikes for Climate *and* Fridays for Future

The scale of climate change and environmental disaster can be gauged from the fact that 'between 2030 and 2050 climate change is projected to cause an additional 250,000 deaths per year' globally (UN, 2020b, p 85), along with irreversible damage to the non-human world. Already, between 2008 and 2018, climate change is estimated to have caused 'an average of 24.1 million people per year' to be forced out of their homes 'as a result of weather events and natural disasters' (UN, 2020b p 83 and UN, 2020a). The Anthropocene is dominated by human activity that is increasingly compromising the future of the planet, and the survival of human and non-human species, with governments prioritizing short-term profit at the expense of environmental sustainability. It is in this context of an environmental and climate emergency that we witnessed the mobilization of school children whose future is under jeopardy. The SS4C and FFF were started by environmental activist and school student Greta Thunberg who began protesting against the Swedish government's failure to meet the targets set in the Paris Agreement (Fridays for Future, 2020; UNFCCC, 2020). Inspired by this lone figure protesting against a government indifferent to her future, and the future of so many children, as images of her protest spread online through social media, school students, parents, activists and allies all over the world joined the movement, organizing 'the most comprehensive coordinated global strike ever' on 15 March 2019, with '1.6 million people in 2000 locations worldwide' protesting for action to mitigate the climate and environmental emergency (Holmberg and Alvinius, 2019, p 79). Students have started organizing protests every Friday until their demands are met. While these demands vary across countries, dependent on the particular policies of national governments, they have largely included holding governments accountable to the Paris Agreement, a halt on fossil fuel production, and making 'ecocide an international crime'. There is also an increasing recognition that 'climate and environmental justice cannot be achieved' without tackling 'social and racial injustices and oppression' (Neubauer et al, 2020).

Campaigns for environmental and climate protection are not new, having been led by Indigenous communities and environmentalists in different parts of the world. This movement is unique, however, in its mobilization of school students across the world in an age of digital communication and social media. The place of children as leaders of this movement is particularly important. Children have often been portrayed as 'vulnerable and victims ... educatable (subjects possible to transform and empower) and as crucial agents for change (for their future – not crucial for those living today, though)' by national and international policy makers (Holmberg and Alvinius, 2019, p 82). The focus has been on their 'potential', where their involvement in youth parliaments is meant to prepare them for future roles. Yet, this movement illustrates the existing power of children and their ability to mobilize, using technology to organize and campaign. The climate movement has resulted in children becoming active participants to ensure that their concerns and their vision about their own futures are not only heard but implemented, especially in a context where time is of the essence. As a result of their political activism, students were invited to the UN's Youth Climate Action Summit in September 2019, at which 'youth climate champions' from 140 countries shared 'their solutions on the global stage' (UN, 2020c) at Davos to discuss their concerns and vision with world leaders, at the 'Voices of Youth' organization, created by UNICEF (2019a; 2019b) as 'a dedicated platform for young advocates to offer inspiring and original insights on issues that matter to them' among other local and global forums.

The movement also provides an important form of learning for students who are walking out of schools and classrooms, collectively holding local and global leaders accountable. It reinforces a 'habit of hope' (Hytten, 2018 as children take the lead. Furthermore, in line with Henry Giroux's philosophy, McKnight (2020, p 53) argues that 'the learning spaces of protests and marches facilitate an opening up to new ideas, a reduction of hierarchy in learning, and the creation of community.' Analyzing the speeches and interviews of participants from SS4C and FFF, she notes how young activists are making links between issues of 'capitalism and colonialism' in their fight for environmental justice. They are beginning to recognize hierarchical disparities that exist in decision-making, where the most vulnerable to the climate and environmental emergency are often the least influential in the local and global power hierarchy. The global hierarchy has historical roots in colonialism and imperialism, a history that needs to be confronted in education systems in the global North and South, a confrontation that is being led by young students who aim to decolonize the curriculum.

Civic and racial justice: a reckoning with history

Local and global hierarchies of knowledge, of what is considered worthy of knowing and learning, is embedded within the education system. This legitimate knowledge is largely Euro-, Western- and white-centric, where the educational traditions of Indigenous communities, of various racial, ethnic, religious or cultural groups, are often undermined or silenced not only within the global North, but also through educational hierarchies in a post-colonial South. The struggle to reclaim one's educational heritage against such hierarchies of knowledge production and legitimation are not new, with anti-colonial and anti-racist movements taking on these challenges (see Said, 2001; Peters, 2015 and 2018; wa Thiong'o, 1986; Ellis, 2009; Shahjahan, 2011). Decolonizing the curriculum and Rhodes Must Fall are a legacy of these struggles led by university students from South Africa to the UK. These began as student campaigns in 2015 by students at the University of Cape Town with the aim to challenge 'the ideological apparatus of white supremacy and colonialism' triggered by the 'particular conditions' and realities of their specific contexts (Pimblott, 2020, p 211). For instance, Rhodes Must Fall began with the demand for free education under the slogan 'Fees Must Fall' which grew to challenge the reality of a post-apartheid South Africa, calling for the removal of the statue of colonialist Cecil Rhodes who laid the groundwork for apartheid, and a demand to decolonize the curriculum (Meda, 2020, p 88; Peters, 2018, p 265; Miller and Pointer, 2019).

The movement gained transnational appeal, being taken up by students at the University of Oxford, in the UK where Rhodes was a 'benefactor'. The students involved in this movement were not only inspired by those in South Africa, but also by student-led movements in other parts of the world, including the 'campaign against caste prejudice' in Indian universities, the anti-racist struggles by students in the USA,[2] building on earlier movements and protests led by 'the Black and Asian Studies Association concerning the representation of Black history within the UK National Curriculum ... among others' (Bhambra et al, 2018, p 1). Decolonization took on a range of meanings from 'rediscovering and recovering' knowledge, 'reconstructing and deconstructing' knowledge to changing the entire structure of the higher education system (Meda, 2020, pp 89–90). One underlying aspect of this campaign is to engage in 'reflexivity' that questions the process by which certain types of knowledge are legitimized: 'It requires looking both inwards and outwards, accepting that there is more than one way of speaking about, thinking about, and researching the complex social and political phenomena bound up within our disciplines' (Saini and Begum, 2020, p 219).

At the University of Oxford, Rhodes Must Fall aims to challenge the 'plague of *colonial iconography*', reform a '*Euro-centric curriculum*' and address the '*underrepresentation and lack of welfare provisions* for black and minority ethnic (BME) among Oxford's academic staff and students' (emphasis in original) (Peters, 2018, pp 265–266). Henriques and Abushouk (2018) highlight how the Rhodes Must Fall movement in Oxford permitted a 'transnational discussion around structural transformation which would force the university, an institution which is highly resistant to change, to be self-reflective and consider learning from both its British and international students' (p 308). The movement was reignited in 2020, spreading to other universities, inspired further by Black Lives Matter protests in the USA (McKie, 2020).

The danger of such movements becoming tokenistic without addressing deeper structures of knowledge production that reinforce hierarchies has been challenged through campaigns such as 'Why is My Curriculum White', spearheaded by the National Union of Students (NUS) in the UK. Sian (2017, p 13) has argued that these 'campaigns illustrate the significance of carving out epistemological spaces for educators and students to engage with "other" knowledges and situate global issues in nuanced frameworks.' These campaigns and movements are important in highlighting how civic participation has evolved in a context of migration and pluralism as communities move across geographical boundaries, redefining and reimagining national identities and ideals of citizenship. They are pushing to reimagine an education system that confronts the history of colonialism and the hierarchies that continue to exist, where Indigenous, racial, ethnic or cultural forms of knowledge and identity continue to be undermined (See Saini and Begum, 2020).[3]

A reimagining of education begins with dismantling such hierarchies that privilege one form of knowledge, instead of focusing on the diversity of human and non-human experiences. It further requires rethinking of the disconnect between 'formal' and 'informal' ways of learning, where communities beyond school and university structures are considered equally legitimate in the learning experience. In short, a reimagining through a critical pedagogy and feminist praxis is central for the futures of education.

Critical pedagogy and feminist praxis – reimagining the futures of education

The SS4C, FFF, Rhodes Must Fall and decolonizing the curriculum protests led by students from schools and universities illustrate the importance of developing an educational ecosystem that cuts across disciplinary or physical borders. The climate crisis is exacerbated by an unequal world system that is embedded in a historical context of colonialism and imperialism, which is yet to be confronted, where taken-for-granted assumptions about knowledge and learning legitimize a Eurocentric world view while cultural, ethnic, Indigenous or religious diversity is reduced to a subject or a class on world cultures, world religions or multiculturalism within the formal education system. In reimagining this system, this chapter proposes a framework that is embedded in local experiences and knowledge and which cuts across the humanities, and natural and social sciences yet engages with different world views and ideologies, while enabling student curiosity towards science and technology and inculcating civic values towards human and non-human equality.

This reimagining begins by expanding the 'situated knowledge' (Yuval-Davis et al, 2017) of local existence through a critical pedagogy:

> Central to any viable notion of what makes pedagogy critical is, in part, the recognition that it is a moral and political practice that is always implicated in power relations because it narrates particular versions and visions of agency, civic life, community, the future, and how we might construct representations of ourselves, others, and our physical and social environment. (Giroux, 2018, pp 84–85)

This pedagogy is located both inside and outside the classroom where educators create conditions that 'rearticulate justice and equality' (Giroux, 2005). It is also through such critical pedagogy that the student as the 'border crosser' is envisioned.

This critical pedagogy is linked to a particular feminist praxis that adopts an intersectional approach to educational practice. This reveals how power is constituted differently within education systems and local contexts. It not only exposes 'multilayered structures of power and domination by adopting a grounded praxis approach' but 'also engages the conditions that shape and influence the interpretive lenses through which knowledge is produced and disseminated' (Cho et al, 2013, p 804). Such an intersectional approach therefore creates an awareness and realization of where power is located and how it is experienced by different groups, human and non-human.

In order to develop a sensibility towards such dynamics of power, an 'ecologically informed intersectional genealogy' is also central. Such 'genealogical sensibilities' permit the possibility of understanding local histories and existing realities around structures of oppression, where racism and environmental exploitation often 'coalesce' in different ways (Tuana, 2019, p 12). These genealogical sensibilities are a first step towards confronting taken-for-granted values and beliefs within a particular community, where the 'goal of genealogical sensibilities is to become attuned to the often silent workings of power' and how it is deployed in different forms 'in order to identify histories of oppressive practices, particularly to silenced or suppressed lineages that often continue to animate oppression' (Tuana, 2019, p 4).

Such a praxis permits the possibility of introspection and interrogation through an education that questions the fundamentals of legitimatized knowledge in different contexts, an introspection already taking place through the student movements that have been highlighted in this chapter. A critical pedagogy exposes students to a diverse curriculum from the standpoint of other communities necessitating a 'pedagogy of difference' where education becomes a 'transformative' learning experience (Giroux, 2005). Both the expansion of borders and the crossing of borders are possible as education creates the conditions for human and non-human connections.[4]

Reimagining the human and non-human connection

In rethinking and resituating our relationship with the human and non-human world, there is an urgent decentring of the individual in relation to the community. Central to this is our understanding of communities and collectivities through a feminist praxis, as Sara Ahmed (2002, p 570) argues:

> [C]ollectivities are formed through the very work that we need to do in order to get closer to others, without simply repeating the appropriation of 'them' as labour or as a sign of difference. Collectivity then is intimately tied to the secrecy and intimacy of the encounter: it is not about proximity or distance, but a getting closer which accepts the existence of distance and puts it to work.

In acknowledging that distance, and the possibility of multiple realities, the futures of education can move beyond a prescriptive ideal. Styres et al (2013) in their work on the 'pedagogy of land' provide an important example of such connections. Pedagogy of land is more than a pedagogy of place as it captures not only the 'materiality' of land but also the 'spiritual, emotional and intellectual aspects of Land' where Land is 'sentient' with a 'history ... a living thing' (pp 37–38). Styres et al propose a 'de-colonizing and indigenizing' of learning that is connected with the histories and realities of the land in relation to communities, 'a holistic perspective taking into account spiritual, emotive, cognitive, and physical elements of human interaction' that are 'ever-changing' (pp 39–40). The need to reorient education where a pedagogy of land is central to human inquiry, is also echoed in the work of Bell and Russell (2000) who highlight the limitations of existing critical pedagogical inquiry in which 'non-human' knowledge is 'peripheral to the core curriculum' (p 192). Drawing on Donna Haraway, they examine how intellectual engagement with the non-human world centres the human experience, where ecological and environmental encounters are defined by a human vocabulary that legitimizes the power and control of humans over non-human 'things' (pp 194–195). Central to this education is the reconnection with the diversity of the land and its various human and non-human inhabitants. It is this diversity that also informs the civic responsibility that is linked to the land and its inhabitants. The ideological borders of citizenship are further expanded, where a connection within and beyond nation states is developed.

Expanding and crossing borders

In reimagining education, the disciplinary boundaries that have ghettoized knowledge and learning need to be dismantled. Learning through an interdisciplinary curriculum, through community-led initiatives and progressive campaigns and movements that continue to evolve in ensuring human and non-human rights, creates the possibility of crossing intellectual and physical borders, creating empathy and strengthening civic and collective action.

In conceptualizing such a 'border crosser' (Giroux, 2005), the pedagogy of land is central. Styres et al (2013) suggest focusing on land-centred narratives and storytelling, with teachers helping students to 'interact with Land in their own teaching' (p 58). This further creates the possibility of expanding disciplinary boundaries, where land as a living thing becomes central to interdisciplinary inquiry.[5] Developing such a pedagogy of land is all the more important at a time where mass migration and displacement continues. The humanities and sciences in such a context provide the possibility of engaging with narratives of migration in relation to the land, focusing on people who have moved, or those who moved across generations, or were natives to the land, locating their relationship not only with each other but also with the land and the ecosystem within and beyond national boundaries (Whyte 2016 and 2018; Styres et al, 2013; Miller and Pointer, 2019). The diversity of the human and non-human experience that is realized through the education system also expands the discourse on rights, where every entity has a right to belong to the land, and exist in harmony, with civic responsibility towards all beings and entities that inhabit the land.

Intergenerational communities of learning

Formal education systems have been following a hierarchical model of education delivery, often undermining local, Indigenous knowledge and learning, where a disconnect exists between the formal school and the larger community. The problem with such a disconnect is further exacerbated when confronted by a global crisis such as the Covid-19 pandemic, which, by April 2020 had affected 94 per cent of learners worldwide that included '1.58 billion children and youth, from pre-primary to higher education, in 200 countries' as educational institutions closed down (UN, 2020d, p 5). If the goal of education is to promote a form of critical pedagogy that develops democratic values of progressive engagement in the human and non-human world, then such a disconnect undermines the entire project of change. It cannot meet the demands of decolonizing the curriculum, SS4C, FFF or Rhodes Must Fall, or the many protests by students against austerity, race, caste, class and citizenship violations in different parts of the world. An intergenerational, community-based model of learning prioritizes the local community as a pedagogical space of learning (see Iyengar and Shin, 2020; Quartz and Saunders, 2020). The critical pedagogy and feminist praxis approach takes this further, drawing on Indigenous methods of learning, where generational memory of involvement with the land becomes an essential part of this community engagement.

An example of such an approach can be found in the developing field of Indigenous Environmental Studies and Sciences (IESS), that focuses on 'Indigenous historical heritages, living intellectual traditions, research approaches, education practices, and political advocacy to investigate how humans can live respectfully within dynamic ecosystems' (Whyte, 2018, p 138). Such emphasis on a community-based approach that draws on Indigenous knowledge will also be instrumental in challenging the hegemony of knowledge production that legitimizes a Eurocentric, largely white-centric epistemology (Rich, 2012). However, in reimagining education, this approach is not simply another field of inquiry, but central to the education process. The institutionalized nature of education needs to evolve as a more fluid model of community engagement. Technological innovation in such a context balances the human and non-human relationship with the land and can be used to create greater ecological and environmental harmony. Civic responsibility will be linked more directly to the needs of the community and, more broadly, to principles of justice and equity, as promoted through a more fluid, community-based approach to education.

Conclusion: the futures await

As the struggle for sustainability continues, with governments reneging on their commitments to environmental and human rights, social movements, particularly those led by students, will be instrumental in holding existing governments accountable and in reorienting and reimagining the future. Such movements provide invaluable insights into reimagining the futures of education that are informed by the demands and concerns of these students. The various crises of the Anthropocene can be dealt with through an education that is localized in allowing deeper introspection and interrogation of structural injustices, while moving beyond the boundaries of the nation state through an affinity to the land and all of its inhabitants.

This chapter, in expanding on a future educational framework of CPFP, draws on existing student movements that have gained transnational appeal, that have highlighted environmental and ecological crises and the social and racial hierarchies that have ignored or silenced alternative forms of knowledge. The reimagining decentres the human in relation to the land; it decolonizes a largely Euro-/Western-/white-centric system of knowledge production by expanding and crossing disciplinary and physical boundaries, where education becomes a holistic experience and where learning is not confined to a formal institution, but equally centres community and generational knowledge. Such a decentring is all the more important in a context of mass migration and displacement, where the land, climate and environment are being ruthlessly exploited, and where local and Indigenous languages are in danger of becoming extinct and with them a rich heritage that celebrates the human and non-human connection with the land. This decentring employs a more interdisciplinary approach to education that locates the importance of natural sciences, humanities and social sciences, emphasizing an education that embraces technological and medical advancement while simultaneously centring narratives of land that contribute to a civic responsibility in protecting those who have been silenced within and beyond the nation state.

Notes

[1] Porta and Mattoni give examples of protests from 2008 to 2014 at different points in Iceland, Ireland, the Middle East, Portugal, Spain, Greece, New York, Turkey, Bulgaria, Brazil and Bosnia. These different protests evolve in response to the specific conditions in which they emerge.

[2] Examples of campus activism include campaigns such as #iTooAmHarvard to highlight the struggles and experiences of 'racially minoritized students' (Pimblott, 2020: 211).

[3] Such reckoning is also happening in other parts of the world, with the BLM movement that has inspired protests in other countries in the global North.

[4] This concept of the border crosser draws on Giroux (2005) and Yuval-Davis (2013 and 2017).

[5] Other examples include Wendy Harcourt's work on using art to develop a process of 'commoning' through which a 'shared political imaginary' is possible in relation to ecological and economic sustainability (Harcourt, 2019) and the Green Leadership Schools in South Africa that focus on Indigenous environmentalism (see Miller and Pointer, 2019).

Disclaimer

This paper was commissioned by UNESCO as a contribution to *Reimagining Our Futures Together: A new social contract for education* (UNESCO, 2021). © UNESCO 2020. This work is available under the Creative Commons

References

Ahmed, S. (2002) This other and other others, *Economy and Society*, 31(4): 558–572.

Angelo, M. (2020) Brazil slashes budget to fight climate change as deforestation spikes, Reuters, available at: reuters.com/article/us-brazil-deforestation-climate-change-a/brazil-slashes-budget-to-fight-climate-change-as-deforestation-spikes-idUSKBN2392LC [accessed 24 January 2023].

Bell, A.C. and Russell, C.L. (2000) Beyond human, beyond words: Anthropocentrism, critical pedagogy, and the poststructuralist turn, *Canadian Journal of Education / Revue canadienne de l'éducation*, 25(3): 188–203,

Bhambra, G.K., Gebrial, D. and Nişancıoğlu, K. (eds) (2018) *Decolonising the University*, London: Pluto Press.

Cho, S., Crenshaw, K.W. and McCall, L. (2013) Toward a field of intersectionality studies: Theory, applications, and praxis, *Signs: Journal of Women in Culture and Society*, 38(4): 785–810.

Climate Action Tracker (2020a) USA, available at: climateactiontracker.org/countries/usa/ [accessed 24 January 2023].

Climate Action Tracker (2020b) Brazil, available at: climateactiontracker.org/countries/brazil/ [accessed 24 January 2023].

Ellis, C. (2009) Education for All: Reassessing the historiography of education in colonial India, *History Compass*, 7(2): 363–375.

Fridays For Future (2020) Our Demands, available at: fridaysforfuture.org/what-we-do/our-demands/ [accessed 25 January 2023].

Giroux, H.A. (1992) Literacy, pedagogy, and the politics of difference, *College Literature*, 19(1): 1–11.

Giroux, H.A. (2005) *Border Crossing. Cultural Workers and the Politics of Education*, 2nd edn, New York: Routledge.

Giroux, H.A. (2018) *The Public in Peril Trump and the Menace of American Authoritarianism*, New York: Routledge.

Harcourt, W. (2019) Feminist political ecology practices of worlding: Art, commoning and the politics of hope in the classroom, *International Journal of the Commons*, 13(1): 153–174.

Henriques, A. and Abushouk, L. (2018) Decolonising Oxford: The student movement from Stuart Hall to Skin Deep, in J. Arday and H.S. Mirza (eds) *Dismantling Race in Higher Education: Racism, whiteness and decolonising the academy*, London: Palgrave Macmillan, pp 297 – 309.

Holmberg, A. and Alvinius, A. (2019) Children's protest in relation to the climate emergency: A qualitative study on a new form of resistance promoting political and social change, *Childhood*, 27(1): 78–92.

Human Rights Watch (2020) EU/Brazil: Delay trade deal pending Amazon crisis response establish benchmarks to address violence, deforestation, available at: hrw.org/news/2020/07/06/eu/brazil-delay-trade-deal-pending-amazon-crisis-response [accessed 24 January 2023].

Hytten, K. (2018) Globalization, democracy, and social movements: The educational potential of activism, in M. Gordon and A.R. English (eds) *John Dewey's Democracy and Education in an Era of Globalization*, New York: Routledge, pp 5–20.

Iyengar, R. and Shin, H. (2020) *Community-based Programs to Tackle Environmental Education and COVID-19: A case study from Millburn*, New Jersey: Prospects.

Jan, A.A. (2019) The students are rising, The News International, available at: thenews.com.pk/print/572314-the-students-are-rising [accessed 23 January 2023].

Ku, A.S. (2020) New forms of youth activism – Hong Kong's Anti-Extradition Bill movement in the local-national-global nexus, *Space and Polity*, 24(1): 111–117.

Martelli, J. and Garalytė, K. (2019) How campuses mediate a nationwide upsurge against India's communalization. An account from Jamia Millia Islamia and Shaheen Bagh in New Delhi, *South Asia Multidisciplinary Academic Journal*, 22, available at: journals.openedition.org/samaj/6516 [accessed 1 August 2020].

McKie, A. (2020) Rhodes Must Fall, Inside Higher Ed, available at: insidehighered.com/news/2020/06/19/britain-campaign-renewed-take-down-statues-cecil-rhodes [accessed 24 January 2023].

McKnight, H. (2020) The oceans are rising and so are we: Exploring utopian discourses in the School Strike for Climate movement, *Brief Encounters*, 4(1): 48–63.

Meda, L. (2020) Decolonising the curriculum: Students' perspectives, *Africa Education Review*, 17(2): 88–103.

Miller, D. and Pointer, R. (2019) Decolonising South African universities: Challenging the Anthropocene and re-centring Indigeneity, *South African Review of Sociology*, 50(3–4): 22–41.

Neubauer, L. et al (2020) Face the climate: Open letter and demands to EU and global leaders, available at: climateemergencyeu.org/#letter [accessed 24 January 2023].

Peters, M.A. (2015) Why is my curriculum white? *Educational Philosophy and Theory*, 47(7): 641–646.

Peters, M.A. (2018) Why is my curriculum white? A brief genealogy of resistance, J. Arday and H.S. Mirza (eds) *Dismantling Race in Higher Education: Racism, whiteness and decolonising the academy*, London: Palgrave Macmillan, pp 253–270.

Pimblott, K. (2020) Decolonising the University: The origins and meaning of a movement, *Political Quarterly*, 91(1): 210–216.

Porta, D. and Mattoni, A. (eds) (2014) *Spreading Protest. Social Movements in Times of Crisis*, European Consortium for Political Research.

Quartz, K.H. and Saunders, M. (2020) Community-Based Learning in the Time of COVID-19, Learning Policy Institute, available at: learningpolicyinstitute. org/blog/community-based-learning-time-covid-19 [accessed 25 January 2023].

Rich, N. (2012) Introduction: Why link Indigenous ways of knowing with the teaching of environmental studies and sciences? *Journal of Environmental Studies and Sciences*, 2: 308–316.

Rootes, C.A. (1980) Student radicalism: Politics of moral protest and legitimation problems of the modern capitalist state, *Theory and Society*, 9(3): 473–502.

Said, E. (2001) *Orientalism*, New Delhi: Penguin.

Saini, R. and Begum, N. (2020) Demarcation and definition: Explicating the meaning and scope of 'decolonisation' in the social and political sciences, *Political Quarterly*, 91(1): 217–221.

Saunders, F.S. (2016) Where on Earth are you?, *London Review of Books*, 38(5): 7–12.

Shahjahan, R.A. (2011) Decolonizing the evidence-based education and policy movement: Revealing the colonial vestiges in educational policy, research, and neoliberal reform, *Journal of Education Policy*, 26(2): 181–206.

Sian, K. (2017) Being Black in a white world: Understanding racism in British universities, *International Journal on Collective Identity Research*, 2(176): 1–26.

Styres, S, Haig-Brown, C. and Blimkie, M. (2013) Towards a pedagogy of Land: The urban context, *Canadian Journal of Education / Revue canadienne de l'éducation*, 36(2): 34–67.

Tuana, N. (2019) Climate apartheid: The forgetting of race in the Anthropocene, *Critical Philosophy of Race. Special Issue: Race and the Anthropocene and Race, Immigration, and Refugees*, 7(1): 1–31.

UN (2020a) Sustainable Development Goals, available at: un.org/sustainabledevelopment/climate-change [accessed 24 January 2023].

UN (2020b) World Social Report 2020: Inequality in a Rapidly Changing World, available at: un.org/development/desa/dspd/wp-content/uploads/sites/22/2020/01/World-Social-Report-2020-FullReport.pdf [accessed 23 January 2023].

UN (2020c) Youth Climate Action Summit 2019. un.org/en/climatechange/ youth-in-action [accessed 22 July 2020].

UN (2020d) Policy Brief: Education during COVID-19 and beyond, available at: un.org/development/desa/dspd/wp-content/uploads/sites/ 22/2020/08/sg_policy_brief_covid-19_and_education_august_2020.pdf [accessed 24 January 2023].

UNESCO (2020) *Visioning and Framing the Futures of Education*, Paris: UNESCO.

UNFCCC (2020) The Paris Agreement, available at: unfccc.int/process-and-meetings/the-paris-agreement/the-paris-agreement [accessed 24 January 2023.].

UNICEF (2019a Youth for Climate Action, available at: unicef.org/ environment-and-climate-change/youth-action [accessed 10 August 2020].

UNICEF (2019b) *Voices of Youth*, available at: voicesofyouth.org [accessed 10 August 2020].

wa Thiong'o, N. (1986) *Decolonising the Mind: The politics of language in African literature*, Woodbridge: James Currey.

Whyte, K. (2018) Critical investigations of resilience: A brief introduction to Indigenous Environmental Studies & Sciences, *Daedalus*, 147(2): 136–147.

Whyte, K.P. (2016) Indigenous environmental movements and the function of governance institutions, in T. Gabrielson, C. Hall, J.M. Meyer and D. Schlosberg (eds), *The Oxford Handbook of Environmental Political Theory*. Oxford: Oxford University Press.

Yuval-Davis, N. (2013) Working paper 2: A situated intersectional everyday approach to the study of bordering, *EU Border Scapes*, available at: euborderscapes.eu/fileadmin/user_upload/Working_Papers/ EUBORDERSCAPES_Working_Paper_2_Yuval-Davis.pdf [accessed 25 January 2023].

Yuval-Davis, N., Wemyss, G. and Cassidy, K. (2017) Everyday bordering, belonging and the reorientation of British immigration legislation, *Sociology*, 52(2): 228–244.

5

British Council Dialogues on Decolonization

Yvette Hutchinson

When we finished the Series, we did an evaluation. ... I said, what's the audacious goal; that the organisation makes a public statement to commit to looking at decolonisation. Sometimes you have to ask for the audacious win; the audacious ask ... [it] must be on the table to be turned down. It's fine if they say no but let's make them consciously say no. It's important that they are aware of what they are saying no to. And they can't say no if you don't ask. ... [It] forces the thought process.

Interviewee A

Introduction

The aim of this chapter is to reflect on grassroots activity and corporate strategy relating to decolonization at the British Council. The first was a staff-led, decolonization webinar series. The second was an anti-racism action plan driven by senior leaders. The chapter begins with an outline of the British Council's role and purpose and the events that took place in the summer of 2020. It identifies themes that emerged from interviews conducted with those involved in the Decolonisation Series and the anti-racism plan and places them within a framework that shows how the process for decolonization at the British Council began.

The British Council

The British Council builds connections, understanding and trust between people in the UK and other countries through arts and culture, education and the English language. The British Council works in two ways – directly with individuals and with governments and partners. Working in English and arts and culture, the British Council connects the best of the UK with the world and the best of the world with the UK. These connections lead to an understanding of each other's strengths and of the challenges and values that we share. This builds a trust between people in the UK and other nations that endures even when official relations may be strained. The British Council has over 10,000 members of staff in offices, teaching centres and libraries in the UK and more than 100 countries and territories worldwide. In 2019–20 we connected with 76 million people directly and with 983 million people overall, including online and through our broadcasts and publications. We are funded by a grant-in-aid from the UK government and with significant additional income from partnership agreements, contracts, teaching and exams. Founded in 1934, the British Council is a UK charity governed by Royal Charter and a UK public body (British Council, 2020a, p 4).

The British Council is often referred to as a cultural relations organization. Cultural relations are understood as:

> reciprocal transnational interactions between two or more cultures, encompassing a range of activities conducted by state and non-state actors within the space of culture and civil society. The overall outcomes of cultural relations are ... mutually beneficial transactions and enhanced sustainable dialogue between people and cultures, shaped through engagement and attraction rather than coercion. (Goethe-Institute and British Council, 2018, p 6)

In an internal British Council global live event in June 2021, Paul Smith, Country Director Germany, supplemented that definition, arguing that we need to see cultural relations as 'the way to describe, distinguish, celebrate the different peoples, societies, communities and network that make our world.'[1]

As in many organizations, the summer of 2020 was a vibrant period of equality and anti-racism grassroots activity at the British Council: 'There was across the organisation, a kind of cry for action, a cry for the British Council to take a position, a kind of grassroots movement which grew up and said how can we not be commenting on [these challenges to racism and colonialism?]' (Interviewee E).

As well as local, in-country events, there was a Black History Month initiative that, within days, became of interest to staff members across the network, with an increasing number of participants from around the globe. There was also a coaching series created and delivered by a minority ethnic staff member for fellow minority ethnic colleagues across the organization. As this was during the first few months of the Covid pandemic, these activities took place online, which opened up the opportunities to more people and made it easier for global activities to take place.

Engaging with decolonization

In August 2020, the British Council held a global webinar series on decolonization. Its target audience was staff in the Cultural Engagement department, made up of the teams who work across the arts, English and education in our offices globally. The idea for the webinars came from a small group of employees who volunteered their time to produce this series to explore decolonization. Such an initiative was groundbreaking as it involved colleagues from across the globe, mainly from lower pay-bands, speaking openly about a topic rarely mentioned at the British Council. The event was also significant because it was an opportunity for those colleagues to speak directly to the organization and to have their views shared openly with senior-leader decision-makers. There were, and have been, long-standing corporate structures in place to address issues of equality and diversity, but those issues were not part of the general discourse across the organization. Colonialism and decolonization were not included in the guidance document and strategies, neither were the experiences of minority ethnic staff candidly discussed and prioritized.

> 'There was a gap. In spite of having a Diversity Unit and an Equality Diversity and Inclusion team which said we should be focusing on these things, and in spite of having a race equality guide [too], it was clear that leadership hadn't been doing what the Diversity Unit had been advocating. Something had to be done.' (Interviewee F)

As an organization, around the same time, perhaps not unrelated to the events in the summer of 2020, the British Council was embarking on its anti-racism action plan, with five sections to address learning, organizational culture, policies and practice, diversity in leadership and products and services. The other major corporate activity was within the Cultural Engagement department, in response to independent research commissioned early in 2020 by the Minority Ethnic Working Group (MEWG) made up of UK-based staff particularly concerned about minority ethnic representation in the UK. The research, later dubbed the Greenwich Report, reviewed minority ethnic staff representation and experiences. The implementation of the report recommendations helped to maintain momentum around these issues directly within Cultural Engagement and by extension across the British Council.

This chapter concentrates on the influence of the Decolonisation Series on the British Council's anti-racism action plan and considers themes that arose as staff-led activism emerged at the same time as the British Council was proposing its corporate aims. While acknowledging that currently there are many arguments about the term decolonization and 'the danger of superficial engagement with decoloniality' (Left of Black and Rodriguez, 2018), the focus of the grassroots activists was to explore decolonization as a means to open debates about colonialism, heritage and practice in the British Council. These debates took place alongside a more formal, corporate initiative whose initial goal was to focus on anti-racism policy. This chapter explores how the volunteer activities appeared from a 'liminal space' led by Black and Brown staff members from across the global network, most of whom had little or no engagement with the initial development of the corporate anti-racism action plan.

This discussion uses Ashcroft's definition of the liminal as 'an interstitial or in-between space, a threshold area' (Ashcroft et al, 2007, p 117). The activists working on the Decolonisation Series came from a 'threshold area' determined by their ethnicity and lower pay-bands. To an extent, discussions around race and decolonization were also on the threshold, or the edges, of the priorities of corporate discourse at the British Council. A group of British Council activists created a new space for dialogue; a 'transcultural space in which strategies for personal or communal self-hood [were] elaborated' (Tiffin, 1995).

Liminality has often been used to frame discourse in post-colonial studies. Caribbean theorist Sylvia Wynter regards the liminal as a 'boundary-category' and suggests that those in that category are 'able to break free of the normative ways of knowing Self, Other and world, mandated by the prescriptive rules' (Wynter, 1990). Homi K. Bhaba (1994, p 4) sees liminality as opening up 'the possibility of a cultural hybridity that entertains difference without an assumed or imposed hierarchy.' In contrast, theologian Barry Stephenson (2020, pp 3 and 6), writing on the limits of liminality, argues that:

> liminality is rarely theorized in relation to normativity. Rather, liminality/anti-structure are often first placed in binary opposition to disciplined, normative practice (to social status, to norms, to structure), and, second, the suspension of rules, transgression/subversion, and creativity are generally valorized at the expense of norms, institutions, and structures … It is not simply that normativity tends to be given short shrift – normativity tends to be positioned as a boogey or straw man.

This chapter aims to demonstrate a call and response between the 'structure and anti-structure', where what might have begun as a 'binary opposition' became an institution's blended approach to challenging inequality. Indeed, Stephenson himself conceded (2020, p 1): 'The goal is not necessarily to flee to and embrace the margins, but to allow greater access to centering institutions, as well as move those worthwhile beliefs, values, and ways of life that may be cultivated or protected at the margins into the center, into "officialdom".'

Based on the responses from the British Council staff interviewed, these definitions of the liminal as a boundary-category subject to 'imposed hierarchy', correspond to how several of the respondents considered their position as employees.[2] Informed by Wynter and Bhaba's work, we will see how those staff members used their own 'cultural hybridity' and the opportunities from the Decolonisation Series to 'break free of the normative'; to open up a new area of discussion. They introduced a unique exploration of decolonization and the beginning of a new approach to how the British Council could define and develop its programmes.

There is also a significant body of research on liminality in management and organizational studies. Söderlund and Borg (2018, p 1) conducted a systematic review of this literature that has 'advanced understanding of the inherent problems and tensions involved in transitioning from one condition and identity to another, and the profound challenges and significant consequences of developing and living with multiple identities and competing value systems.' Their review showed that the literature on liminality falls into three categories: as process, position and place. These provide a helpful way to frame the themes that emerged during analysis of the interviews discussed later in the chapter.

The liminality of the activists is in contrast to the role and position of those who commissioned the anti-racism action plan: established senior colleagues who represented and were supported by the corporate machinery of the British Council.

Positionality and methodology

As an African Caribbean woman and British Council employee involved in its Minority Ethnic Working Group, I acknowledge my own commitment to what Patricia Hill Collins describes as 'lived experience as a criterion of meaning.' With that in mind, I invoke those lived experiences in 'selecting topics for investigation and methodologies used' (Collins 2000, pp 257–258). Accepting Greene's (1994, p 539) observation that 'the self of the qualitative evaluator is acknowledged to be present in the inquiry, a presence that permeates all methodological decisions and penetrates the very fabric of meaning constructed,' I have included the notion of 'having skin in the game' in my own reflections and observations as well as those of the contributors. Equally, I acknowledge what April-Louise Pennant identifies in her PhD research, that 'the identities, experiences and feelings of the interviewer and interviewee ... are imbued in this method and greatly shape the direction of the interviews, what is shared within them and how the data is interpreted' (Pennant, 2019, p 103). My interactions with the interviewees have been informed by my own experiences as a Black woman employee experiencing that liminal space. It has also been influenced by my commitment to the aim of decolonization and my support and admiration of the colleagues who volunteered to design a grassroots decolonization activity that later informed a corporate priority. However, I have been mindful of the four factors of researcher motivation, description of research methods, strategies to establish rigour and the researcher's role in data analysis that Liu (2016) identified as the methodological foundation for the generic inductive approach.

To examine the topic, I reviewed the following British Council documents, all of which were written within the last two years and were chosen because they represent the organization's position specifically on race equality and anti-racism, rather than the more general and guidance on equality diversity and inclusion:

- British Council New Narratives report on a programme designed to help contribute to changing reciprocal perceptions between Africa and the UK (March 2020)
- *The Greenwich Report*, Minority Ethnic Staff Representation and Experiences in the Cultural Engagement SBU at the British Council (June 2020)
- British Council Summary and Evaluation of the Decolonisation Series (September 2020)
- Race equality through anti-racism guide (March 2021)
- British Council Anti-Racism Action Plan (May 2021)
- 'Decolonisation, Cultural Relations, and the British Council: Exploring Africa-UK Relations', a collaborative piece of research commissioned in July 2021

Using an inductive approach, I chose purposive sampling to conduct semi-structured interviews with seven British Council colleagues, four of whom were based in the UK. The two males and five females were located in four of the seven regions and two of them were on the senior management pay-scale. They defined themselves as: Queer Black British cis female; mixed race; African Asian mixed race; African; Middle Eastern; white male; Black with white English (African born). All of the interviewees had contributed to or were involved in the anti-racism action plan, the Decolonisation Series, Black History Month 2020 events, the New Narratives programme and the coaching plan. They are referred to as Interviewee A to G. Based on their responses, three major themes were identified that relate to the Decolonisation Series and the development of the anti-racism plan:

1. The process of development
2. The personal and professional
3. The spaces created and the support networks

Later in the chapter, I place the themes within the three stages of liminality and draw some conclusions on the ways in which the grassroots and corporate activities intertwined.

The following section provides an overview of the Decolonisation Series, the anti-racism action plan and the three major themes that emerged. It includes an analysis of Söderlund and Borg's (2018) categorizations of liminality and how they relate to these two British Council events.

The Decolonisation Series

The Decolonisation Series of six online events took place in August 2020. The aim was to start conversations, consider new approaches and respond to the global movement for equality. The British Council works across a variety of platforms, some of which include engaging with educators and artists who are also thinking critically about the issue of decolonization. Thus, while the Series was about starting conversations within the British Council, the theme of decolonization was important for many British Council partner organizations, and the aim was also to equip staff to engage in those discussions with external agencies.

The development of the Series brought about a transition from a situation where issues of race, identity, culture and colonialism were rarely discussed in open forums to opportunities for such dialogue across disciplines, pay-bands, cultural identities and socio-economic and political positions. The purpose was for this global organization to engage 'staff with lived experience ... to help shape what we as an organisation should be doing [about decolonisation] and shaping our understanding' (Interviewee D).

The genesis of the idea for the Decolonisation Series came about after a summer induction programme in 2019. The programme took place in the UK and provided an opportunity for individuals working in arts teams from a range of British Council country offices to meet together in the London headquarters. During the induction, they shared an understanding of the British Council's arts portfolio. They also visited different cities, historical locations and artefacts in the UK and learned about UK cultural institutions. A troubled Jamaican colleague noted the beauty of the buildings and wealth that came from the enslavement of their ancestors. The colleague found the experience of seeing the magnificent architecture and the celebration of those institutions harrowing; they expressed their concern to the leaders of the induction programme. The discomfiture coming from this 'racial erasure' (Sriprakash et al, 2020) was discussed among the group, and other colleagues on the programme began to express similar concerns. In particular, they noted that, in their experience, the issues of racism and Britain's colonial past were never examined, either in the British Council UK or in their own country offices.[3]

Months later, after the murder of George Floyd and the subsequent resurgence of Black Lives Matter, the leader of the induction programme communicated with the participants to resurrect the discussions from

2019. This began a debate on decolonization that they wanted to explore more fully with others in the British Council. Contributing to this discussion was what they believed to be the British Council's invidious position as a cultural relations organization and its role in the teaching of the English language. As such, the British Council had been a part of the British Empire's colonial project and this, they argued, was a huge issue for the organization to manage. Despite recent commitments to promote multilingual education (British Council, 2019), the British Council's role in teaching English around the world was also regarded as an element of the organization's colonial past and present. The interviewees said that the organization should look critically at issues of colonialism, power and empire; to acknowledge the historical legacies that inform the realities of relationships between the British Council and other countries. With these concerns in mind, 26 colleagues from offices across the British Council launched an online series to explore decolonization. The production team developed the theme, agreed the content, identified speakers and contributors and managed each webinar.

The sessions were a mixture of external and internal speakers, discussions and reflections on British Council programmes, assets and artefacts across the areas of arts, English and education. The Series also allowed colleagues to showcase work that was already happening, such as the Africa/UK New Narratives programme,[4] 'designed to contribute to changing reciprocal perceptions between Africa and the UK' (British Council, 2020c, p 2).

By highlighting topics such as North-South partnerships, land ownership and the use and role of museums, the Decolonisation Series showed how British Council cultural products, artefacts and assets could be explored from a 'decolonised lens'. The Series also encouraged colleagues to think about how the British Council shared expertise, how it privileged certain types of knowledge and particular voices, while not providing a similar opportunity for others. In the evaluation report, the writers outlined the benefits of the series: 'By initiating this series, and empowering colleagues to raise challenging issues through the crowd sourced approach, the organisation was taking an important and welcome step forward in acknowledging the importance of hosting difficult conversations and encouraging organisational self-reflection' (British Council, 2020b, slide 21).

As the Series continued, the momentum around the topic of decolonization drew 'bystanders', supporters, senior leaders and key decision-makers to attend. They listened and participated in discussions that began to take place across the organization. Despite having to adjust to Covid-19 lockdown demands and its associated pressures, the need for these discussions became evident as the content of the Series and the opportunities to discuss culture, race and equality issues drew more people to participate. All the sessions allowed time for discussion and open dialogue, and what began as a series for one department of the British Council became a global event with over 500 total attendees from over 30 countries.

The Anti-Racism Action Plan

The British Council Anti-Racism Action Plan (March 2021) was created through ongoing consultation to address racism and how it would be challenged across the company. The British Council has a Diversity Unit that has consistently challenged the organization to improve performance in the areas of equality, diversity and inclusion. Balancing the role of support and challenge, the unit had produced toolkits and guidance as well as speaking directly to the leadership on actions and accountability. The development of the anti-racism plan was seen as both a continuation of the work of the Diversity Unit and a corporate response to recent global movements against racism and the ongoing legacy of colonialism. The process began in the Autumn of 2020 and was 'signed off' by senior leaders in the following statement in May 2021:

> Based on the experience and expertise of our Diversity Unit, research and feedback, we have set the following five priorities as a starting point:
>
> 1. Improving our learning and understanding about racism/s and its impact
> 2. Supporting a more inclusive organisational culture that prioritises anti-racist actions and behaviours, leadership development, and improved ways of listening to and acting on colleagues' feedback and concerns
> 3. Human resource policies and practices that are reviewed, revised and undergo equality screening and impact assessment to ensure they promote inclusion and antiracist principles
> 4. A greater diversity of nationality and race in our global leadership
> 5. Programmes, products and services that are deliberately anti-racist and inclusive in their development and delivery, consistent with our commitment to *decolonise* our work. (Emphasis added)

In the document's joint introduction from the senior leadership team and the anti-racism task force,[5] it was clearly stated that 'The Anti-Racism Action Plan is an addition to the range of interventions that have supported and will continue to support our Equality Diversity and Inclusion work.' Discussion with the interviewees revealed that the initial aim of the plan did not include decolonization but had its focus on reiterating the British Council's commitment to inclusion and making clear that anti-racism had to be a significant part of that pledge. As the consultation continued, the plan had to ride the waves of opinion, frustration and solidarity that groups were expressing. Having invited the comments of individuals and groups, it was clear that the issue of decolonization was becoming increasingly important. Finally, as a result of the Decolonisation Series and subsequent grassroots activities and events, the writers had to broaden the aims so that the British Council's anti-racism plan included decolonization as its fifth priority.

From the inductive approach taken to this study, three themes emerged that reflect the issues identified by those working on the Decolonisation Series and those involved in the development of the anti-racism action plan. While these themes arose for those involved in the Series from a liminal 'boundary-category' (Wynter, 1990), for those leading the corporate initiative, they related to the themes in distinctly different ways.

Decolonization from the grassroots

Theme 1: The process of development

For some of the interviewees, the Decolonisation Series fitted into Söderlund and Borg's definition of liminality as process: 'various types of transgressional events that destabilize identification and that trigger the co-creation of some means to resolve the ambivalence' (Söderlund and Borg, 20178 p 8). For them, the Series was 'transgressional', as the act and process of launching the Series circumvented the corporate bureaucratic systems in order to respond immediately to the need to discuss racism and decolonization. These interviewees saw a more organic, almost anti-bureaucratic approach as a strength of the Series. They talked about not having to wait 'on an18-month plan' (Interviewee B); a wry comment on the length of time it can take for an idea to become a plan and then become established practice in the organization. There was a sense in which the very systems and processes that were a central feature of the organization were being disrupted to achieve immediate engagement with colleagues.

Crucially, part of the process was the nature and structure of the grassroots activities themselves: a decolonized approach that Interviewee A called 'enabling unheard voices'. In their insightful essay 'Is Decolonising the New Black?' Left of Brown and Jenny Rodriguez (2018) state: 'Decolonising work sets out to destabilise epistemic understandings, building consensus among the marginalised. ... As such, its aims are always collective, collaborative and anti-competitive.' This collective collaboration was evident in the way in which the Decolonisation Series was organized and in who was involved in the programming: 'Like a crowdsourced idea, not top-down. We've got actually in-house experts with academic, intellectual and lived experience. It was decolonising how we did things' (Interviewee D). Interviewee D further outlined the approach they agreed to use in organizing the webinar:

'Let's make this democratic. Let's invite people to step up to present if they feel comfortable in doing so... Let's not do it in the typical British

Council way, which is people with fancy job titles telling everyone what they should be doing. Let's do it in a way that's more inclusive. … I think what I found powerful was that there were people running, producing [the Series], at lower pay [grades], talking about some of these issues. … That was in itself powerful and 'uncorporate.' (Interviewee D)

The 'transgressional act' of the Series itself, along with the crowdsourced approach, was reflective of the values and ambitions of those who developed the programme.

Under this first theme of process, unlike the Series activists, those leading the British Council's anti-racism action plan did not see bureaucracy as a barrier. They saw bureaucracy as valuable; an enabler to embed the ambitions of the plan into corporate systems: 'The plan is well-circulated and translated into [performance management targets] for each member of the global leadership team which will be published on the British Council's intranet and embedded into the corporate structures, processes and quarterly business reviews' (Interviewee F).

Another interviewee recognized the importance of using the checks and balances of British Council management procedures as an inclusive tool; a way to allow the voices of those in the 'border category' to be a part of the process:

'When the intent was articulated to develop the Plan, it came with a governance process through which the Plan would happen; a Task Force [a corporate implementation group] as well as a Challenge Group [a group of colleagues from across the global team who were invited to review and critique the different versions of the action plan]. The first task was to assemble that Challenge Group. We expected 50 people across the network, who would register as our consultation group – we had more than 170.' (Interviewee E)

The process was important to those involved in the anti-racism action plan, as they developed their approach in response to a recent project on 'New Narratives', which sought to change reciprocal perceptions between Africa and the UK. That influence, along with the innovative creation of the Decolonisation Series, led them to an awareness of the richness of the views and discussions from local staff associations, different job functions and pay-bands that would then inform the way the consultation process was managed (Interviewee E).

Theme 2: The personal and professional

Of the three themes identified, the most poignant came from interviewee reflections on the personal and often emotional cost of raising issues around race and the experiences of minority ethnic staff. Söderlund and Borg identified this liminality of position as complexities of the 'blurred volunteer-practitioner boundaries' (Söderlund and Borg, 2018 p 100). The interviewees said that they felt they had to volunteer their time to create activities relating to decolonization. Some interviewees pondered whether they should take on the Decolonisation Series and then did so somewhat reluctantly, knowing that it would require 'huge emotional labour and intensity. ... I am glad I did it, because it's been a journey for me as well and I can see the value that I bring, but I think it's important to acknowledge that it was hard' (Interviewee D).

These concerns notwithstanding, overwhelmingly, the interviewees recognized that the personal costs also had benefits to themselves as individuals as well as to their work and to the British Council: 'Something I find generally in activism, specifically anti-racism which is grassroots ... [requires] people using their extra time ... a lot [of commitment] at the time but worthwhile, really rewarding to see the engagement [of colleagues], shining a little light can help them with their path' (Interviewee C). The personal cost went beyond volunteer time and engaging in topics that have a personal impact. One interviewee saw the Decolonisation Series as a contribution to the history of struggle for Black people within the British Empire:

'It's an honour and privilege to do the work. It's not just skin in the game, I carry my family with me, those who have gone before us, those who have fought for us to have these opportunities to continue the good work. ... Generations before and behind you when you do this work, that keeps you going. ... I didn't expect to personally have the emotive response to the work that I did and that surprised me. [As did] how much it meant to be able to connect with new colleagues globally, over a really important issue that we were interested in.' (Interviewee A)

From a professional point of view, while none of the interviewees mentioned enhancement of their professional profiles, by being involved in the Series, many of them were introduced to a global British Council audience and their abilities were showcased across the organization. For some, recognition of their skills and abilities outside their immediate teams helped to raise their profiles and increased the professional respect they received within their own teams.

Under this theme of the personal and professional, those working on the anti-racism action plan were not required to volunteer their time and had corporate sanction to establish teams and commission reports. However, personal cost and professional impact became an important theme as those who developed the plan realized the pressure of volunteerism and the dangers that it posed to the organization's minority ethnic staff. Interviewee E commented on the need for work around anti-racism and decolonization to be a corporate commitment that was not dependent on those who were personally invested in seeing these changes: 'Through the process of developing the Plan and engaging [with colleagues from across the organisation] I am convinced more than ever, that we need a corporate response [to decolonisation]. We can't leave it to individuals.'

Theme 3: The spaces created and the networks

Liminality as place is described by Söderlund and Borg (2018 p 14) as 'giving rise to new possibilities for the creation of alternative organizational arenas.' Applied to decolonization activities in the British Council, the Series opened spaces for conversations from which new possibilities could emerge. In her essay 'Decolonising Education: A pedagogic intervention', Carol Azumah Dennis (2018, p 202) concluded with ten pedagogic approaches to decolonizing education, and the first is particularly pertinent to this theme: 'Establish a space within which it is possible to speak about decolonisation. This may require a rejection of the most readily and easily available spaces, necessitating the deliberate cultivation of an otherwise space.' The Series itself was a new space for the topic of decoloniziation, and, equally important, it created openings for colleagues to share their views and value the existence of fellow minority ethnic colleagues:

> 'That learning of not Westernising your thinking, of decolonialisation, is really important. It reinforced how important it is for us to be able to create a safe space to talk about difficult things; a safe space because we work in a complicated organisation and we actually enjoy talking about those things. There was a whole new space where I could be with other people who are ME [minority ethnic] colleagues.' (Interviewee A)

In addition to the value of spaces to discuss decolonization was the parallel development of support spaces that buoyed and energized activists. 'I had white colleagues saying you shouldn't be doing this. ... It wouldn't have been possible without Xxx and Xxx, I need[ed] that emotional support. It was hard' (Interviewee D). While interviewees named particular (minority ethnic) colleagues who were sources of support, it was the development of systems of support and networks that was a crucial enabler.

In Azumah Dennis' ten pedagogic approaches (2018, p 202), the final suggestion particularly defined what became a source of strength for the grassroots activists:

> Develop and nurture sacred spaces and protected narratives. Work to ensure a strong support network comprising of white allies, Black colleagues and friends. This network will act as your sacred space of

sanctity. ... Such spaces provide an opportunity to engage in forms of narrative protected from the dehumanizing violence of the White World. These are narratives with which to theorise, decode, de-stress in relative safety and to reaffirm one's humanity.

The Diversity Unit's role of challenge and support foregrounded much of the activity and solidarity on which new groups were built. The British Council's Minority Ethnic Working Group was already established and had commissioned the Greenwich Report on minority ethnic career progression and experiences. Following the Decolonisation Series, Black History Month activities and the coaching programme, a global ethnically diverse group was established with a huge membership across the organization. As colleagues began to relax into these 'safe spaces', a monthly meeting, 'Team Strength: A space for us, by us', became their 'sacred space'.

One of the new networks came from the changed relationship with senior leaders. It was surprising that most interviewees commented on the importance of senior leadership backing and support. Interviewees acknowledged the importance of managerial endorsement – 'that this was a valid way to spend time' (Interviewee A). They also noted that having shared the idea of the Decolonisation Series with leaders, they felt that those senior leaders went beyond expectations and 'mandated' the grassroots activists to complete their work (Interviewee D). This endorsement of their activities opened the door for further discussion about decolonization, not just as an activity led by a few colleagues, but as a movement within the British Council that needed to be adopted by corporate leaders and embedded into the organization's work and programming.

Under the third theme of creating spaces and networks, this became an important element of the process of the action plan development and, indeed, was written into the second pillar of the plan itself; to promote improved ways of listening to and acting on colleagues' feedback and concerns.

Regarding networks, the Decolonisation Series gave the activists a chance to speak to senior leaders and receive endorsement for their work. As one would expect, those leading the anti-racism action plan, talked about being fortunate to have been given the task by members of the senior leadership and global leadership teams who were committed to the plan. For them, the process of the wide consultation and the engagement with task forces and challenge groups also gave rise to new networks. These new networks allowed those leading on the plan to expand their engagement with different groups across the organization and crucially to hear from a variety of colleagues: '[We had]lots of engagement from pay-bands 5 and 6 as well as senior colleagues. We made sure that the plan had their inputs. We [involved] a much wider group than had been envisaged [and it was] all the better for it' (Interviewee F).

Conclusion

My aim in this discussion was to consider how the British Council – the UK's international cultural relations organization – negotiates and continues to respond to calls for a discussion about decolonization. One month after the webinars took place, the evaluation of the Decolonisation Series made eight recommendations, one of which asked for a global call for colleagues to suggest practical ways to 'decolonise thinking'. Interviewee A, whose comments open this chapter, challenged the team to consider what might be the 'audacious goal'. The activists were amazed when, through their discussions and subsequent contributions to the action plan consultations, they saw the realization of their audacious goal: a public commitment to decolonize British Council programmes and products.

Recognizing Stephenson's challenge that 'normativity tends to be positioned as a boogey or straw man' (2020, p 6), this chapter has illustrated how these grassroots and corporate activities repositioned normativity for the British Council. The process of repositioning required, and continues to demand, organizational reflection and review. For those involved in the Decolonisation Series with 'skin in the game', this reflection was also personal. As the sociologist Árpád Szakolczai (2009, p 166) acknowledges: 'while liminal situations and positions can contribute to creativity or the renewal of institutions and structures that have become oppressive or simply tired, liminality also implies deep anxiety and suffering for all those entering such a stage.'

Since conducting these interviews, the British Council has commissioned more research on 'Developing the British Council's Understanding of Anti-racism in the Context of its Cultural Relations Strategy and Programming'. The aim is to further the exploration of decolonization by suggesting working definitions and how they can be applied to programming. This will enable the British Council to begin the process of putting the commitment into action. However, there are still significant challenges: 'One thing that I've really learned and has made me very sad, is how UK-centric this organisation continues to be. That message keeps on coming through and that's going to be a difficult one to address, in the way we think, work and how English language is a part of that, as well' (Interviewee F).

The British Council continues to navigate the territory of teaching English in a way that equitably values other languages. It also has to balance its role to promote UK expertise at the same time as it endorses different ways of knowing and doing as part of the process of decolonization. Indeed, as the chapters on reparative futures in the third part of this book will show, in order to decolonize our institutions, we also have to recognize the impact, repercussions and symbolism of an imperial and colonial past.

There is also the matter of fulfilling the raised expectations of minority ethnic staff. As the anti-racism action plan has committed to 'greater diversity of nationality and race in our global leadership', there is an opportunity and a challenge to increase the number of minority ethnic staff in senior positions. For those involved in the Decolonisation Series, and indeed those who contributed to the consultations on the action plan, they have ambitions for the organization and wish to hold the British Council to account. At the same time, they want to work within the organization to effect the changes they wish to see. The British Council will need to consider how this can be achieved without adding the 'burden' of decolonization on staff members whose personal commitment and enthusiasm has added significantly to their current workloads.

This exploration of the grassroots actions of a group of staff who, in many ways, were on the sidelines of corporate actions and decisions, has illustrated how the 'audacious aim' of a small group of individuals can effect lasting change in a global organization's policy and actions. The encounter between these grassroots and corporate activities will have a lasting effect on the future of decolonization at the British Council. As Interviewee E optimistically concluded: 'Even if [the action plan] doesn't cover every little thing, it will inspire, energise, trigger other grassroots actions and they will feed off each other.'

Notes

1   British Council Global Live Event, 23 June 2021, 'What makes a great Cultural Relations project?'
2   The notion of the' imposed hierarchy' in this context relates to two factors. The first is the fact that there are very few minority ethnic staff in leadership positions. The second is to do with the imposed hierarchy of ideas and topics that such a monocultural leadership creates.
3   One interviewee pointed out that there was a general recognition that colonialism and its ramifications were problematic elements of the British Council's existence and its activities and needed to be addressed.
4   The British Council New Narratives programme commissioned the Research, Insight and Evaluation (RIE) team at M&C Saatchi World Services to undertake a comprehensive investigation into how young people in the UK and African countries perceive each other and their countries. The investigation had five objectives:
    1. Identify the source and nature of dominant narratives, messages and themes that frame the UK in Africa and Africa in the UK.
    2. Map how young people in the UK and Africa engage with, share, and resist the dominant narratives, messages and themes.
    3. Establish the extent to which these narratives contribute to moulding perceptions that 18–35-year-olds across both places have of each other.
    4. To understand the ways, if any, that 18–35-year-olds feel these narratives affect their willingness to network across both places to social, economic and political ties.
    5. Highlight the less dominant narratives that 18–35-year-olds across both places would like the other place to have access to, such as: What would a young African want the UK to know about Africa?
5   The anti-racism task force was a group of staff members from across the globe who managed the consultation and document development process.

References

Ashcroft, B., Griffiths, G. and Tiffin, H. (2000) *Post-colonial Studies: The Key Concepts*, London: Routledge.

Azumah Dennis, C. (2018) Decolonising education: A pedagogic intervention, in G.K. Bhambra, D. Gebrial and K. Nişancıoğlu (eds) *Decolonising the University,* London: Pluto Press, pp 197–207.

Bhaba, H.K. (1994) *The Location of Culture,* London: Routledge.

British Council (2019) English language and medium of instruction in basic education in low- and middle-income countries: a British Council perspective, https://www.teachingenglish.org.uk/sites/teacheng/files/K068_EMI_position_low-and_middle-income_countries_Final.pdf.

British Council (2020a) Annual Report and Accounts 2019–20, available at: britishcouncil.org/sites/default/files/annual_report_2019-20.pdf [accessed 25 January 2023].

British Council (2020b) Exploring Decolonisation Series, Evaluation Report, September 2020.

British Council (2020c) New Narratives Report, March 2020, https://www.britishcouncil.org/sites/default/files/new_narratives_report_summary.pdf.

Collins, P. (2000) *Black Feminist Thought: Knowledge, Consciousness and the Politics of Empowerment,* 2nd edn, New York: Routledge.

Goethe-Institut and British Council (2018) Cultural Relations in an Age of Uncertainty Report, November, 2018, https://www.britishcouncil.org/sites/default/files/cultural_relations_in_an_age_of_uncertainty_en.pdf

Greene, J. (1994) Qualitative program evaluation, in N. Denzin and Y. Lincoln (eds) *Handbook of Qualitative Research,* Thousand Oaks, CA: Sage, pp 530–537.

Left of Black and Rodriguez (2018) Sista Resista Is Decolonizing the New Black? July 12, 2018 https://sistersofresistance.wordpress.com/2018/07/12/is-decolonizing-the-new-black/

Liu, L. (2016) Using generic inductive approach in qualitative educational research: A case study analysis, *Journal of Education and Learning,* 5(2): 129–135.

Pennant, A. (2019) Look, I have gone through the education system and I have tried damn hard to get to where I am, so no one is gonna stop me!: The educational journeys and experiences of black British women graduates, A thesis submitted to the University of Birmingham for the degree of Doctor of Philosophy, School of Education, University of Birmingham.

Simpson, J. (2019) English language and medium of instruction in basic education in low- and middle-income countries: a British Council perspective, British Council.

Söderlund, J. and Borg, E. (2018) Liminality in management and organization studies: Process, position and place. *International Journal of Management Reviews,* 20: 880-902. https://doi.org/10.1111/ijmr.12168.

Sriprakash, A., Tikly, L. and Walker, S. (2020) The erasures of racism in education and international development: Re-reading the 'global learning crisis', *Compare*, 50(5): 676–692.

Stephenson, B. (2020) The limits of liminality: A critique of transformationism, *Liminalities: A Journal of Performance Studies*, 16(4):1–23.

Szakolczai, A. (2009) Liminality and experience: Structuring transitory situations and transformative events, *International Political Anthropology*, 2(1): 141–172.

Tiffin, H. (1995) Postcolonial literature and counter-discourse, in B. Ashcroft, G. Griffiths and H. Tiffin (eds) *The Post-Colonial Studies Reader*, London: Routledge, pp 95–99.

Wynter, S. (1990) *Do Not Call Us Negros*, San Francisco: Aspire.

6

Decolonizing the University: A Perspective from Bristol

Alvin Birdi

Introduction: decolonizing what?

Like many universities, the University of Bristol is engaged in a process of examining its complex links with a colonial past.[1] The University's relationship with slavery, for example, is memorialized in the names of some of its buildings and facilities and it has benefited from investments derived from slave labour, such as tobacco, chocolate and sugar. The process of reckoning with the university's heritage involves a broad range of work that is being coordinated by a high-level strategic committee chaired by the provost.

Acknowledging past injustices and incorporating them into the story that universities tell of themselves makes a contribution towards reparative justice as argued by Walters (2017) in the context of Brown and Harvard universities. Indeed, as was the case with both of these US universities, research into the past and its legacy is one way to understand the structural injustices that persist into the current day and inform actions that might improve the lives of those who continue to be harmed as part of this legacy.

This pursuit of intergenerational equity is one of the features that brings decolonization into alliance with climate justice. Colonial injustice, like climate injustice, involves inequities that play out over many generations. In the case of climate, current extractive activities may impose significant costs on future generations. In the same way, colonial injustice persists through time because of its deep embedding within economic, educational and social institutions and within cultural norms and power relationships. Injustice, in other words, may be passed between generations even in the absence of any intentional activity unless it is explicitly identified, countered and dismantled. In both cases, of climate and colonial injustice, inequities can be obscured by the fact that oppressor and oppressed are not always contemporaneous.

This chapter concentrates on intergenerational manifestations of coloniality without wishing to hide contemporaneous injustice so as to limit the focus on a specific aspect of education, that is, what Pinar et al (1995) define as the culture-preserving aspects of curriculum over time. They write that an educational curriculum is 'what the older generation chooses to tell the younger generation ... [the curriculum] is intensely historical, political, racial, gendered, phenomenological, autobiographical, aesthetic, theological and international. It becomes the site on which the generations struggle to define themselves and the world' (pp 847–848). This temporal transmission involves the preservation and replication of epistemic injustice, the undervaluing, exclusion and silencing of certain types of knowing.

Decolonizing the curriculum is a way of interrupting this temporal logic by scrutinizing and arresting the transition of culture from one generation to the next. Despite a considerable literature and public discussion about decolonization, however, practical examples of what is entailed in decolonizing within higher education are rare. One reason is that the term, decolonizing, 'involves a multitude of definitions, interpretations, aims and strategies' (Bhambra et al, 2018, p 2). Equally, the object of the decolonization is often fluid, moving freely between the 'curriculum', 'education' or even the 'university'. This fluidity has also led to some confusion about the scope and focus of activities aimed at decolonizing.

As a result, there are a wide variety of practices that are regarded as decolonizing activities in universities worldwide. These include efforts to reform local course content and teaching practice, scrutiny and rewriting of reading lists, institutional efforts to address racial attainment and promotion gaps, promotion of staff and student diversity, the renaming of buildings and facilities, fostering of external partnerships and diversification of procurement. In turn, these activities can be initiated by and involve academic staff, professional services staff, university leaders and students. They might also involve external stakeholders. There is, in other words, no shortage of activities that might be considered constituent elements of decolonizing in a university. Indeed, to the extent that decolonizing should ultimately be concerned with social and reparative justice, its remit cannot be contained within the narrow confines of, say, the taught curriculum and it is therefore unsurprising and welcome that it permeates across the various divisions and functions in a university. To be sure, the university is itself too limited a frame in which to contain decolonization, which is, above all, a global social and civic mission to address injustice.

This chapter focuses primarily on decolonizing the curriculum, delimiting this from wider initiatives aimed at decolonizing the university and the even broader challenges of impacting society beyond the academy. The intention is to provide an overview of what might be *practically* involved in decolonizing the curriculum, a phrase that is widely used but variously understood. I argue that decolonizing the curriculum necessarily involves engaging with wider issues in a university (and beyond), but, at the same time, decolonization cannot succeed in the absence of potentially significant curriculum changes. There is a synergy and mutual dependence between these two dimensions of decolonization.

Decolonizing the university and decolonizing the curriculum

Decolonization necessarily poses some foundational questions for a university about its position and function in society, its values, how it conducts its core work and the role it can play in transforming society. Specifically, decolonizing the university involves acknowledging and discussing the part played by universities in bolstering coloniality throughout the project of modernity and in establishing various epistemic divides, hierarchies and exclusions in the contemporary academy. The continued manifestations of colonial injustices can be seen across university institutions, for example in the lack of diversity in many institutions' staff and student populations, in their procurement practices, their valorization of certain types of research and publication, their inherited estates and funding streams and their memorialization and veneration of individuals and organizations with connections to colonial trades.

There has been a moderately strong focus on addressing these kinds of issues in many universities worldwide. A survey of 128 universities by *The Guardian* newspaper in June 2020 found that around a fifth had committed to high-level initiatives around decolonizing.[2] What that survey reveals is that there is a risk of decolonization becoming lost in the midst of equality-based initiatives. As Tuck and Yang (2012) and Moosavi (2020) remind us, various actions purportedly aimed at decolonizing can run a risk of emptying decolonization of any specificity, capturing it within a range of other improvement projects that universities have already committed to, such as inclusivity and diversity strategies. As such, decolonization activities may simply amount to rebranding existing initiatives.

Such dangers are also implicit in attempts to specifically decolonize the taught curriculum, presumably a more tightly defined task than the decolonization of the university as a whole.[3] Take, for example, the introduction of more plural reading lists with inclusion of authors and voices from the global South. Moosavi (2020) points to the danger that such curriculum decolonization efforts might re-silence voices from the global South by homogenizing or essentializing their contributions to knowledge. He explains that 'essentialisation would occur if one were to allude to an intellectual from the global South and claim that *the* global South perspective had been acknowledged' (pp 343–344), thus falling into the trap of a colonial generalization and riding roughshod over the plurality of voices that one wishes to include. A related danger is the uncritical glorification of scholars from the global South based purely on identity rather than the scrutiny or intellectual disruption that could come from their inclusion, a risk that Moosavi refers to as 'nativist decolonisation'.

A related risk with pluralism is what Bowles and Carlin (2020, p 208), in a different context, have called 'pluralism by juxtaposition' whereby different voices are brought together purely because pluralism itself is seen as a virtuous pedagogic imperative rather than as a means of challenging or throwing a critical or corrective light on mainstream or dominant perspectives. An equally damaging risk stems from the expectation that plural knowledges should only be valued if they enable students to reflect critically on mainstream perspectives and not because they offer valuable insights on the world in their own respect. The dangers inherent in the practice of decolonization are therefore extensive and local practice is beset with immense difficulties. It is therefore not surprising to find in university departments a willingness and passion to engage with the task of decolonization but without a clear sense of how to proceed.

Yet, while these many university- and curriculum-level actions may come with the risk of losing a connection to critical decolonizing practices, they do, nevertheless, contain the potential to be part of a decolonizing project. It is, after all, difficult to conceive of anything called decolonizing that does not consequently extend educational opportunity, raise the diversity of the staff and student body, introduce more pluralism into the curriculum or address structural inequalities in attainment, for example. The important question is how these various activities can be given an overarching rationale within a practice of decolonization and how the various risks discussed above can be mitigated in a university setting.

It is argued here that a project of decolonization in an institution as large and complex as a modern university requires the drawing together, by mutual critique and cross-fertilization, a wide and potentially disparate range of equality-oriented practices that in themselves may seem inadequate to the task of progressing epistemic or reparative justice. Without this, multiple localized efforts in the university or within disciplinary curricula can seem unrelated and piecemeal. In other words, decolonization should be conceived as multifaceted, manifesting at local and institutional levels simultaneously. It is a complex and unordered process that gains its potential impact from the creative collision and collective power of diverse practices. It is attended by many potential pitfalls, some of which were sketched earlier, but is nevertheless propelled by a joint imperative to correct injustices that universities help to sustain. In de Sousa Santos' (2018) terms, the different scales of 'micro' and 'macro' need articulating together in order to draw out their potential for change.

Given this imperative, it is welcome that many universities worldwide, including Bristol, have announced, and are currently involved in, resourcing and implementing institution-wide decolonizing initiatives. But there is also a risk that, in a financial context where corporate and financial pressures necessitate the use of performative indicators of success to rationalize resource allocations, universities may choose to see decolonization as a strategic and finite programme in which the metrics of success can be predetermined and progress measured against them. This runs the risk of seeing decolonization as an identifiable state to be achieved. It is near impossible, however, to define what such a state would entail to any degree of performative accuracy. What level of plurality would exist in the curriculum? What levels of participation by disadvantaged communities would there be? What kinds of impact would we need to see in the wider society and employment that universities have influence over?

Such questions cannot be easily answered. Instead, decolonization must be seen as an ongoing and somewhat unpredictable process of change and critical reflection that moves universities and the wider society continually towards repairing some of the epistemic and material injustice that colonialism created. Universities, including their students and staff, do not have a privileged position from which they can identify and rectify the many explicit and implicit negations, exclusions and suppressions of coloniality. Indeed, to presume so would be to repeat a gesture reminiscent of colonialism. As Mignolo and Walsh (2018) put it: 'There is no master plan and no privileged actors for decoloniality' (p 125). They *almost* go so far as to suggest that coloniality is the decolonizing university's unconscious (see p 140) with the implication that coloniality is ever-present in the functioning of a university. Indeed, what needs doing in decolonization can only become known through an ongoing and authentic procedure of reflection, dialogue and transparency, that is, through the very process that brings it about. In other words, decolonization must become an embedded mode of operation for a university in which it both decolonizes and learns what it is to decolonize through reflecting critically on that practice.

Mignolo and Walsh (2018) argue that decolonial practice is not about changing the 'enunciated' or content of knowledge but the 'enunciation' or the terms within which it takes place (p 144). Similarly, we might argue that the defining structures and processes of the university, its composition of divisions and disciplines, its ways of evaluating and rewarding knowledge, staff and curricula and its contributions to civic society are what are at stake in decolonization rather than any plans or strategies that might take place within these structures.

With these issues in mind, this chapter charts a range of work towards decolonization being undertaken across the University of Bristol. In particular, it considers the task of catalysing and offering critique to various initiatives around the institution, bringing together the top-down with the bottom-up, in such a way as to avoid the risks mentioned earlier, that of misidentification with other equality objectives and the presumption that a programme of successful change can be identified in advance. I argue that decolonizing the curriculum is a necessary process of local change that gains its impact through articulation with processes at the institutional level. Decolonizing the university and decolonizing the curriculum are synergistic and mutually dependent endeavours.

The experiences recounted here are necessarily situated within the specificities of the University of Bristol, a research-intensive UK university with complex entanglements with coloniality and the transatlantic slave trade. Nevertheless, Bristol's experience may offer some insights into how decolonizing education may be conceptualized and turned into practice elsewhere too.

What does it mean to decolonize the curriculum?

This section focuses closely on what decolonizing the curriculum entails, building on the discussion of decolonizing education in Chapter 1. Both the term, 'decolonization', as well as its object, 'curriculum', are difficult to define closely so that other terms and concepts sometimes stand in for them.

It is useful to consider Bhambra et al's (2018) description of the term decolonization as comprising two elements. The first is the situating of knowledge and knowledge practices within the context of colonial and racial history so that the influence of colonialism and its effacements can be traced. The second is to offer 'alternative ways of thinking about the world and alternative ways of political praxis' (p 2). While views of decolonizing are varied, they tend to fall somewhere in the broad domain of these two elements.

De Sousa Santos (2018, p 276) similarly describes two sides of decolonizing as firstly redressing 'absence' (or, as discussed in Chapter 1, what he terms 'epistemicide') and secondly fostering the 'emergence' of 'latent and potentially liberating sociabilities'. At a very general level, we might say that decolonizing involves understanding the past and its legacy as well as finding ways to transform the future. As noted previously, there is an important sense in which decolonization involves thinking about equity and justice across time.

One could attempt a crude delineation of activities that fall on one or other side of this two-element characterization of decolonizing. For example, the diversification of reading lists and the inclusion of previously ignored or marginalized viewpoints is one way of addressing the impact of colonialization on current teaching and knowledge practices. Activities such as funded scholarships for students in communities impacted by a colonial past or diversifying procurement might be conceived of as attempts to decolonize society for the future. In other words, various decolonizing activities that take place in a university may be situated along a continuum between understanding the legacies of the past and attempting to address their contemporary and future manifestations. Of course, the two sides of the definition are closely related because it is the knowledge of how colonialism affected the academy that informs how injustices are manifest today and what reparative justice might look like.

At the risk of some simplification, it can be argued that the work of transforming teaching and learning so that it addresses coloniality is being done locally by staff and students within academic departments interrogating their courses and modules, and by allied professional services staff such as those in libraries. Indeed, the impact of this intellectual work on students and staff involved may be profound, and the implicit hope must be that staff and students will carry this critical frame of mind to their future civic lives and their employments so there is a sense in which the second, change-oriented, element of De Sousa's description of decolonization follows naturally from the first.

There are aspects of the second element, however, that are best pursued by the university as a whole. After all, it is at this institutional level that strategic scholarships are often created and where questions of the nature of civic engagement, the values of the university and the framing of its priorities are considered. And it is at this level where the agency exists that can bring the various decolonial activities taking place around the university into critical and productive dialogue with each other. For example, the disciplinary basis of universities makes certain interdisciplinary discussions about coloniality difficult. The issue of reparations is at once a matter of (at least) economics, politics, ethics, social policy, geography, accounting and law, and such discussions can be narrow or omitted because they do not always fall into disciplinary homes. It is only at institutional level that the possibility might exist for the creation of an interdisciplinary lens in education, perhaps through special modules or options.[4]

In a related vein, de Sousa Santos (2018) speaks of 'potentialities, latencies and possibilities of resistance' that occur on concrete or local terrains – what he calls the 'micro level'. But, he says, whereas these micro practices are valuable across times and places, the emergence of new and decolonial practices in education must also take place at the 'macro' level. He suggests that 'the sociology of emergences has to be transscale' (p 251), by which he means that we must be capable of translating local practice into terms that enable us to see their relevance for global hegemony: What challenge do these practices impose at a different scale of analysis? How can they enable us to think differently? Although de Sousa Santos is discussing sociology and the struggles of communities across the world, his insights are nevertheless important in complex university settings too. For example, what does the use of more inclusive pedagogies and pluralistic ways of knowing in individual departments mean for the way that a university prioritizes its research activity, or its partnerships with students, or the possibilities of co-creating the curriculum with stakeholders from outside the university?

The university leadership is critical to bringing these various micro activities together in a way that might create meaningful decolonial change. Barnett (2022, p 184) rightly cautions against seeing university leadership as consisting of a group with a clear and effective corporate agency separate from the disparate community of staff and students. He suggests that we make a clear distinction between the function of corporate management and leadership. Both, he says, are important, but the implication is that a university leadership team may err more towards corporate management rather than leadership. Management, for Barnett, is the art of the possible, of managing complexity successfully, such as in recent efforts to move learning online during the Covid-19 pandemic. Leadership, on the other hand, is a process of encouraging debate and dialogue in the university community and manoeuvering through the resulting, often discordant, competing discourses to 'glimpse new possibilities' for the university (p 187). Decolonial practice, in other words, is a question of leadership. It happens both from the bottom-up and the top-down simultaneously in a process of creative dialogue that is characterized as much by dissension as agreement.

As with 'decolonizing', the term 'curriculum' may also be understood in (at least) two ways.[5] The first is as a description of what is being taught and assessed in a programme, for example its constituent modules. In this form, it may be captured in writing, in a programme document for example. As a definitive textual document about course content and pedagogy, the curriculum can function as an orienting guide for both staff and students, but it can also function as a quality-assurance instrument by which internal and external agencies can influence or evaluate university education. It can also be used as the basis of a consumer-based legal contract between students and universities. The curriculum as a description of constituent elements is somewhat additive and fragmentary, made up of a number of parts that together form a degree programme.

The second interpretation of 'curriculum' is what Barnett (2022) describes as an 'expression of pedagogical responsibility' (p 130), which depicts the terrain over which choices are made during the process of education. In this interpretation, the curriculum merely contains an outline intention, an overarching purpose and design within which an emerging and open process of situated learning takes place. For Barnett, the objective of a curriculum is to envisage and demarcate the kind of 'being' that emerges through education, and how that being embodies understanding and acts in the world. This interpretation stresses synoptic rather than piecemeal understanding. Rather than fragmentary modules and credit points, the curriculum is seen as a process where a student 'becomes' over time through bringing together learning, critical reflection and experiences drawn from the university's taught programmes, its pastoral opportunities, its civic environs, its staff and other students. Just as with the term decolonizing, the curriculum has an aspect that is oriented towards defining and delimiting a programme of what is to be taught and an element that is oriented towards a transformative and experiential process of learning that opens the possibility for a potentially different and more just future. In this second sense, the transformative potential of the curriculum resides both within a critical-orientation of the taught material and with the broader environment of the university experience.

The purpose of raising these definitions here is to suggest that practical decolonization will consist of activities situated within interpretations of both the terms decolonization and curriculum. Such an ecosystem of activity may appear somewhat chaotic in its variety because the definitions of these terms are broad. Some activities may involve staff and students interrogating the complicity of disciplinary frameworks in the colonial project or in tracing the effacements of Indigenous and plural knowledges. Other activities will take the form of encouraging reflection and debate on the content taught and the pedagogical methods used. Yet others will be concerned with the forms that transformative curriculum change might take through partnerships and opportunities inside and outside the university. Many of these actions will be organic, for example reading groups or reading list scrutiny groups instigated by students and staff within local areas. Others will be introduced as decolonization initiatives by the educational leadership. Others will result from committed activism and political groups. We find all of these levels of activity in a university such as Bristol. The following section describes this heterogenous ecology, its emergence and some of its properties.

Decolonizing at the University of Bristol: local practices and praxis

Individual scholars at the University of Bristol have been researching and teaching on aspects of decolonization for many years, but the work has mushroomed in the past couple of years. In 2018, the university's Bristol Institute for Learning and Teaching (BILT) convened a learning community[6] around internationalization and decolonial thought as it pertained to the curriculum. This learning community consisted of around ten scholars drawn from all parts of the university. The group was one of four learning communities based around themes that BILT had identified as of increasing strategic importance at Bristol. The aims of the learning communities from the university's point of view were to foster cross-disciplinary working and to develop intellectual capacity in these emerging strategic areas. From the perspective of the participants, the value was in personal and professional development and the opportunity to build working relationships with academics that they would not necessarily have come across in their usual disciplinary settings. At this stage of inception, there were no students or professional services staff involved in the group as BILT had been instituted primarily as an academic staff institute.

The learning communities were modestly funded and, as is usual with such communities, aims and objectives were not set out in advance but were to emerge organically through the interests of the members. To an extent, a shared desire for decolonization and racial justice animated the group so that the broad aims of the group were consonant. At the time, decolonizing the curriculum had not become a formal part of the university strategy, partly because the strategy in operation had been created some years prior. The productive combination of a central institute of the university organizing and bringing together staff already thinking about or engaged in decolonization without setting out predetermined goals was novel, at least in the educational space of the university. As a model for how a university might work with localized interests and activities in the process of decolonization, it has proved extremely valuable, and key elements of its approach still characterize the work of decolonization in the university today.

In spring 2019, the learning community organized a week-long visit to the university by Professor Bonaventura de Sousa Santos, a well-known scholar of decolonization, particularly as it pertains to universities. The week consisted of seminars and round-tables involving staff and students from across the university. The practice of involving external voices within the decolonization efforts of the university has continued since.

The origins of the strategic decolonizing work of the university in the scholarly work of an interdisciplinary group of academics is important because it situated decolonization within the university as borne out of intellectual pursuit, discovery and critique. When the learning community morphed into the university-level Decolonizing the Curriculum Group (DCG) in 2020, it brought decolonial practice into its existing space of intellectual dialogue. The mix of disparate practical decolonization activities from around the university and theory-laden critique has characterized the university's approach to decolonization ever since. The theoretical perspectives of the staff in the DCG have been brought together with the local practices in existence around the university in a way that affords critical perspectives on both practice and theory. As Mignolo and Walsh (2018) write: 'Praxis without theory is blind; theory without praxis is sequestered' (p 138).

As the work of decolonization has proceeded in the university, it has become clear from consultations during workshops and recent surveys that many staff and students feel their ability to work on decolonization is constrained by a sense that they lack the relevant knowledge and expertise they feel is necessary to engage in this work. The DCG has nevertheless proceeded on the basis that sharing of emergent practice from around the university together with theory-based reflections create a process of mutual learning through which practice is refined on an ongoing basis. This is in opposition to the more traditional mode in which expert leaders drive practice to ensure success.

Recent initiatives by the DCG have included the construction of a large group of staff from around half the schools within the university in a mutually supporting group where plans, actions and outcomes are being shared in a process of communal learning. We return to this schools' decolonization project later.

The DCG reports to the high-level strategic committee co-chaired by the provost called the Anti-Racism Steering Group (ARSG). The DCG's work on decolonizing the curriculum comprises the teaching and learning (curriculum) workstream within a broader set of workstreams aimed at racial justice, which include naming (of buildings and facilities), governance, HR, research and civic engagement and student admissions. Nonetheless, the teaching and learning strand retains considerable autonomy over its own programme of activities and is not convened as a formal committee. It has largely continued to function as a community of practice and does not see its work as coordinating or leading the numerous activities that are taking place across the university. Rather, it has sought to bring visibility and awareness to the various ways in which decolonizing is being practised in the university, with a view to creating an ongoing dialogue about decoloniality, why it is necessary and what it might entail.

In late 2020, the DCG began to record its reflections on decolonizing into a practically oriented course on the *Futurelearn* platform entitled *Decolonising Education: From Theory to Practice,* which went live in January 2021.[7] It brought together academics, students and many external contributors, including de Sousa Santos, and provides an intellectual source for academics and others who wish to find a practically oriented but theoretically informed account of decolonization. Importantly, the course enacts what the decolonizing group had set out to do – to highlight many of the strands of decolonizing work underway in the university and bring them into creative dialogue with others as well as with the theoretical literature around decolonization.

What is clear from the *Futurelearn* course is that there is a great diversity in the work being done on the ground across the university. In the Medical School and in the School of Sociology, Politics and International Studies, for example, student groups have worked with key staff to initiate reviews of many modules in terms of their coverage as evidenced by the course descriptions. In terms of the characterization of the curriculum, this kind of activity is focused on curriculum seen as a guiding definitional document rather than a terrain for open learning. By putting it together with a range of other approaches to decolonization, as well as theoretical conceptions of the curriculum, its value for others as well as its limitations can be brought out clearly. For example, the methodology articulated by the student groups in these schools is currently being used by other schools. At the same time, there is a greater understanding that changes to curricula at the level of written documents (such as reading lists and course outlines) may have limited impact on what goes on in the classroom or in what students are actually encountering in the module content, which may be more open-ended than the documentation allows. Some of these approaches have led to local academic resistance, which limits their impact. An increased focus on classroom pedagogies and student agency may serve to address some of these issues, for example by allowing students more choice in what they are assessed on or giving them more agency within their learning so that they are equipped and motivated to challenge the material they are presented with. Some of these changes may require facilitation centrally in the university, which, if enacted, may in turn influence practice more widely.

Other approaches to decolonization include those that engage with groups and organizations outside the university, either through bringing external voices into the classroom, by partnering with external organizations on specific projects or by learning from anti-colonial struggles and activism in the global South. One collaboration of note is with school teachers from around Bristol and the creative organization CARGO led by Bristol poet Lawrence Hoo. The collaboration, which involved the Bristol School of Education, created History lesson plans that incorporate narratives from individuals of African and African diaspora descent for the city's schools at Key Stage 3, an initiative known as CARGO classroom.[8] The collaboration with CARGO also produced some resources for use with incoming students to provide them with an induction that situates the university within Bristol city by emphasizing the communities of Bristol through narratives of their lives.[9]

Some approaches have been more strategically planned and resourced, such as that undertaken in the Management School, in which formal school committees have sought to embed decolonization as part of the curriculum development and assurance stages of its education, including through formal accreditation from the AACSB and its Assurance of Learning framework. In Law, decolonization efforts have partly revolved around the creation of a specific unit on 'Law and Race' and within Economics, certain module leads have independently revised their units to incorporate more intellectual diversity.

The *Futurelearn* course continued the DCG's original orientation around scholarship as a key component of decolonial practice. It is now being followed by the development of seminars and articles that will form the content of an edited volume on 'decolonization as praxis'. Alongside the seminars, disciplinary resources have been created to help orient staff who are engaged in decolonial practice. The development of these intellectual resources alongside the university's decolonization efforts allows those involved to take stock and reflect on the progress and direction of the process. These developments form both a retrospective account, a theorization and a critical reflection of Bristol's pursuit of decoloniality and they are intended to be 'living' documents, changing as more is learned about the practice of decolonization. In addition, whereas the original BILT learning community consisted of members of academic staff, contributors to the latest stage of work include students, professional services staff and external participants such as CARGO or academics from other universities, broadening the work of decolonization to bring in the voice of the external community. In a recent workshop, two external academics as well as CARGO were present at cross-school discussions in the university and offered their own critique of what they witnessed. As the interest in decolonization intensifies across the university, there are more and more examples of activity developing within academic schools that can be drawn upon and learned from.

As noted earlier, a recent development is the creation of a large grouping modelled loosely on a community of practice. This is the Schools' Decolonisation Project, which consists of heads of school and representatives from a number of schools in the university. The group also contains students and professional services staff. The group is relatively new, having been convened in late 2021. Integral to its success will be ensuring that it does not reduce to a mere juxtaposition of various practices in a kind of smorgasbord or menu from which an academic might select a least-cost fix to the problem of coloniality. Avoiding this trap will rely on bringing a critical focus to decolonial activities through the lens of varied practical experience from around the university as well as theory. As an example, the inaugural event for the group, held in December 2021, involved a survey of practice, a round-table and an external panel in which theoretical and critical considerations were invited on the range of practices discussed. These critical reflections are essential to ensure that practice evolves and does not become ossified, limited or inwardly focused.

Through these reflections, we have learned about the usefulness and limitations of certain activities in specific contexts. For example, we have learned, through some of the work in Bristol, that there are implicit risks involved with common decolonization practices that are solely, or even predominantly, oriented towards the diversification of knowledge content within taught courses, such as in diversifying reading lists. Much decolonial practice instigated by students and staff often begins here. One risk of this practice is that diversity of perspectives may come to stand in for decolonizing. This risk arises partly through interpreting curriculum in an overly limited way, as discussed previously. There is, after all, no guarantee that readings and content that are added to formal written curricula are afforded serious attention within the actual practice of teaching a course or programme. Such are the limitations of an overly legalistic and assurance-based view of the curriculum. There is, in other words, an incompleteness to the written curriculum in that it cannot prescribe within its terms how seriously the subject matter prescribed is approached, taught or valorized. As a result, changing the written curriculum may have no effect at all. At worst, there is the risk of essentialism, tokenism and appropriation (see Moosavi 2020) by the mere inclusion of authors who may be simply placed alongside other perspectives within a course but without any intellectual challenge to orthodox perspectives – what Gopal (2021) calls 'a glib pluralism' and what, following Bowles and Carlin (2020), we might call 'juxtapositional' plurality.

The University is also learning from working with student partners the importance of student agency in the curriculum as a decolonial pedagogy. For example, a risk of concentrating efforts on diversifying knowledge sources in a curriculum is that it stops short of considering how pedagogy animates the way that students encounter and engage with knowledge. Decolonization must enable students to challenge orthodoxy and canonical approaches to knowledge, but the pedagogical literature informs us that this challenge is likely to be most effective where students internalize it and exercise agency; that is, where they are invited and equipped to reflect, research and evaluate knowledge themselves. Barnett (2022, p 141) describes a process of 'energising' the student to impart a 'will to learn' so that they are not merely given command over a discipline as if they were repositories of knowledge. Challenge and plurality are much less effective if merely 'voiced' by an instructor as a range of discrete alternatives. Indeed, they will be most effective if the 'will to learn' is accompanied by pedagogic changes that encourage challenge and discussion in classes.

In Barnett (2022), the process of energizing students is described as providing inspiration (p 114), which is much easier where a curriculum is perceived by a student as relevant to their life or frame of reference. In thinking about whether teaching is relevant for the students in a class, a teacher is compelled to think about whose reality is being ignored, avoiding thereby a characteristic gesture of colonialism where certain interests are marginalized. So, we are also learning about the specifically decolonial uses of authentic pedagogy and assessment.

Decolonizing the university: a whole-institution approach

When the learning community on decolonization and internationalization was set up in 2018, it was not clear that the model of partnership between the university and its complex and diverse communities of staff and schools was one that would work outside the small community of practice. However, as discussions progressed within that community of practice, and particularly once it became the DCG as part of the ARSG strategic committee, it became clear that the model of the community of practice fitted well with the sense the members had developed of decolonization. The process needed to invite multiple viewpoints and practices and that progress would be most likely as an outcome of dialogue and critical and reflective scrutiny. It needed to involve students, staff and communities outside the university, and it needed external links with movements aimed at restorative justice globally wherever possible so that it avoided becoming insular in scope.

The University, through its leadership team and BILT, has been an important facilitator in the work of decolonizing the curriculum. Importantly, it has delegated authority for the leadership of decolonizing the curriculum to the DCG, which in turn has taken a leadership approach of fostering dialogue and engagement following Barnett's (2022) description of leadership. This has enabled the DCG to achieve a balance between bottom-up initiatives coming from academic schools and the dissemination, sharing and dialogic activities organized across schools. In addition, through its strategic ARSG, the university has created a mandate and culture in which decolonization across the institution is encouraged.

Other aspects of this cultural shift can be seen in other parts of the work of the ARSG. It is, for example, taking the issue of memorialization seriously, as noted at the outset of this chapter, by directly addressing the story that Bristol tells of itself and its past. Bristol has, through various actions, begun to acknowledge the issues surrounding the naming of some of its buildings and facilities that relate to slave owners or those who benefitted through colonial trades in tobacco or sugar. A Chair in the History of Slavery and the Memory of Enslavement was established in the university and there is now a centre for Black humanities as well as the Perivoli Africa Research Centre and a Black scholarship programme at undergraduate and postgraduate levels. The University is planning to apply for a Race Equality Charter award. These kinds of commitments at the university draw resources into decolonization efforts. They also help to signal that the university is serious about its commitment to racial justice and that the problem of coloniality is one that affects the whole institution and requires a whole institution response. There is, to be sure, no guarantee that these actions constitute the foundations of successful decolonial practice, but, as a totality, they increase the likelihood of positive change.

Conclusion: a work in progress

Bristol's approach to decolonization is characterized by local practices complemented by institutional leadership by colleagues with a long-standing interest in decolonization. It has pursued a deliberate policy of decolonizing the curriculum supported by wider initiatives for decolonization of the university, recognizing the synergies between the various local and institutional activities. This has involved sharing practices, critical dialogue and theoretical reflection.

There has been an attempt to mitigate and understand risks through dialogue, scholarship and extensive participation of staff, students and external stakeholders. It might be considered a process of encouraging experimentation, debate and challenge that does not try to define the contours of what decolonization should look like in advance and likewise has no discernible end-point. Despite some of the successes we have seen through this approach, there are inevitably shortcomings, and this section highlights some of the challenges that Bristol faces as it progresses this work.

It is no surprise that a significant part of the work on decolonization has engaged at the level of the written or formal curriculum, namely the content that is being taught. This has concentrated on addressing gaps in knowledge and dealing responsibly with the provenance, context and relevance of what is taught. These considerations have, however, sometimes avoided an explicit focus on pedagogy and assessment that may be more difficult to shift where practices of instruction are long-embedded in the culture of teaching. A pedagogy that gives students agency in their learning and assessment is a broad challenge that may require more work, perhaps training, than reconsidering the content of the curriculum.

A further significant challenge is creating space within what, in many disciplines, is an overly full curriculum. This remains a problem in decolonization, not only because plurality and context can only be introduced where there is room to do so, but because the reluctance to remove content may signal the persistence of canonical knowledge that refuses to be challenged.

Finally, Bristol's complex relationship to coloniality, still evident in some of its estate and inheritances as well as the relative lack of representative diversity in its staff and students, remains an ongoing challenge to negotiate, and any successes in decolonizing the curriculum will ultimately be limited by the extent to which the university itself is able to embed decolonization permanently in its structures and processes.

Notes

[1] Glasgow University's pledge of £20m to set up a joint centre for research with the University of the West Indies as part of a programme for restorative justice, has been well publicized. See: theguardian.com/uk-news/2019/aug/23/glasgow-university-slave-trade-reparations.

[2] 'Only a fifth of universities say they are "decolonising" curriculum', *The Guardian*, 11 June 2020.

[3] In the *Guardian* survey, some 84 universities said that they were undertaking curriculum-specific decolonization work.

[4] An example is a recently created module at Bristol open to students from various disciplines called 'Decolonise the Future'.
[5] See Fraser and Bosanquet (2006) on differing conceptions of the curriculum among staff and students.
[6] The concept of 'learning community' is here considered as a heterogeneous community of teaching and research staff brought together with a broadly shared sense of purpose and oriented around collective inquiry through regular interaction. The idea of a professional learning community has been discussed in the literature for some decades. See Graves (1992) for an early account of the concept and its practice within educational settings. See also Li et al (2009) for an account of how the concept of learning communities evolved into the later notion of 'communities of practice'.
[7] See futurelearn.com/courses/decolonising-education-from-theory-to-practice.
[8] See cargomovement.org/classroom.
[9] See universalcity.co.uk.

References

Barnett, R. (2022) *The Philosophy of Higher Education: A critical introduction*, London: Routledge.

Bhambra, G.K., Gebrial, D. and Nişancıoğlu, K. (eds) (2018) *Decolonising the University*, London: Pluto Press.

Bowles, S. and Carlin, W. (2020) What students learn in economics 101: Time for a change, *Journal of Economic Literature*, 58(1): 176–214.

de Sousa Santos, B. (2018) *The End of the Cognitive Empire*, Durham, NC: Duke University Press.

Fraser, S.P. and Bosanquet, A.M. (2006) The curriculum? That's just a unit outline, isn't it?, *Studies in Higher Education*, 31(3): 269–284.

Gopal, P. (2021) On decolonisation and the university, *Textual Practice*, 35(6): 873–899, DOI: 10.1080/0950236X.2021.1929561.

Graves, L.N. (1992) Cooperative learning communities: Context for a new vision of education and society, *Journal of Education*, 174(2): 57–79.

Li, L.C., Grimshaw, J.M., Nielsen, C. et al (2009) Evolution of Wenger's concept of community of practice, *Implementation Science* 4(11).

Mignolo, W.D. and Walsh, C.E (2018) *On Decoloniality: Concepts, analytics, praxis*, Durham, NC: Duke University Press.

Moosavi, L. (2020) The decolonial bandwagon and the dangers of intellectual decolonisation, *International Review of Sociology*, 30(2): 332–354.

Pinar, W.F. et al (1995) *Understanding Curriculum: An introduction to the study of historical and contemporary curriculum discourses*, New York: Peter Lang.

Tuck, E. and Yang, K. (2012) Decolonization Is Not a Metaphor. Decolonization. 1. 10.25058/20112742.n38.04.

Walters, Lindsey K. (2017) Slavery and the American university: discourses of retrospective justice at Harvard and Brown, *Slavery & Abolition*, 38(4): 719–744.

7

Decolonizing the Curriculum in English Secondary Schools: Lessons from Teacher-led Initiatives in Bristol

Terra Glowach, Tanisha Hicks-Beresford and Rafael Mitchell

Introduction

School teachers in England are in a problematic position with respect to the 'decolonizing the curriculum' agenda. On the one hand, they have some scope to determine what they teach in terms of content and methods, and are not prohibited from engaging in such initiatives, as evidenced by the wide-ranging work underway (for example, Moncrieffe, 2020; Gandolfi, 2021; Glowach et al, 2023). On the other hand, England has what we might term an 'unconducive policy environment' for this work. The Department for Education does not endorse such initiatives and external accountability measures do not incentivize them. Despite the government's expressed aim to 'eliminate discrimination [and] advance equality' in education (DfE, 2014), its reforms to the national curriculum have been widely criticized for 'nationalistic ideologies, with monocultural and Anglocentric emphases on exclusively British literature and propagandist history' (Cushing, 2020, p 429). National policy actors have little appetite to acknowledge or address well-documented curricular biases towards the perspectives and contributions of white men (for example, Lais, 2017; Parkin and MacKenzie, 2017; Bain, 2018; Belas and Hopkins, 2019; Watson, 2020; Moncrieffe, 2020; Smith, 2020; Tikly, 2022). Indeed, the government has responded with hostility to calls for a more diverse and representative curriculum. While in post, the influential schools minister Nick Gibb rejected calls to make the teaching of Black history compulsory, arguing: 'We will not create a more harmonious, tolerant and equal society through promoting a curriculum based on relevance to or representativeness of any one group. ... A curriculum based on relevance to pupils is to deny them an introduction to the "best that has been thought and said"' (*The Guardian*, 2021).

English schools operate in an unconducive environment for the kinds of decolonizing work advocated in this book. Such work is neither forbidden nor encouraged, but it is undermined by enduring legacies of colonial, racial and patriarchal domination. In this context, this chapter highlights the critical role of teacher agency in initiatives to decolonize the curriculum. 'Agency' refers to intentional, creative acts that run counter to social norms and expectations, and which may challenge the status quo (Priestley et al, 2015). As we see in this chapter, teachers have various, interrelated motivations for engaging in this kind of work, from the desire to enrich teaching and learning in their subject to fostering critical thinking among learners and countering racist and colonial narratives. Teacher agency in this area is informed by teachers' experiences (both personally and professionally) and is oriented towards the future, intending 'to bring about a future that is different from the present and the past' (Priestley et al, 2015, p 24). It is this motivation to *transform* the existing state of affairs that signals the importance of teacher agency for the decolonizing agenda in English schools. Acts of agency involve teachers drawing on knowledge, values, experiences and other resources as a basis for exercising professional judgement.

Rather than viewing agency as a personal attribute or capacity, agency is best considered from an ecological perspective, as a phenomenon that emerges from teachers' interactions with their wider environment (Biesta and Tedder, 2007), which includes the regulatory and material conditions of their work, school and departmental cultures, formal and informal professional networks and relationships with colleagues, students, parents and other relevant groups. As such, teacher agency is not solely a matter of individual concern, but something that may be enabled or constrained by environmental factors. As demonstrated in this chapter, teacher agency may be strengthened through intentional processes of professional learning and collaboration, which has important implications for the decolonizing agenda.

This chapter reports on practical examples of the kinds of teacher-led work on decolonizing the curriculum that is currently underway in English schools, based on presentations made by two of the chapter's authors, Terra Glowach and Tanisha Hicks-Beresford, at a continuous professional development (CPD) event held in Bristol in the summer of 2021. Both teachers recount critical engagement with the 'processes by which knowledge is validated and selected for inclusion in the curriculum', a condition of decolonizing work described in Chapter 1 of this book. The following section provides some background on the Bristol context, after which are edited versions of the talks. The final part of the chapter reflects on themes raised by these presentations and draws wider lessons for those seeking to advance policy and practice in this area.

The context

The English city of Bristol has a progressive image. The hometown of Banksy and street art, Massive Attack and the trip hop scene; the first UK city to receive the European Green Capital award (2015); and first European city to elect a Black mayor, Marvin Rees (2016). In June 2020, Bristolians toppled the statue of the slave-trader Edward Colston, bringing international media attention to the city and visually recalling the removal of Cecil Rhodes from the University of Cape Town five years previously. Nevertheless, beneath its progressive image, Bristol is 'a city divided', ethnically, economically and educationally (Elahi et al, 2017). An influential 2017 study by the race equality think tank Runnymede Trust uncovered inequalities that shocked many working in education in the city: the gap between the average attainment of young Black learners and their white peers was among the largest anywhere in the country.[1] In accounting for this, the report highlighted 'the unrepresentativeness of the curriculum, lack of diversity in teaching staff and school leadership, and poor engagement with parents' (Elahi et al, 2017, p 1).

In response to the Runnymede report, a series of 'City Conversations' were convened in Bristol to stimulate debate and action on issues identified by the study (*Bristol Post*, 2018a). These conversations brought together teachers, school leaders, council and community members, activists, academics, artists and others, and sparked a number of initiatives across the city. These have included efforts to increase the recruitment and retention of Black teachers (*Bristol Post*, 2018b); the launch of One Bristol Curriculum[2] and CARGO,[3] school curriculum projects that centre Black perspectives and contributions; a secondary History textbook that explores the impact and legacy of Bristol's involvement in transatlantic slavery (Kennett et al, 2021); and numerous other interventions, such as the activities at May Park Primary School described in Chapter 8.

Against this backdrop, in June 2021, around 60 primary and secondary teachers participated in an online event titled 'Decolonising the Curriculum in Bristol: Across the subjects, from school to university'. It was organized as part of Teacherfest, an annual CPD festival hosted by the Bristol Education Partnership, which included presentations from six teachers and a representative of the One Bristol Curriculum.[4] To provide insights on the event itself, and examples of the kinds of teacher-led initiatives there have been in the city as a basis for wider reflection and learning, this chapter includes presentations by two teachers. At the time of the event, Terra and Tanisha worked at the same state-funded secondary school in the city. Terra is a white Canadian, who had significant international experience teaching in Canada, Ethiopia, India, Japan and elsewhere in England before joining the school as an English teacher. Tanisha is a Black British early-career teacher of Citizenship, who joined the school in a pastoral capacity before training as a teacher in post. She attended a state school in Bristol and a Pan-African supplementary school.

Terra Glowach: Incorporating Somali poetry in the English curriculum

I want to start by addressing a common concern: 'Why decolonize the school curriculum? Isn't it just about *diversifying* a curriculum?' It's important to challenge first of all some misunderstandings about what decolonizing of a curriculum is. It's not about taking anything away; it's about taking the blinders off. As an English teacher of 20 years, the best CPD I've had has been in the last couple of years; doing research with my own communities and engaging with literature that I would not otherwise have encountered because it's not in the canon.

Decolonizing the curriculum is about *critical intellectual engagement* – not just with our colleagues and with our disciplinary matter but also with our students and our wider community. It not only involves gaining knowledge but also challenging the framing around our subjects. It involves a critical, investigative approach that we're modelling to our colleagues, as well as to the children in our classrooms; and it increases the capacity of teachers as informed, expert curriculum developers. As professionals with a commitment to our chosen subjects, the research and collaboration involved in decolonizing the curriculum is a sustained and impactful form of CPD. Because it's not just a whim, or a top-down initiative that inspires fleeting compliance when you are observed, it's hard-won knowledge that is embedded in the curriculum.

I'm working in an inner-city school in Bristol, where recent government statistics show that, as a city, we're significantly behind the rest of the country in terms of Black African students' GCSE attainment (see, for example, DfE, 2021). Of course, 'Black African' is a diverse group, and the government should really be breaking this down, but I can say that, in my school, that means our Somali cohort, which is by far our largest cohort of African-heritage pupils.

Looking at these statistics and having a think about the work that I could do in my school, in 2019, I invited some of our Somali students to teach Somali phrases to our teachers at lunchtime. Following this, I continued reading around the subject and learned that Somalia is known as the Nation of Poets. I decided then that I was going to do some research by reaching out to our community. This is what I'm referring to when I say 'the best CPD I've experienced in 20 years of teaching.' See Figure 7.1.

When I started researching Somali poetry, I got in touch with Ugbaad Aidid (then an MSc Education student at the University of Bristol) who generously sent a number of academic articles that I could read to better understand the form of Somali poetry, because it is diverse and complex and it comes from a long tradition. What I learned quickly was the relevance of Somali poetry in our Key Stage 3 curriculum. Just as a knowledge of Aristotle and the fundamental dramatic concepts can inform students' understanding of Shakespeare, studying the Somali tradition enriches their understanding of poetry itself. What I realized very quickly is that by *not* teaching Somali poetry and *not* teaching where this tradition comes from, we're doing a disservice to our students and ourselves as professionals.

The other person I talked to was Abdihakin Asir, a former Director of Education in Mogadishu, and I had the opportunity to sit down and have coffee with him. He talked me through the perspectives of the Somali community in Bristol, which is sometimes positioned by schools as a 'hard-to-reach' community. Abdihakin told me exactly where most schools go wrong when they try to contact and work with Somali families and parents. These discussions often fail to acknowledge the high expectations of Somali parents, which are not always mirrored by the expectations of teachers. He advised me on the ordering of content within a scheme of work on Somali poetry, and one thing he said that was really powerful was that for every poem I teach, the students should be writing a poem, because the Somali tradition is democratic – 'There's a poet in every family and so students shouldn't feel like this is an elitist practice that they can't quite reach; they should feel inspired to write a poem for every one they read,' which I think is really important for creative development.

This conversation led me to Abdullahi Haji, an academic who sat down with me over coffee and shared fascinating traditional poems and their contexts. And finally, Warda Yassin, with whom I recorded an interview which I use in Key Stages 3 to 5. She talked about her process of writing poetry, and about the importance of context and form.

Finally – and this is important, as many Black experts, professionals and artists are asked to do this work for free – all of the contributors mentioned above were paid for their time and contributions. Most were compensated by the One Bristol Curriculum, and Warda Yassin's fee came out of my school's English budget.

Now, all of these things are about inclusion, and engaging intelligently with our Somali community. That is important for demonstrating respect for all our learners, teaching empathy, and also teaching white students in particular how to study and navigate in a diverse world. It is also important for students'

Figure 7.1: A slide from Terra's presentation, with images of contributors Aidid, Asir and Yassin

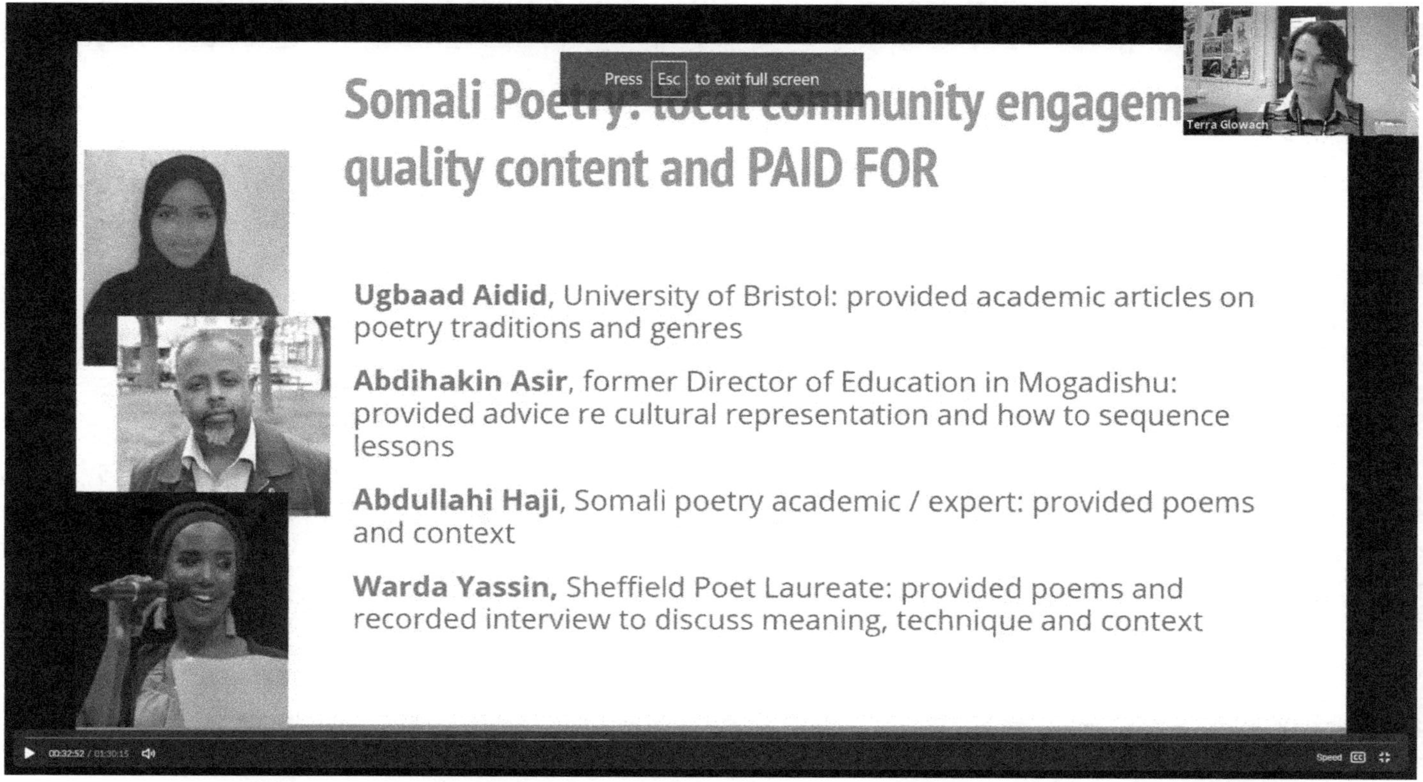

Progress 8 attainment, because they are learning complex poetry skills related to form, context, language and structure that are essential for GCSE poetry. The Somali poetry tradition delivers on all fronts and encourages students to develop their own voice at the same time. Essays by Year 8 students across a range of ethnicities demonstrated a confident understanding of the links between context, form, purpose and language. Previously reticent Somali students took starring roles when delivering original poetry to their class.[5]

Tanisha Hicks-Beresford: Reflexive questions for an anti-racist Citizenship curriculum

'Good, bad, or indifferent, [school] helps to define our collective reality. And if a child grows up never seeing themselves represented as successful or as the hero, then they are the anomaly if they succeed and the expectation if they fail.' (adapted from a speech by Yara Shahidi)

For me, this is a great reminder of why it is imperative for all schools to decolonize the curriculum. One of the many reasons I wanted to become a teacher was to inspire. This has to be embedded across all aspects of practice – it is not genuine if it is limited to isolated moments. How can I truly inspire my Black students if they are denied opportunities to see reflections of themselves being great and doing great things? The repercussions of ignoring this are 'expected failure'.

I have the pleasure of serving as the lead Citizenship teacher at my school. It is an exciting subject and I enjoy teaching it because it develops students' understanding of how to become active citizens while they are at school and in the future. The Citizenship curriculum addresses important issues such as individual liberties, diversity, community cohesion and multiculturalism. But it is not perfect. Just like any other curriculum area, there are elements that are missing and need adapting. As a result, when carrying out lesson planning and longer-term planning, I have four questions that I consider:

1. How does this unit help my students to learn more about themselves and others?
2. What histories am I unearthing that widen students' perspectives of themselves and the world around them?
3. How can I share Black joy or strength?
4. Are there any racist ideologies or privileged perspectives in the unit that would make students feel inferior?

The first question concerns how I can encompass the cultural experiences of those in the class and the wider community, and how the other students will experience this. The second question is about perspectives; about looking back to see if there are any historical perspectives that the unit or topic may have omitted. My third question refers back to the opening quotation on representation – ensuring that joy, strength and success are also shared in my lessons. The final question involves reflecting on the unit or topic and asking: 'What issues might be raised that could lead my students to feel inferior?' It is all about foresight and thinking ahead.

This is how it looks in practice when I teach 'British values – democracy, rule of law, individual liberty and mutual respect and tolerance'.

- In relation to Question 1, we look at the current make-up of British society and the impact of diversity on their school community, the city of Bristol, and nationally – helping the students to appreciate the world that they live in.
- In relation to Question 2, we look at different rulers and forms of governance globally through time. What values underpin these societies? Although sometimes challenging, it is important to share multiple aspects of historical events, especially in safe environments, such as the classroom. This enables students to discover cultural truths.
- In relation to Question 3, we utilize members of the community as role models, for example politicians, artists, historians and talk about events in Bristol such as St Paul's Carnival, St Marks Road Eid Festival and the Bristol Black Lives Matter movement. At every opportunity, pictures on slides are reflective of our contemporary society and shown from a positive perspective. This enables Black students to experience the joys of being Black directly in their own classroom. Unfortunately, this cannot be relied upon in the wider world where students are regularly confronted with news about Black people being assaulted and abused, most recently in the case of Child Q (Gamble and McCallum, 2022).
- In relation to Question 4, we consider racist ideologies. This involves analysing the term 'British values' and challenging the misconception that these values solely belong to those who identify as, or are, British. Students are encouraged to share values from their own communities, which enables quality discussions about the richness of all cultures within our classroom and beyond. See Figure 7.2.

The questions themselves originate from my own childhood experiences in the education system, and not seeing myself in *any* part of *any* school curriculum; not seeing any of my heritage or cultural background in anything when I was growing up. Ngũgĩ wa Thiong'o (1986) talked about a 'cultural bomb' leading to the annihilation of a people's self-belief, and that is exactly what it felt like. As a teacher, I have always tried to help Black students feel more fully engaged within the education system, rather than

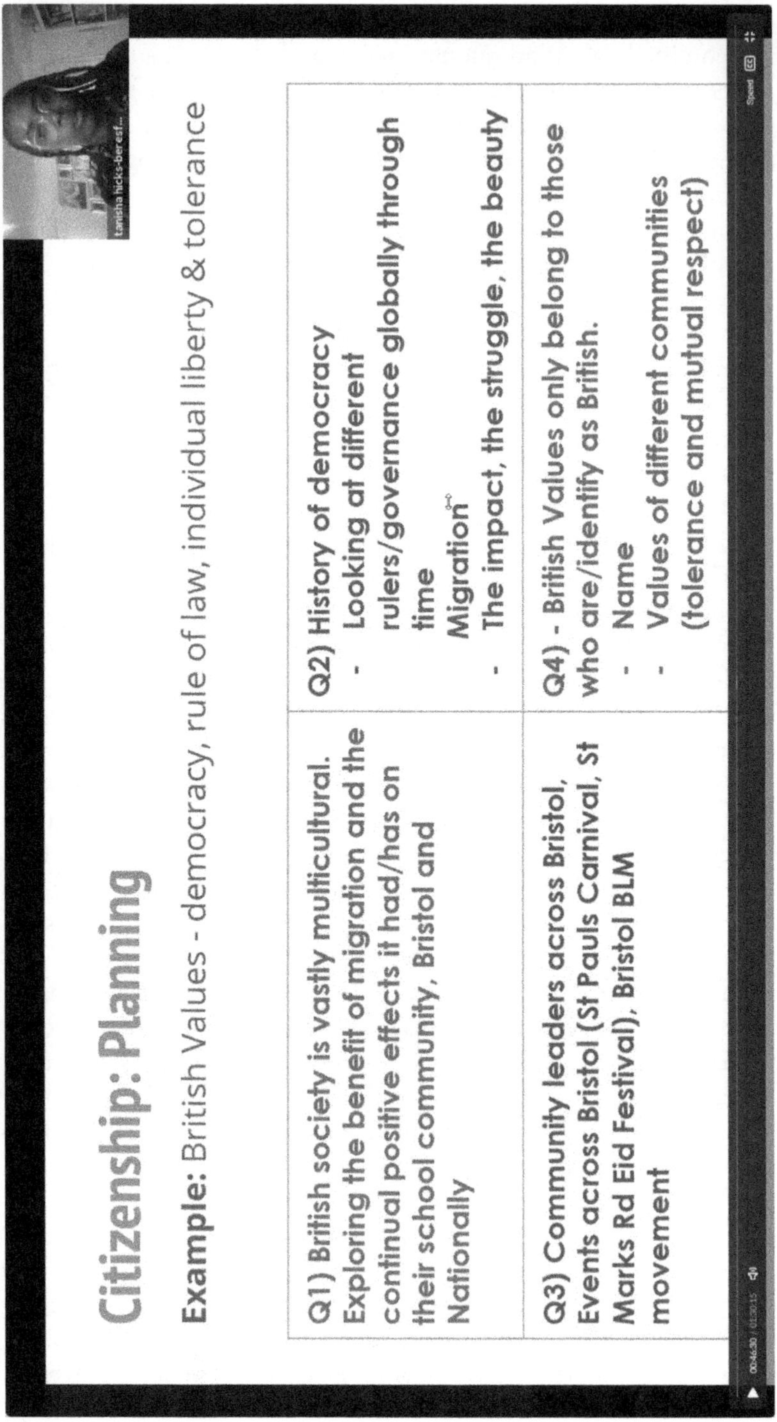

Figure 7.2: A slide from Tanisha's presentation on Citizenship lesson planning

feel that education is something that is done *to* them. This was reignited during the George Floyd protests and the Black Lives Matter movement. But these reflexive questions are not just important for our Black cohort, but for all the students I teach. All of our students will leave our school and engage with a society that is very diverse. As a Citizenship teacher, I see it as my role to develop our students so that they are skilled in understanding different viewpoints and are able to live harmoniously with others.

Beyond informing my curriculum planning and teaching, this set of questions helps me to reflect on what I can do to make a difference on a daily basis. I believe that, in everything that we do, including in meetings with colleagues, we should be thinking: What racist assumptions may these discussions uncover? How can I share Black joy? How can I widen the perspectives of all? Can I bring another viewpoint? If we can take these questions forward into our discussions with teachers and others, then I believe we will progress further in our path to decolonizing our education system.

Discussion and conclusion

In this closing section, we reflect on the teacher-led initiatives described in this chapter to draw tentative lessons for those seeking to advance decolonizing and anti-racist agendas in education, whether as teachers, school leaders, teacher educators or researchers. The initiatives themselves vary significantly in terms of their focus, rationale, forms and intended outcomes, and so, drawing on the notion of teacher agency raised in the introduction, we organize this discussion around the *motivations* for this work, and the *means* by which it is pursued.

Motivations for teacher-led decolonizing initiatives

The initiatives described here are a means of promoting the subject-related knowledge and understanding of *all* students (in English and Citizenship, respectively) and improving the quality of education for all by localizing, updating and in other ways enriching the taught curriculum. At the same time, these initiatives specifically seek to redress the historic erasure of Black lives in English curricula (Bain, 2018; Moncrieffe, 2020), challenge structures of white supremacy (Tikly 2022; Sriprakash et al, 2022) and improve educational experiences and outcomes for Black students.

Despite significant differences between these initiatives, a common feature is that they are self-directed, reflecting the perspectives, concerns, priorities and *agency* of the teachers involved and drawing on the resources that are available to them. The push for this work does not come from national policy actors or those with formal positions of leadership in school, but results from the intentional and creative acts of teachers who aim 'to bring about a future that is different from the present and the past' (Priestley et al, 2015, p 24). For those seeking to advance the decolonizing agenda, this prompts discussion around the question: How can teacher agency in this area be supported and strengthened?

Although the national policy environment is unconducive for this kind of work, there is local support for decolonizing activities within Bristol, including from the council, subject teacher communities and grassroots networks of practitioners and activists. Key factors that contributed to this enabling environment were 'City Conversations' on the quality of provision for young Black learners (*Bristol Post*, 2018a) which were prompted by the publication of statistical evidence on educational disparities (Elahi et al, 2017). The Runnymede report, which proved so influential, is nothing more or less than a four-page policy brief containing tables and infographics; and Terra refers to this, alongside government data, as a motivator for her work with the Somali community. The process of community-based research she employs echoes Sriprakash et al's vision of 'reparative remembering', allowing the co-creation of 'new resources for interpreting individual life stories and group histories' (see Chapter 10). For the decolonizing agenda, this suggests the value of researching educational inequalities, sharing evidence in an open and easily accessible way and promoting broad public and professional dialogue around this.

That said, Tanisha's presentation illustrates that not everyone will require statistical evidence in order to recognize the problem. Tanisha's practice is informed and motivated by her own lived experiences of alienation as a student at a school in Bristol, where she did not 'see' herself or her cultural background 'in *any* part of *any* school curriculum'. To redress this, Tanisha seeks out and seizes opportunities to represent Black joy and achievement in the classroom, in ways that echo the work of Black educators elsewhere in the world (for example, hooks, 1994; Givens, 2021). Like the Somali community's rejection of the 'hard-to-reach' label, Tanisha's presentation demonstrates the need for those working in the sector – particularly those without personal experience of structural racism – to commit to listen to and learn from the voices and experiences of those who are marginalized by existing provision (Wenham, 2021).

Approaches to decolonizing the curriculum

To date, there has been no 'state of the nation' survey or audit of the kinds of decolonizing the curriculum work being undertaken in English secondary schools. As such, we cannot comment on the prevalence or representativeness of the initiatives described in these presentations, or locate them alongside others on the smorgasbord of existing approaches. Nevertheless, we can identify some areas of convergence and divergence.

On the face of it, the initiatives are quite different. The approach reported by Tanisha involves reflexive questioning as a means of interrogating and challenging curricular norms that reproduce harmful assumptions and inequitable power relations; while Terra's initiative involves collaborative action, learning and curriculum development with members of a community that has historically been marginalized within the English school system. A common factor is that both approaches entail some form of professional development on the part of the teachers involved, referring to the formal or informal processes through which teachers acquire or enhance their knowledge, skills and attitudes for improvements in practice (Mitchell, 2013). Professional learning appears to be a necessary condition for teacher-led initiatives of this kind. Terra refers to her Somali poetry initiative as 'the best CPD I've experienced in 20 years of teaching.' Her work involved collaborative action and learning: fostering relationships with members of the wider community in order to draw on knowledge *outside* the teaching profession and incorporate this within the curriculum. In Tanisha's example, professional learning results from the use of strategic questions to support ongoing processes of reflection and adaptation (Schön, 1983; Brownhill, 2021). Such reflexive questioning has been used by others seeking to promote anti-racist education in the UK. For example, it is the basis of the National Education Union's 'Framework for developing an anti-racist approach' (NEU, 2020), which has been proposed as a school self-evaluation instrument to assess the extent to which racial inequalities are being challenged, or reproduced, in school. The evidence considered in this chapter suggests that decolonizing initiatives necessarily involve some forms of learning (or unlearning) on the part of teachers. It is important to recognize this, rather than assume that progress in this area can be achieved simply through the provision of curriculum resources and other materials.

A final point of comparison between these projects is their visibility. The initiative described by Terra – a senior, white practitioner – is overt, undertaken in collaboration with others inside and outside the school, and with financial support from the English department and the One Bristol Curriculum. Conversely, the approach described by Tanisha – an early-career Black teacher – is covert in the sense that it does not draw on additional resources beyond the individual teacher and is not necessarily visible to other staff in school or reliant on their support or permission. As such, Tanisha's approach echoes Givens' (2021) account of 'fugitive pedagogy', a term coined to describe the covert practices of 20th-century Black educators in the USA who, denied a formal means of resisting narratives of white supremacy in the classroom, covertly introduced stories of Black achievement through proscribed textbooks and other resources.

The evidence considered in this chapter signals the importance of raising the visibility of decolonizing initiatives in order to mobilize capacities that are distributed across schools and other settings. This requires creating or opening up spaces for dialogue, establishing new connections and relationships, sharing resources and undertaking collaborative inquiries, action and learning (Mitchell et al, 2020; Glowach et al, 2023; Walker et al, 2022). The Teacherfest session itself is one example of this, which led to the establishment of the Bristol Decolonising Network. Similar formal and informal professional learning networks exist across the country, often aimed at specific regions or subject communities. We encourage teachers and others seeking progress in this area not to labour in isolation, but seek collaborators within and beyond your own institutions.

Notes

1   According to the most recent data (DfE, 2021), Bristol is the second worst-performing English city (after Bradford) for Black students' attainment at GCSE level.
2   See onebristolcurriculum.org.uk.
3   See cargomovement.org and Chapter 6.
4   A recording of this event is available at: https://bit.ly/3uOdlQd.
5   Further details on the Somali Poetry Scheme of work are available elsewhere (Glowach 2019, 2022). The resources are available on request by contacting Terra directly via Twitter (@TerraGlowach) or email (T.Glowach@uwe.ac.uk).

References

Bain, Z. (2018) Is there such a thing as 'white ignorance' in British education?, *Ethics and Education*, 13(1): 4–21.

Belas, O. and Hopkins, N. (2019) Subject English as citizenship education, *British Educational Research Journal*, 45(2): 320–339.

Biesta, G.J.J. and Tedder, M. (2007) Agency and learning in the lifecourse: Towards an ecological perspective, *Studies in the Education of Adults*, 39: 132–149.

Bristol Post (2018a) First City Conversation announced as part of Bristol's Year of Change, available at: bristolpost.co.uk/news/bristol-news/first-city-conversation-announced-part-1510162 [accessed 26 January 2023].

Bristol Post (2018b) We only have 26 black teachers out of 1,346 in Bristol, and that's a problem, available at: bristolpost.co.uk/news/bristol-news/black-teachers-bristol-schools-only-1958455 [accessed 26 January 2023].

Brownhill, S. (2021) Asking more key questions of self-reflection, Reflective Practice, DOI: https://doi-org.bris.idm.oclc.org/10.1080/14623 943.2021.2013192.

Cushing, I. (2020) The policy and policing of language in schools, *Language in Society*, 49(3): 425–450.

Department for Education (2014) Equality objectives, available at: gov.uk/government/uploads/system/uploads/attachment_data/file/368325/DfE_Equality_Objectives.pdf [accessed 8 December 2021].

Department for Education (2021) GCSE Results (Attainment 8), available at: www.ethnicity-facts-figures.service.gov.uk/education-skills-and-train ing/11-to-16-years-old/gcse-results-attainment-8-for-children-aged-14- to-16-key-stage-4/latest#data-sources [accessed 26 January 2023].

Elahi, F., Finney, N. and Lymperopoulou, K. (2017) Bristol: A city divided? Ethnic Minority Disadvantage in Education and Employment, Centre on Dynamics of Ethnicity, The Runnymede Trust.

Gamble, J. and McCallum, R. (2022) Local child safeguarding practice review Child Q, City & Hackney Safeguarding Children Partnership, available at: chscp.org.uk/wp-content/uploads/2022/03/Child-Q-PUBLISHED- 14-March-22.pdf [accessed 27 Apr. 2022].

Gandolfi, H.E. (2021), Decolonising the science curriculum in England: Insights from decolonial science and technology studies to secondary school science, *Curriculum Journal*, DOI: https://doi.org/10.1002/curj.97.

Givens, J.R. (2021) *Fugitive Pedagogy*, Cambridge, MA: Harvard University Press.

Glowach, T. (2019) Somali poetry: Resources for a SOW, available at: theteacherist.com/2019/10/05/somali-poetry-resources-for-a-sow [accessed 27 January 2023].

Glowach, T. (2023) Belonging in literature, Decolonising and Diversifying the Curriculum Series, online course, Chartered College of Teachers, available at: my.chartered.college/module-5-belonging-in-literature.

Glowach, T., Mitchell, R., Bennett, T., Donaldson, L., Jefferson, J., Panford, L., Saleh, A., Smee, K., Wells-Dion, B. and Hemmings, E. (2023) Making spaces for collaborative action and learning: Reflections on teacher-led decolonising initiatives from a professional learning network in England, *The Curriculum Journal*, 34, 100–117, https://doi.org/10.1002/curj.186.

The Guardian (2021) Schools minister rebuffs calls to decolonise English curriculum, available at: theguardian.com/education/2021/jul/21/schools- minister-rebuffs-calls-to-decolonise-english-curriculum?CMP=Share_ AndroidApp_Other [accessed 26 January 2023].

hooks, bell (1994) *Teaching to transgress: Education as the practice of freedom*, Routledge.

Kennett, R., Thorne, S., Allen, T. et al (2021) *Bristol and Transatlantic Slavery: Origins, impact and legacy*, Bristol Books CIC.

Lais, H. (2017) As a history teacher, I'm horrified by the whitewashing of my curriculum – I'm being told to teach that colonialism was good, The Independent, available at: independent.co.uk/voices/black-history-month- colonialism-history-teacher-whitewashing-selective-past-a8025741.html [accessed 26 January 2023].

Mitchell, R. (2013) What is professional development, how does it occur in individuals, and how may it be used by educational leaders and managers for the purpose of school improvement?, *Professional Development in Education* 39(3): 387–400.

Mitchell, R., Wals, A. and Brockwell, A. (2020) Mobilising capacities for transforming education for sustainable futures: Opening spaces for collaborative action and learning, TESF Background paper, DOI: https://doi.org/10.5281/zenodo.4134931.

Moncrieffe, M.L. (2020) *Decolonising the History Curriculum: Euro-centrism and primary schooling*, Cham: Springer Nature.

National Education Union (NEU) (2020) Framework for developing an anti-racist approach, available at: neu.org.uk/media/11236/view [accessed 27 January 2023].

Parkin, C. and MacKenzie, S. (2017) Is there gender bias in Key Stage 3 textbooks? Content analysis using the Gender Bias 14 (GB14) measurement tool, *Advanced Journal of Professional Practice*, 1(1): 23–40.

Priestley, M., Biesta, G.J.J. and Robinson, S. (2015) Teacher Agency: What is it and why does it matter?, in R. Kneyber and J. Evers (eds) *Flip the System: Changing education from the bottom up*, London: Routledge.

Schön, D.A. (1983) *The Reflective Practitioner: How professionals think in action*, New York: Basic Books.

Smith, L. (2020) Top ten texts: A survey of commonly taught KS3 class readers, Teaching English, NATE.

Sriprakash, A., Gerrard, J. and Rudolph, S. (2022) *Learning Whiteness: Education and the settler colonial state*, London: Pluto Press.

Tikly, L. (2022) Racism and the future of antiracism in education: A critical analysis of the Sewell report, *British Educational Research Journal*, 00: 1–19.

wa Thiong'o, N. (1986) *Decolonising the Mind: The politics of language in African literature*, Woodbridge: James Currey.

Walker, S., Bennett, I., Kettory, P. et al (2022) 'Deep understanding' for anti-racist school transformation: School leaders' professional development in the context of Black Lives Matter, Curriculum Journal, DOI: https://doi.org/10.1002/curj.189.

Watson, M. (2020) Michael Gove's war on professional historical expertise: Conservative curriculum reform, extreme Whig history and the place of imperial heroes in modern multicultural Britain, *British Politics*, 15: 271–290.

Wenham, L. (2021) *Misunderstood, Misinterpreted and Mismanaged: Voices of students marginalised in a secondary school*, Peter Lang: Oxford.

8

Little Voices: Embracing Difference in Bristol Schools through Engaging Learner Voices

Ben Spence

Introduction

In June 2020, when the statue of Edward Colston was toppled, Bristol became the centre of the Black Lives Matter movement in the UK. The international protests had come close to home, and educators in the city felt compelled to respond. Leaders started to look at developing anti-racist policies and shifting the culture of schools beyond Eurocentricity. These policies demanded a review of the curriculum. The showcase of children's work in this chapter sets out to reveal the challenges faced by primary educators in introducing diverse narratives into the curriculum, and highlights the demand for this action by the children themselves. It also demonstrates the critical themes the children identified when they explored the concept of decolonizing the curriculum. Finally, the chapter addresses what one primary school intends to do in order to answer the 'call to action' from its children.

Primary and secondary: demands and opportunities

The Black Lives Matter movement really struck a particular chord with the teachers at my school. Our inner-city primary is based in Bristol. The school population is over 60 per cent Black, Asian or Minority Ethnic pupils. It has a three-form entry, ranging from nursery to age 11 and is large enough for 680 pupils. Despite serving a very diverse community, one that echoes the BAME population of the school, our teaching staffing is predominantly white British. Only 14 per cent of the teaching staff is from a BAME group: four teachers from the 29 members of staff. Prior to my tenure as principal, only

5 per cent of the team came from non-white British groups. For us, during that summer of 2020, Bristol felt like the epicentre of the UK movement. Within education, the movement was particularly vibrant. Activities and discussions that had already been taking place in schools, colleges and universities were being revitalized in classrooms and staffrooms across the city.

There were resources flooding in across all education networks: book lists, lesson ideas and suggestions on how to 'decolonize the curriculum' were everywhere. Except for the book lists, however, most other resources felt decidedly secondary-school based. The more in-depth curriculum changes seemed to depend on the more specialized subject knowledge that secondary teachers possess. Secondary educators were able to investigate and share ways to decolonize the curriculum through detailed subject plans and curriculum changes. They were able to utilize the international zeitgeist to apply pressure on senior leaders to approve these changes across schools. The secondary curriculum began to amplify the voices of secondary children. This was especially evident in the secondary school that is part of our Bristol Academy Trust. Staff and students were making demands for the decolonization of their curriculum and school experiences. They introduced an equality staff working group, made changes to the History curriculum and created an anti-racist policy swiftly and efficiently.

As a primary school, we felt unable to respond to the question of decolonization in the same way, as the knowledge required to change the curriculum in a profound and meaningful way was not prevalent within our staffing team. There was a lack of supporting resources for primary teachers outside book lists and limited lesson plans. We realized that we would have to source and adapt existing materials to create our own opportunities for our children's voices to be heard alongside the perspectives of their secondary counterparts. We lacked the detailed knowledge required to develop resources from scratch, so, as primary practitioners, we would need to act as intermediaries between existing resources and primary-aged children. So, the questions were what to do and how to do it in a way that was appropriate for primary-aged children.

I am a secondary-school-qualified science teacher. I taught in an inner-city secondary school for 16 years and served on the senior leadership team for ten years before leaving to take up the position as a principal in a large inner-city primary school in September 2019. For most of my career, I have been quite content to teach my subject. Like most of my secondary counterparts, I rarely had the opportunity to teach outside my subject and, if I did, I often took to it reluctantly. My knowledge of the curriculum was limited to similar disciplines such as Mathematics and Engineering. When I ventured into the humanities, the content was firmly driven by the subject head and those far more qualified. Decolonization happened in silos, each secondary area adapting and changing the curriculum to meet the needs of the students until it became a whole-school focus. As a Black senior leader in the secondary phase, I did not have to drive this change. My previous school had started to look at reflecting its community through its curriculum, especially in terms of the History being taught in Key Stage 3. My secondary colleagues understood the need to have children reflected in the curriculum as the children themselves were demanding this of them.

I thought this model might be easily transferrable to the primary curriculum. I thought I could discuss the idea of decolonization with staff and then they would be able to implement the changes required to achieve the goal. I had not considered the interdisciplinary nature of primary educators and the resulting impact on specific curriculum knowledge. I also did not anticipate that the children's voices would be so quiet and their demands for change so softly spoken. They had not reached the same crescendo as at secondary school and, as a result, the drive and impetus for change was not as pressing.

Part of this initiative came from my instinct that my pupils wanted change but they needed help to find the language to articulate the changes they wished to see and a supportive space to explore their ideas. I realized that the drive would need to come from me, and I would need to provide the space and security for staff and children to explore challenging and complex themes so that everyone could find their voice. Now the initial barriers in primary could be converted into advantages over secondaries. The primary sector already provides excellent opportunities for cross-curricular work, with teachers able to weave already-mapped knowledge throughout a variety of disciplines. Our work could exploit this interdisciplinary mechanism. In addition, the primary timetable allows for merging subjects and themes. For example, English can be taught through a study of a historical non-fiction text. This ability to adapt the daily timetable is of particular benefit as meaningful discussions need not be abandoned mid-sentence due to having to move to the next teacher's lesson. I recognized that this could provide an excellent opportunity to explore complex themes.

Galvanized by Black Lives Matter, and as part of our ongoing initiatives to create learning spaces that suit the histories, narratives and lived-experiences of the school's diverse children and families, we decided to conduct workshops and interviews to enable our pupils to discuss what decolonizing the curriculum meant to them. Alongside these workshops, we had made changes to other curriculum elements, intending to use resources to reflect our pupils' diversity. Using the flexibility of the primary curriculum and the teacher's skills at introducing complex themes through literature, we facilitated spaces for children to express, in their own voices, their thoughts about what was important. We started during Covid-19 lockdown with an online writing project centring on the poem 'If' by Lawrence Hoo with Year 6 pupils (aged 10 and 11). This was followed by two further workshops with Year 5 (aged 9 and 10) and Year 6 when pupils had returned to school after lockdown. Our final workshop emerged as a response to the themes that arose from the sessions around 'If'. They provided an opportunity to explore recurring themes in depth.

Lockdown project – 'If'

This session was teacher-initiated and pupil-led and directly responded to the Black Lives Matters movement. The children were introduced to the task and left to navigate and define the answer for themselves. The poem was set as a lockdown writing project for children aged 10 to 11. The children were asked to watch Lawrence Hoo's recitation of his poem and then plan and write their interpretations. They were encouraged to examine what they would ask of, or perhaps what they wanted from, their education and to consider the extent to which the curriculum represented their hopes and dreams. Once the work was completed, pupils were invited to post their responses on the school's communication platform. In the first lockdown, where this work was produced, there were significant technological constraints and pressured home-working conditions. Lockdown placed pressure on digital resources at home. Most homes had some devices with online capabilities, but these were often unsuitable for online learning. Phone screens, for example, were too small for reading shared documents or supporting engagement with the whole class. There were also some concerns relating to access: children and parents were sharing devices, with highest demand from both peaking at the same parts of the day. This issue was exacerbated in homes where there were multiple school-aged children, all attempting to attend live lessons or complete the tasks set online. Parents had to prioritize the use of devices between siblings, with the eldest child often getting the most time. These individual domestic arrangements were not always at times that would allow participation in a live lesson. Alongside these issues within pupils' homes, our school was rapidly learning to deliver lessons online. This was not completely full-time, so there was less supervised learning. As a result, the children explored their responses with very little input or oversight by the teaching staff. Nonetheless, the poems below are examples of what the children produced: our children's demands for their future education.

I Wish
I wish I could learn about space,
And how the planets and galaxies race,
I wish I could learn about tradition,
And know there *[sic]* yearly celebrations,
I wish I could see food from many places,
Trying food from different races,
I wish I could learn outside for a bit.

AB (February 2021)

I wish for more equal rights,
I wish for more animal habitat,

I wish for more education?
I wish for less pollution,

MM (February 2021)

I wish …
To travel all over the world and see places
I have never seen,
I wish … equal rights for everyone no matter
Where they have come from or have been.
Animals are safe and need to be cared for,
The environment does too? cos *[sic]* that's what were *[sic]* here for
If we do not take care of nature and our earth,
If we do not realise what it is all worth,
Then we might as well not be here at all
I wish … for a better place for everyone and everything
That's all.

OE (February 2021)

The themes that emerged from the written pieces produced in remote learning during lockdown covered equality, the environment and a sense of wanting to understand and discover the wider world. When we read the poems, while we expected the responses to consider equality, we were surprised by the extent to which environmental issues were part of the pupils' written responses. When asked to work out their own wants and wishes for the future, there was careful consideration of self, humanity and environment, as evidenced in OE's plan for his poem 'I wish …':

I wish …
• Equal rights for everyone – everyone to have the same chances in life no matter where they're from or how rich or poor they are
• I wish to travel to different countries and visit ancient places
• I wish for people to be better, for the world to be healed from what humans have done, for there to be no more war!
• Wildlife: more conservation, make hunting illegal, make everyone respect them … stop their habitats from being destroyed

OE (February 2021)

The work in subsequent workshops included far more adult facilitation, and, sadly, the echoes of the environment disappeared from the work created by the children. For our children working during the lockdown period, their natural response to the task was to align environmental outcomes and decolonization. Their wishes for education included a reflection of self, increased knowledge of the world and protection of the Earth.

The new world – post-lockdown response

September 2021 signified a new start for schools, with the spectre of Covid continuing to loom over us. It was back to business as usual for schools, but alongside track and trace, isolating staff and daily school restructuring. Learning did not stop during the pandemic. Staff were delivering lessons online, in school and visiting children at home. However, the suspension of statutory tests and external inspections meant that teachers and staff could meet and discuss deeper ideas on the curriculum. Teachers had more capacity to consider and discuss these wider educational issues, such as increasing knowledge acquisition and retention in the primary curriculum. Once school restarted in earnest, in autumn 2021, it felt as though the space we had been given during the pandemic to reconsider the school curriculum's shape was removed. The work on decolonizing the curriculum seemed to slow in terms of our national narratives.

More locally, the work continued with teacher-led organizations leading the way. Most of these grassroots organizations still appeared to focus on older pupils. Our work at school now concerned a new cohort of pupils and staff. The Year 6 pupils involved in the lockdown project left in July 2021, and the school experienced the natural staff turnover at the end of the academic year. There was a shift in momentum – it had slowed. I felt that revisiting the original 'If' project could amplify the children's voices and once again move decolonization back to the forefront of the conversation. Our workshops with Years 5 and 6 were designed to find out whether the new Year 5 and 6 children shared the same views as their predecessors. We decided to replicate the 'If' project, but, first, I started our exploration of decolonizing the curriculum by examining representation in literature and History. Before our first Year 5 workshop in autumn 2021, I invited five children for a discussion about the importance of representation in the curriculum. The discussion also gave me the opportunity to evaluate the impact of work that had taken place in the previous academic year; chiefly the introduction of texts and changes to the areas studied in our Enquiry curriculum to represent our diverse cohort. The following extracts are from the conversation I had with my Year 5 group. The key comments from Hameedah and Zakariye focus on representation in the curriculum and the sense of belonging.

Ms Spence:	Over to you, right? Do we think it's [inclusion of BAME voices] important and why? ...
Hameedah:	Yes, yes, we can as well. [Although] There's more African children in this school, [it] doesn't really mean that we shouldn't include other people histories. ...
	It's important that all Africans, we might want to learn about other histories more than our own. You [other children] might be curious as well.

Here Hameedah is commenting on the introduction of the Kingdom of Benin into the History curriculum at May Park. We replaced the Aztecs with the Kingdom of Benin as one of our ancient civilizations studied. We did this to reflect our school community. Over 30 per cent of our pupils are from a Black African or Black Caribbean group, but only 4 per cent of pupils identified as coming from South America. Hameedah is explaining that, even though our school has a number of African pupils, this should not exclude the histories of others. I thought that it was interesting that she does not champion a complete overhaul of the curriculum to include only African voices. She implicitly understands the need for balance.

When Zakariye is asked about the inclusion of Somali voices in the curriculum, however, his response is more personal. Zakariye is expressing the desire to have the curriculum value the contribution of voices that reflect his own culture and other diverse cultural voices so that a sense of normalcy occurs. I interpreted this normalcy as meaning 'belonging'. So, in other words, 'If you value the contributions of people like me on the curriculum, I stop being othered; I belong.'

Ms Spence:	So, if I taught you something like a poem, and when we're doing lots of poetry and then we had a poem, one poem that was by somebody who was Somali or British Somali, how would that make you feel?
Zakariye:	It will make me feel normal.
Ms Spence:	Yeah, why?
Zakariye:	Because, 'cause I'm Somali ...?
	...
	Like I said, people should be contributing from their area, so if Somali people contributed in that poem, it shows their contributions. And then if other people [from diverse backgrounds] want to contribute, they [feel like they] can if they want to.

Our discussion showed that the children remained clear in their message. They understood the need for their identities to be reflected in the curriculum. This was echoed in broader class discussions where Black Lives Matter was still a key message for our children despite it not being an overt intention in our curriculum. In our workshops, the children reiterated this key message with a focus on equality for all (Figure 8.1a, b and c).

It was often not the main parts of the children's work that gave insight into how they felt. The sessions included in-depth discussion, which was far more extensive and with more teacher facilitation than in the lockdown project. This is because children often want a structure to

Figure 8.1a: Students' creations focusing on equality: 'Be Equal!'

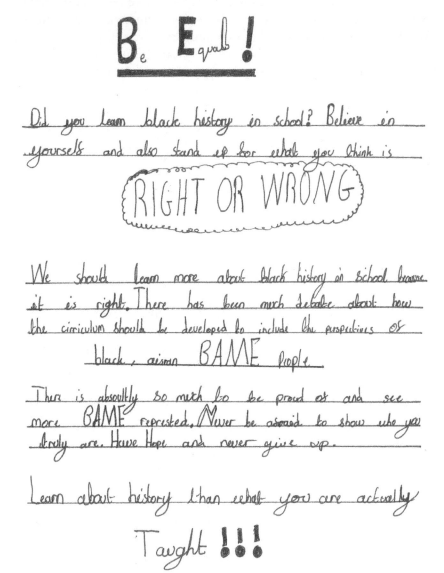

the work that they produce. They want the 'right' answer. We wanted a record of the children's responses in their own words, so the written tasks were used as evidence of the sessions. The children requested a structure for their work, so several outcomes were suggested, such as posters, poems or pamphlets. When I looked at the children's work, however, their personal messages were often hidden in the decoration or appeared as peritexts: the spaces where structured work desists. The

Figure 8.1b: Students' creations focusing on equality: 'Equality Inclusion'

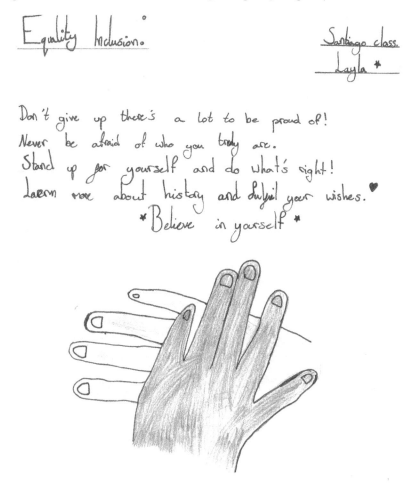

main body of the work conveyed the main messages, but the peritexts seemed to have more emotional and reflexive responses. Figure 8.2, for example, is the border for a larger piece.

Figure 8.3 is a small sentence that was tucked under the main poem on a poster.

A Black child created the poster in Figure 8.4 during the same workshop. I personally found this poster difficult to read. From the title 'My Dream' to the tiny word 'hope' hidden in the corner, this piece seems to be impressing on the reader the need for us to reframe Black narratives for children. When selecting work to include here, I struggled with showcasing this piece as the language is forthright. My colleague who delivered this workshop had no such reservations. She selected this piece as one of her favourites. When

Figure 8.1c: Students' creations focusing on equality: 'Equality BAME'

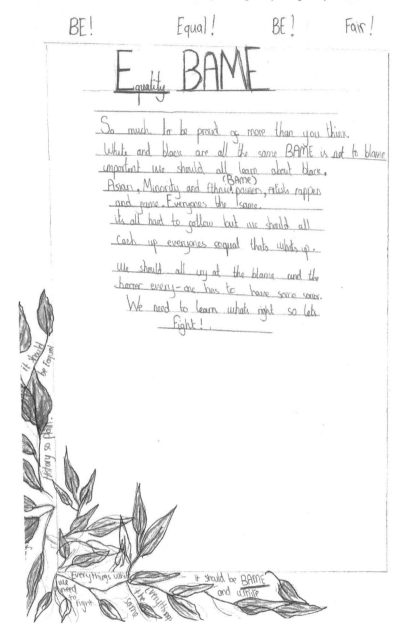

Figure 8.2: A student's drawing and poem

Figure 8.3: A fragment of a student's poem

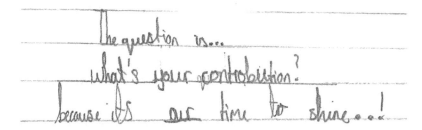

Figure 8.4: A student's poster titled 'My Dream'

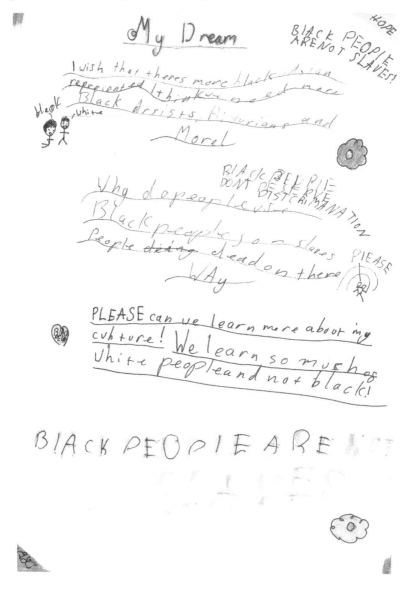

I read it, it causes me as a Black educator to question why I feel the need to soften my language when dealing with the issue of race. This poster demands that we tackle these issues head-on.

The poster work highlighted a key issue: the children and the adults both really struggled with the concept of decolonizing the curriculum. This meant that some of the poems and posters contained misconceptions

Figure 8.5: An example of misconceptions and ill-formed concepts

or ill-formed concepts (see Figure 8.5). Some posters highlighted the children's lack of knowledge about the transatlantic slave trade, which is not surprising as it is not on the primary curriculum and is usually taught at Key Stage 3 in the secondary phase. They also focused mainly on Black voices despite the cohort containing Asian and other minority ethnic groups. I discussed earlier the impact of lack of specificity of subject knowledge on decolonization at primary school. I feel that these examples show in detail the difficulties that teachers had in challenging misconceptions in children. Despite using the poem 'If' to support the conversations, the staff that facilitated the sessions stated that they themselves struggled with the concept of decolonization.

In answer to this conundrum, we decided to unpick the term 'decolonization' away from source material such as Laurence Hoo's poem or well-publicized world issues. In our next workshop, we asked the children to create their own definitions.

Decolonizing the curriculum: what does it mean?

'My definition of decolonising the curriculum is that rules are made from one leader/ruler. I think instead of making rules amongst themselves they should be more open minded and ask for various opinions.' (Rayan, Year 6)

I have opened this section with my favourite pupil definition because it speaks to me as a leader. Decolonizing the curriculum is embracing the voices of others. Our workshop with the children explored their interpretations of the term decolonization and ideas for how it could be achieved. The results were interesting. There were popular ideas, such as culture days and a wider range of languages, but the children also included surprising elements around health, science and outdoor learning (Figure 8.6a, b and c).

The children enjoyed constructing the spider diagrams and idea maps, and, as with the earlier activities, the teachers tried to give as little explanation as possible. However, at the end of the session, in our staff debrief, we discussed the difficulties in breaking down the concept of decolonization for the children, with staff admitting that they did not have a fixed definition for decolonization themselves. This is a problematic issue for primary educators; one that is more easily overcome in the secondary phase. At the primary level, teachers cover a number of subjects that may not be their specialism in terms of knowledge, so, despite the teaching opportunities provided by this interdisciplinary approach, identifying opportunities to include alternative voices to the mainstream requires a comprehensive subject knowledge, and this can be difficult. In addition, the school workforce is not diverse, so this monoculture means that there is little systemic change. In carrying out these workshops, the teachers began to reflect on their lack of knowledge.

Figure 8.6a: Interpretations of 'decolonizing the curriculum': spider diagram

Decolonize the curriculum
Learn about non-European languages such as Arabic, Somali,
Languages
Culture Day we need to have the chance to learn about other peoples cultures
Decolonize
Cooking
trips
Culture Day!
I also think we should include cooking so the kids can learn how to cook and we could have it like weekly food tech.

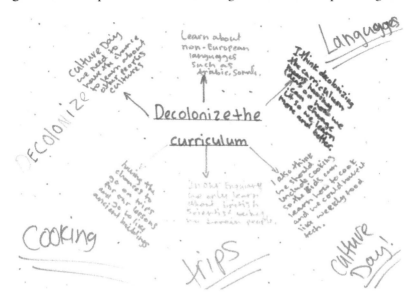

Figure 8.6b: Interpretations of 'decolonizing the curriculum': thought map (1)

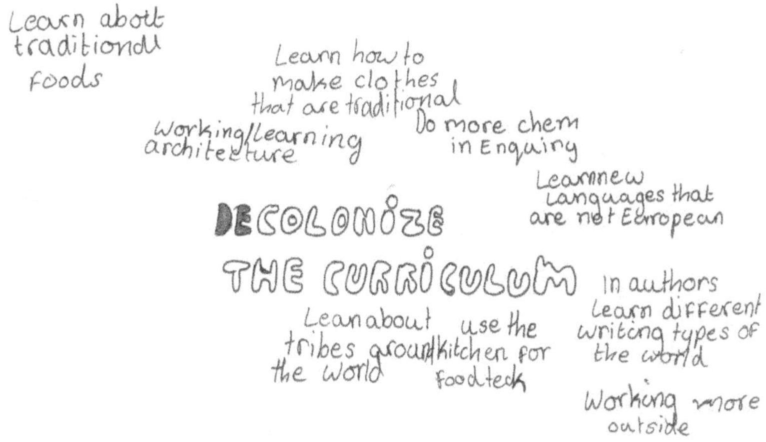
Learn about traditionall foods
Learn how to make clothes that are traditional
Working/Learning architecture
Do more chem in Enquiry
Learnnew languages that are not European
DECOLONIZE THE CURRICULUM
In authors
Learn about tribes around the world
use the kitchen for Food teck
Learn different writing types of the world
Working more outside

Figure 8.6c: Interpretations of 'decolonizing the curriculum': thought map (2)

Curriculum wish list

The final workshop involved the children writing letters to the then Secretary of State for Education in England, Nadim Zahawi. The premise for this activity was, 'In terms of decolonizing the curriculum, what would be on your wish list if you could write directly to the Education secretary?'

> Dear Mr Zahawi,
>   I am writing to you because I believe some things should be included in the Primary curriculum. Everything a child learns in school is a part of the curriculum. Although

foundation subjects such as Art, Science and Geography are mostly based on European culture and some things being taught should be more diverse.

The following are ideas of mine:

- More food tech/cooking (a useful skill)
- Trips related to learning
- Revision on lessons not understood
- Learning about more diverse culture.

Food can make any child happy especial if they made it; it is also very resourceful.

Kim, Y6

Dear Mr Zahawi,

I am writing to you because I have a few ideas to decolonise the curriculum. My ideas may be postponed depending on the time of the year.

My first idea is to do more outdoor learning (you could do this throughout the summer) because children enjoy hot weather and fresh air. This may reduce bad moods during the afternoon. Sometimes, kids can get distracted easily, so you can do this with older students.

Next, I have is to do with more cultural learning: more education on cultures. I think you should do this because when someone learns or hears something about their culture, they feel more at home. These cultures can include the people in class: they can teach everyone their culture. Popular cultures: India, Pakistan etc.

Creativity is expressed in many ways: art, pictures, words and sculptures. It is better to put art into lessons. An example of this would be maths posters and colourful fact files. These things can be put on a board or wall. Many subjects can be used for art. Examples are English, Maths, Science and languages.

Finally, students should learn Science closer to modern time. I think that because people should know what's happening currently. But I think it could be a mix. Both should be learnt, so students get a good education.

Unsigned, Y6

Dear Mr Zahawi,

I'm writing to implore you to decolonise the curriculum and give you some ideas on how to do it.

My first idea is that you focus on different cultures. You could change the art curriculum so that we use cultural drawings. You could also change your Science curriculum, so we learn about cultural scientists.

> My second idea is that we do more outdoor learning about nature because we do learn about nature, but it would be better to know about it whilst around it. For example, we could do it outside when we are drawing plants instead of picking them and bringing them indoors. It will also give us a better understanding and experience.
>
> My third idea is that we have a culture day. On a culture day, we dress up in clothes from our culture and bring food from other cultures. On those days, we can address all cultures as a whole.
>
> For me decolonising the system because there is colonising in the real world. Colonising a country is when people force people to obey their rules and follow their ideas. I do not think this is right.
>
> Elio, Y6

Conclusion: what did we learn?

We learned that children are passionate about equality. They want the opportunity to explore and discuss concepts such as decolonization and equality. Discussions of these concepts prompt debate and increase engagement. Children enjoy exploring and expressing their own values and beliefs. They feel heard. Children also feel quite strongly about seeing themselves reflected in the curriculum; it increases their sense of belonging and value.

For the staff, these activities highlighted gaps in their knowledge and the limited access they had to appropriate resources for the agenda of decolonizing the curriculum. However, the high pupil engagement and enjoyment in curriculum aspects that are a part of the decolonizing agenda has spurred staff to overcome these barriers. An example would be the decision to include the ancient Benin kingdom in our curriculum. It is more difficult to find resources for, and teachers have less prior knowledge than a possible alternative such as the Aztec kingdom, but teachers have persisted in developing their own resources in order to deliver a topic that really engages the pupils. As a leader, I have also had to recognize that this work is difficult, and it is not always a natural driver for teachers. The workshops were delivered by staff who were invested in the delivery despite not always having the language or knowledge. They were willing to learn, and have continued to embed this learning in their practice.

Finally, we learned that children see decolonization, equality and sustainability as one conversation. This was a surprising outcome from the work with the pupils because, as educators, we often miss the intersections and direct associations across these topics.

What next?

The letters written to the Education Secretary will never reach him as they were merely an exercise. They have, however, connected with me.

As a leader, it is my responsibility to ensure that the needs of the children in my school are met. It is also my responsibility to ensure the continuing professional development of my staff. In order to embed decolonization in our teaching practice, we must first decide what it means to us. We need to make it a question we ask as we plan every part of our curriculum. It needs to become embedded in our ethos.

Our children have given us the visible parts of the curriculum that we need to change, but, in order to change the narrative, the majority of the work is beneath the surface. The change starts with demystifying decolonization. We need to broaden the scope to include narratives beyond the transatlantic slave trade. As educators, we need to recognize and promote a more global view of the knowledge we teach so that our children can see themselves in all aspects of the curriculum.

I have learned that the ebb and flow of popular views can really galvanize social action, but the sustained impact can be challenging to maintain because, as yet, the decolonization agenda is not statutory. It fights for its place in the curriculum. In primary schools, the voice of the child needs careful nurturing and facilitation from their educators. This is required at this earlier stage of education to provide a safe space for children to discuss their views and have any misconceptions addressed. We also need to teach our children to demand the change they wish to see at secondary school. We need to prepare children by giving them the language to use. Literature is ideally placed to support this facilitation, and we plan to continue to use it on our journey. Using poems and stories to introduce challenging themes provides staff and children with narratives and ideas as a basis for quality discussions. This negates the need for deep subject-specific knowledge, and the focus can be on emotional responses to the text. Most importantly, we plan to make space for the work to elevate the status of decolonizing the curriculum beyond the zeitgeist of popular movements.

PART III

Education's Reparative Possibilities: Responsibilities and Reckonings for Sustainable Futures

9

Indigenous Education and Activism: Dignity and Repair for Inclusive Futures

Tarcila Rivera Zea

This chapter reprints in English and Spanish (versión en español disponible abajo) the contributions of Tarcila Rivera Zea to the UNESCO CIRE seminar series. She spoke in the session entitled 'Education's Reparative Possibilities: Responsibilities and reckonings for sustainable futures' held on 24 February 2020. In the session, Rivera Zea argued that reparative and healing education must be based on dignity and dialogue across differences to repair the harms of colonization and discrimination, sharing her experiences as an Indigenous rights activist.

Tarcila Rivera Zea is an Indigenous Quechua activist from Ayacucho, Peru, and founder of CHIRAPAQ (Centre for Indigenous Cultures of Peru). She is a member of the United Nations Permanent Forum on Indigenous Issues and, in 2011, received the Visionary Award from the Ford Foundation.

Ñañaykuna, Turiykuna, ukun sunquymantam rimaykamuychik llapankichiqta. Runasimi rimaqmi kani, Inkakakunapa wawanmi kani, tawantinsuyumanta hamun. From the bottom of my heart, with my sincerest regards, I greet you all in my mother tongue, Quechua, which is the language of the Incas. Globally, we have to allude to the Incas because this is the civilization we come from in this part of the world where I am speaking to you from. I want to thank the organizers for this opportunity to share some words, thoughts and hopes. I also want to congratulate the university and its partnership with UNESCO for creating a broader and global space for discussion that is possible thanks to online technologies.

Indigenous people are more than 480 million of the world's population divided into seven geo-cultural regions, and this is how we participate in the United Nations. In the American continents, we are nearly 60 million people. Since colonial times, Indigenous people have gone through all kinds of attempts to dissuade us from being who we are. We have been through invasion, colonization, evangelization, ideologization and politicization. More recently, colonies started to dissolve, and states, nations and republics began to form. We have also participated in these developments with the hope for freedom to gain our legitimate rights in a new state – a democratic state, at least, theoretically. However, the establishment of republics and countries in our traditional land areas has not brought about the acknowledgement and legitimization of rights for the people and cultures preceding colonization.

If we link this process of the development of nation states and countries with education, we are faced with education systems grounded in ethnocentric or Eurocentric approaches and Western hegemony. This type of education neglects diverse cultures and peoples who also are part of this society and geographical area. Therefore, attempts through education to 'make us better people' or 'civilize' us have instead hurt and undermined our humanity. They have limited our opportunities to be human beings with dignity and the freedom to contribute and make public what we know, our ways of thinking, to share our ways of coexisting with nature and others. This is the first barrier for us that makes education exclusive and contributes to creating hierarchies and status.

Therefore, many Indigenous peoples have witnessed only how society unfolds, how power is exercised, and how those power structures leave us behind. In the last 20 years, we have come to realize that, around the world, states have systems in place to exert power in racist ways, expressed through discriminations and exclusions. We see this, for example, in the exercising of power that is deeply patriarchal, racist and discriminating.

We find several barriers within the public education sphere, which Indigenous people also have the right to access. Unfortunately, when we enter the classroom, we find that this is a place where we, as 'the other', find that our existence, contributions and values are negated. Indigenous women, for example, have identified that the worst forms of violence that we face in our societies are racism and discrimination. Why? Because upon entering the classroom – where our language is not spoken, where our attire is not validated, where our cultural expressions and values, our knowledge and our resources are excluded – we start to lose our self-esteem. We start believing that we genuinely do not have the same rights as the others because the classroom – the space seen as the site of knowledge and where a person grows and learns – is precisely where we are being delegitimized. This has been my experience. I was monolingual (Quechua speaking) until I was ten. But, after my negative educational experiences, I acquired new skills that made me stronger and made me say: no, we cannot submit to what they say we must do. Our dignity is the only and most important thing that moves us to keep experiencing the world differently.

Therefore, in the late 1980s, in the context of an internal armed conflict, we started to develop our proposals from CHIRAPAQ, an Indigenous organization, and we began with an initial exercise. We started with the question: What do we need to transmit to our people in order to share with society subsequently? Based on that, we developed the concept of 'looking towards ourselves'. What does it mean? It asks: How can we heal the pain that we have accumulated as a result of the various exclusions, discriminations and negations of self that we have experienced? We had low self-esteem and did not have consciousness of our rights, since they had been denied to us for so long. Hence, when we started looking inwards, we started thinking: How could we heal from that suffering, from that denial to our dignity to express who we really are, what we really have and what we really want to be in society?

Thanks to the process of looking inwards, we were able to say: no more resentment, no more victimization. Instead, we were able to bring the heritage from our ancestors to the fore. However, this contribution has still not been reflected in the formal educational curriculum. Hence, we developed some proposals. For instance, in contexts of political violence, with refugee children, we asked how we could respond in ways that acknowledge the need for recognition and reaffirmation of our identity. And I can tell you, dear people of the world, that we have examples of men and women whose only trajectory in life had been to accept oppression and therefore to take a wrong path in their marginalized condition. But now, we have young people, men and women, with positive leadership skills, with open minds – but still Quechua, still Aymara – and they bring that dignity and assured self-esteem as they open themselves to the world.

When we think about a healing and reparative education, I believe that the most crucial aspect should be an education that genuinely guarantees a respectful relationship between human beings and across differences. We need to create opportunities to exercise power based on respect and the rights of the other. It is crucial that power, big or small, is used well for politics that dignify people, dignify human beings and positively contribute to the development of the human being in the classroom and, beyond it, to other training spaces.

We say this because, when we look at global phenomena, we see an arms race, a race to struggle for power, a race to demonstrate who has the strongest economy and is most capable. Those winning this 'strength race' are dehumanizing others. We consider that formal and informal education spaces have considerable responsibility for changing mentalities not only about accessing new technologies to improve economies, but accessing new technologies to develop knowledge and democratize opportunities. That is what we dream of as an education that can make peace sustainable.

We, Indigenous peoples with critical thinking, or organized groups, are often referred to as disharmonious people, terrorists and people who are always in opposition. Still, people don't see that we are only reclaiming rights that have been denied to us, formally denied to us, because the official structures of our states do not include us in their political, economic, social or cultural life. We may not have the same opportunities that others have. However, we have the right to speak and raise our voices. Fortunately, we have not lost our critical awareness of what constitutes injustice.

Going back to the healing and reparative function of education, I think that, from an educational perspective, healing and repair must be linked to our 'being', our humanity. Of course, when the state wants and accepts that we must have quality education, in a historical and reparative manner, they must invest in educational spaces that are appropriate, as well as in teacher training. In that sense, we think that all human beings must have the right to access opportunities. We are not suggesting that we all should be the same. We cannot be. But we should all have the opportunities to find spaces for dialogue where different manifestations of knowledge can have a pleasant conversation and serve as the basis to build peace among us all. We do not oppose technological or scientific advancements but demand equal access.

We, Indigenous women, are committed to education and a new generation. We want our children – from different Indigenous groups – to be global citizens. Still, we also want them to feel that their cultural values, expressions and heritage are a source of pride and dignity. We want them to enter the global stage to dialogue across diversity, respecting differences. What will give us sustainability is this: educating new generations that grow up believing that the one who is different from me is knowledgeable and has something to contribute, and not thinking of them as 'backwards', or third-class citizens, or ignorant. We keep discussing that, and we really hope for a change.

In this context, imagine how Indigenous women in our states and our societies are miseducated; for example, educated into machismo or patriarchy. The very vertical understanding and exercise of power also reaches Indigenous women and harms us in many ways. For instance, Indigenous women's education is often not regarded as a priority, leaving them without opportunities to grow and be themselves, constantly subordinated in power relations that position them as second class. This means that Indigenous women do not have the same opportunities as men, neither within Indigenous societies nor outside them. Why? Because colonization processes have made us believe that our role is to be wives and domestic workers. Hence, the denial of any opportunities for us, alongside low self-esteem, our poor economic conditions, as well as our status as Indigenous women, put us in a worse situation.

Fortunately, we are recovering images of Indigenous women who have fought for rights and freedom through history, who lifted their heads to speak and gained strength, and we are sharing these examples with the new generations. We demand the end of oppression. Education must be dignifying and strengthen our souls, emotions, and visions to coexist with mother nature, who has given us life, gives us life and feeds us. We must leave aside the race for depredation and consumption, the ambitions of power, and the continuous harm caused to the communal space we all live in: the world, nature and the natural environment. We need a healthy climate. A reparative and healing education can support us in our path towards this vision.

Capítulo 9 Educación Indígena y Activismo: Dignidad y reparación para futuros inclusivos – *Tarcila Rivera Zea*

Este capítulo reproduce en inglés y español (versión en inglés disponible arriba) la contribución de Tarcila Rivera Zea a la serie de seminarios coordinado por el Centro de Investigación acerca de Educación Comparada e Internacional (CIRE, por sus siglas en inglés) y UNESCO. Tarcila habló en la sesión titulada 'Las posibilidades reparadoras de la educación: responsabilidades y posibilidades/ potencialidades para futuros sostenibles' llevada a cabo el 24 de febrero de 2020. En dicho evento, Rivera Zea sostuvo que una educación reparadora y sanadora debe basarse en la dignidad y el diálogo entre quienes son diferentes si genuinamente se busca reparar los daños de la colonización y la discriminación.

Tarcila Rivera Zea es una activista Indígena Quechua de Ayacucho, Perú, y fundadora de CHIRAPAQ (Centro de Culturas Indígenas del Perú). Ha sido miembro del Foro Permanente de las Naciones Unidas para las Cuestiones Indígenas y en 2011 recibió el Premio Visionario de la Fundación Ford.

Ñañaykuna, Turiykuna, ukun sunquymantam rimarimuni llapaykipaq. Runasimi rimaqmi kani, Inkakunapa wawanmi kani, tawantinsuyumanta hamuni. Con todo cariño les mando un saludo desde el fondo de mi corazón en mi lengua madre, Quechua, que es la lengua de los Incas. A nivel global, tenemos que hacer referencia a los Incas porque de esa civilización venimos en esta región del mundo donde me ubico. Agradezco la oportunidad de poder compartir palabras, pensamientos, esperanzas y felicito a la Universidad por esta articulación con la UNESCO para llegar a un espacio más amplio y global que la tecnología hace posible.

En el mundo, las personas que pertenecemos a los pueblos Indígenas somos más o menos 480 millones, nos dividimos en 7 regiones geo culturales y así participamos en las Naciones Unidas. En las Américas estamos llegando casi a alrededor de 60 millones. Desde la colonización, los pueblos Indígenas hemos sido objeto de acciones encaminadas a cambiar nuestras formas de vida. Hemos vivido invasiones, colonizaciones, evangelización, ideologización y politización. Esto ha ocurrido también en los últimos tiempos, cuando comenzaron a desaparecer las colonias y se empezaron a formar Estados, naciones y repúblicas. También en esta época, los y las Indígenas participamos con la esperanza de tener libertad, de adquirir derechos legítimos en un Estado nuevo — teóricamente con mayores condiciones para la democracia. Sin embargo, el establecimiento de las repúblicas y países en nuestras tierras originales no ha significado el reconocimiento y la legitimación de derechos de esos pueblos y culturas preexistentes a las colonias.

Entonces, relacionando este proceso de establecimiento de naciones, estados y países con la educación, como ustedes lo saben, se implanta un sistema de educación totalmente etnocéntrico y eurocéntrico desde una hegemonía occidental, sin tomar en cuenta las expresiones de las diversas culturas y pueblos que somos también parte de ese medio social, de ese medio geográfico. Todas estas formas de querer convertirnos en 'mejores personas' o 'civilizadas' nos han ido dañando. Nos han limitado la oportunidad de ser seres humanos con dignidad y con libertad para aportar, compartir lo que sabemos, lo que pensamos y, compartir nuestras formas de convivir con la naturaleza y entre nosotros mismos.

Para nosotros, esa es una primera barrera que hace que la educación, vista como un privilegio, contribuya a crear jerarquías y estatus. Por eso, pasamos muchos pueblos a ser sólo observadores de cómo la sociedad se desenvuelve, cómo se ejerce el poder y cómo las estructuras de ese poder nos han ido dejando de lado. Llegamos a comprender en estos últimos tiempos — quizá los últimos 20 años — en general, que tenemos estados con sistemas de ejercicio del poder en una forma totalmente racista que se expresa en las discriminaciones y las exclusiones; llámese, ejercicio del poder sólo desde un sector, llámese ejercicio del poder en una forma totalmente patriarcal, pero también en una forma totalmente racista y discriminadora.

En la educación pública, que es a la que también tenemos derecho los pueblos Indígenas, nos encontramos con una serie de barreras cuando entramos al aula, ese lugar es donde lamentablemente se legitima una forma de negar la existencia, los aportes y los valores del otro. Las mujeres Indígenas, por ejemplo, hemos definido que la peor forma de violencia a la que nos enfrentamos en nuestras sociedades es el racismo y la discriminación. ¿Por qué? Porque al entrar al aula — donde no se habla tu idioma, no se valida tu vestimenta, no se toman en cuenta tus expresiones culturales, de conocimiento, de recursos, de lo que traemos como carga cultural —empezamos a perder nuestra autoestima. Empezamos a creer que verdaderamente no tenemos los mismos derechos que otros; porque el espacio que es visto como el espacio del saber, del desarrollo de la persona, de adquirir nuevos conocimientos, nos va deslegitimando. Esa es la experiencia que yo he tenido. He sido monolingüe hasta los 10 años. Entonces después de mis experiencias negativas en la educación estatal, adquirí otras herramientas para ser más fuerte y decir: no, no podemos ceder a lo que dicen que debemos ser cuando en realidad nuestra dignidad es lo único y más importante que nos mueve para seguir mirando el mundo de otra manera.

En este sentido, a finales de los años 80, en el contexto del conflicto interno armado, cuando empezamos nuestras propuestas desde CHIRAPAQ, una asociación Indígena, hicimos un primer ejercicio. Nos preguntamos, ¿qué es lo que tenemos para transmitir a nuestro pueblo, para compartir con la sociedad? Entonces, ideamos un concepto que se llamaba 'hacia nosotros mismos, hacia nosotras mismas'. ¿Qué quiere decir? ¿Cómo podríamos sanar esos dolores que traíamos como efecto de las formas de exclusión, discriminación o negación de nosotros mismos? Teníamos autoestima baja sin conciencia de derecho porque nos la negaban. Entonces, cuando empezamos a mirarnos a nosotros mismos dijimos: tenemos que curarnos de ese dolor, de esa negación de nuestra propia dignidad para luego transmitir lo que realmente somos, lo que realmente tenemos y lo que realmente quisiéramos ser en la sociedad.

Haciendo el camino hacia nosotros mismos dijimos: no más resentimiento, no imagen de víctima; sino sacar todo lo que heredamos de nuestros ancestros, y esto, hasta el momento, aún no se refleja en los contenidos educativos formales. Entonces, iniciamos propuestas, por ejemplo, en contextos de violencia política con niños/as refugiados/as, indagando sobre cómo podíamos responder en espacios de formación a la necesidad de reconocernos y autoafirmarnos. Les cuento, queridas personas del mundo, que tenemos ejemplos de hombres y mujeres cuyo único camino era aceptar que es un oprimido y escoger el camino no correcto en sociedades marginales. La generación que participó en los talleres de afirmación cultural y fortalecimiento de autoestima, ahora son jóvenes, hombres y mujeres con liderazgos positivos, abiertos de mentalidad al mundo pero que siguen siendo Quechuas, que siguen siendo Aimaras, y van con esa dignidad y esa autoestima afirmada abriéndose al mundo.

Cuando imaginamos una educación sanadora y reparadora, considero que tenemos que pensar que el aspecto más importante de reparación y sanación tiene que ser una educación que realmente garantice una relación de respeto entre nosotros, entre las diferencias. Que haya oportunidades de ejercer poder justamente basado en el respeto y en el derecho de los demás; que el poder, pequeño o grande, sea usado de buena manera para políticas que dignifiquen a las personas, a los seres humanos, y contribuyan de forma positiva en la formación de ese ser humano que transita del aula a otros espacios de formación.

Decimos esto porque cuando nos ponemos en el escenario global, donde la carrera armamentista, la carrera de pelea por el poder, de quién tiene más poder económico, y quién puede más nos está deshumanizando. Consideramos que, por eso, la educación formal y no formal tienen bastante responsabilidad, justamente, en el cambio de mentalidades que no sea solo para tener acceso a nueva tecnología como economía, sino a nueva tecnología para desarrollar el conocimiento, desarrollar valores, democratizar oportunidades. Eso es lo que soñamos: una educación que pueda hacer sostenible la paz.

Muchas veces a los pueblos Indígenas que tenemos capacidad crítica, nos relacionan con gente conflictiva, terrorista, que estamos siempre en contra de todo, pero no se ponen a pensar que estamos reclamando derechos negados, y negados formalmente, porque la estructura de nuestros estados todavía no nos incluye ni en la vida política, económica, social ni cultural. Entonces, aunque no tengamos las mismas oportunidades que otros, tenemos el derecho de usar nuestra palabra, de usar nuestra voz porque, felizmente, no hemos perdido la capacidad crítica sobre situaciones que son injustas.

Volviendo a la función sanadora, reparadora de la educación, pienso que el aspecto de reparación, sanación desde la perspectiva educativa, tiene que estar más relacionado a nuestro ser, a nuestra humanidad. Por supuesto que el estado, cuando quiera y acepte que debemos tener educación de calidad como forma de reparación histórica, también tiene que invertir los presupuestos públicos en espacios de educación apropiados y en la formación de docentes. En ese sentido, creemos que todos los seres humanos tenemos el derecho a igualdad de acceso a las oportunidades. No estamos diciendo que toditos vamos a ser iguales. No podemos ser todos iguales. Pero sí tener la oportunidad de encontrar espacios de diálogo donde los conocimientos de unos, los saberes de otros puedan dialogar armónicamente y puedan servir para construir justamente la paz y la relación armónica entre nosotros. No nos oponemos al avance científico, tecnológico, pero pedimos que todos tengamos oportunidad de acceso a ello.

Nosotras, las mujeres Indígenas que hacemos formación y estamos comprometidas con la educación y la nueva generación, sí queremos que nuestros hijos de diferentes pueblos Indígenas sean ciudadanas y ciudadanos universales, que sus expresiones y la carga cultural que tienen de sus culturas de origen sea un motivo de orgullo, de dignidad y que puedan también entrar en el escenario donde se dialoguen las diversidades respetando las diferencias. Creo que lo que más nos debe dar sostenibilidad es esto: la formación de nuevas generaciones que crezcan teniendo esta mirada de que el diferente algo sabe, algo tiene que compartir y no verlo como alguien que es el atraso de la sociedad o son ciudadanos de tercera o que son ignorantes. Hasta ahora es algo que discutimos y esperamos que cambie.

En ese escenario, imagínense la situación de las mujeres Indígenas. En estados y sociedades machistas, patriarcales, racistas y discriminadoras son maltratadas e impactadas en sus vidas. Toda esta imagen de ejercicio de poder tan vertical también nos salpica y nos daña triplemente. Por ejemplo, las mujeres Indígenas suelen ser consideradas en segundo lugar para tener acceso a la educación, dejándolas sin oportunidades para seguir creciendo y ser ellas

INDIGENOUS EDUCATION AND ACTIVISM

mismas, sometiéndolas a una relación de poder de segunda clase. Entonces, desde niñas ni dentro de la sociedad Indígena actual ni fuera de ella tienen las mismas oportunidades que los varoncitos. ¿Por qué? Porque como hemos pasado por todas estas formas de colonizar creemos que solo somos para el marido o somos para el trabajo doméstico. Con las oportunidades negadas, con la autoestima baja, sin acceso a oportunidades, por ser Indígenas, por ser mujeres y por ser pobres, nos encontramos en peor situación.

Afortunadamente, estamos recuperando las imágenes de mujeres Indígenas que lucharon por derechos y libertades a través de la historia, que levantaron la cabeza, que adquirieron fortaleza, transmitiendo sus enseñanzas a las nuevas generaciones. Entonces, basta de opresión. La educación tiene que ser dignificadora y fortalecer nuestro espíritu, nuestra emocionalidad y nuestra visión de convivencia con la madre naturaleza que nos dio vida, nos da vida, nos da todo para comer, alimentarnos. Tenemos que dejar de lado esta carrera consumista basada en la depredación, de la ambición de poder desmedido y de dañar el espacio común que es el mundo, la naturaleza y el medio ambiente. Un ambiente sano, una educación reparadora y sanadora puede apoyarnos en el camino hacia esta visión.

10

Learning With the Past: Racism, Education and Reparative Futures

Arathi Sriprakash, David Nally, Kevin Myers
and Pedro Ramos-Pinto

Introduction

This chapter discusses the importance of historical thinking for futures-oriented policy in education. It proposes that a concept of 'reparative futures' can be a generative basis for knowledge and learning, not only in formal educational institutions, but in community organizations, workplaces and in all sites of cultural exchange. The idea of reparative futures signals a commitment to identify and recognize the injustices visited on, and experienced by, individuals and communities in the past. It understands that these past injustices, even when they appear to be distant in time or 'over', will continue to endure in people's lives in material and affective ways unless, and until, they are consciously and carefully addressed. Although there are certainly different languages and forms of reparative address, we suggest that critical practices of historical thinking can offer a vital starting point for critiquing and reformulating the interrelations of past, present and future.

The discussions focus specifically on the importance of acknowledging and seeking justice for enduring histories of racial and colonial domination. We argue that UNESCO's present programme on the futures of education needs to be underpinned by a concept of the future that is reparative if it is to challenge rather than reproduce such systems of domination. The historical thinking that we propose for this work involves the creation of educational relationships that are centred on processes of dialogue and exchange and which proceed explicitly from an anti-racist position of fundamental human equality. Such modes of education, and the radical humanism they embrace, are foundational to, and are indeed a necessary precondition for, imagining and realizing futures that are just.

Most attempts to build better futures have proceeded along different lines. In the first part of this chapter, we examine UNESCO's efforts at the end of the Second World War to identify and install through education a new 'universal' humanism, one that might dispense with hierarchies of 'race thinking'. We show, however, how UNESCO's search for a new humanism rested on norms of social evolution that denied the 'coevalness' of others and assumed a kind of tutelary power over peoples and territories that needed to 'catch up' with the West (Fabian, 1983; Lorenzini, 2019). Busy identifying deficits and filling gaps, experts associated with UNESCO's activities rarely interrogated their operating assumptions or addressed the racialized violence that structured the global economy and rendered their curative interventions 'necessary'. Couched in benevolent, colour-blind rhetoric and favouring planning instruments that promoted abstraction and simplification, they set about working on a future premised on the need to govern and 'develop' the lives of 'backward' populations (Li, 2007). We discuss this as the 'chronopolitics' of development, and show through a case study of UNESCO-led activity in this period how such technocratic projects tended to negate, or at least radically simplify, the past. In doing so, these futures-oriented policies in education, under the guise of universal humanism, enabled colonial and racialized modes of domination to endure.

How might UNESCO's present effort to formulate futures-oriented policy in education address this history? In the second part of the chapter, the practices associated with reparative futures are set out in greater detail. The focus here is on the epistemic and dialogic conditions of reparation – that is, its educational premise. This does not displace or diminish juridical or material forms of reparation; rather, we take collective learning – particularly through historical thinking and practice – as a necessary basis for any form of reparative redress. An education for reparative futures would be alive to the structures of power that animate social life and have produced deeply uneven opportunities for individuals and communities to flourish. It would involve attending to the epistemic erasures and active silences, political interests and interpretive closures of the production and legitimization of knowledge through educational and historical practice itself. After all, these are the knowledge-politics that have shaped past and present racialized hierarchies, including judgements of whose histories are considered important to know and to learn.

We propose that an education for reparative futures would embed the practice of asking ongoing and difficult questions with the past: cultivating spaces to remember, create, explore and discuss injustices; fostering an ethics of listening and dialogue capable of generating new perspectives; seeking to understand the histories, voices and experiences that have been silenced or erased through assimilative forms of education; and grappling with the irresolvable difficulties of redemptive thought (Simon, 2005). It is an education that, like the abolitionist thinking of Black feminism, is defined by its imaginative potential rather than by the constraints of predetermined or delegated outcomes. It is dedicated to building new relationships of reciprocity and modes of collaborative interpretation and collective organization to imagine life beyond all forms of injustice (Olufemi, 2020). Learning with the past – particularly past struggles over the future – is crucial, we argue, for holding open education as a mode of critique, rather than allowing it to sustain systems of domination.

Racism and the chronopolitics of development

While all past authorities have in some sense attempted to plan for the future – to realize opportunities or sidestep catastrophic events – the 'Age of Internationalism' born in 1945 marked a distinctive turn towards a more centralized, globally oriented, and 'vertical' style of futures-thinking (Urry, 2016; Andersson, 2018). The Bretton Woods institutions and the newly minted UN agencies, in particular, were mandated to steer the future of human welfare globally – addressing, for example, acute hunger and agriculture poverty (FAO), disease and ill-health (WHO), unemployment and economic hardship (ILO), and the educational needs of children and society (UNESCO) (Mazower, 2012; Neizen and Sapignoli, 2017).

The futures-oriented institutions of this era consciously sought to set goals and intervene in specific geographies to 'ready' communities to receive and absorb their new planning orthodoxies. 'International development', as this project has been more commonly called, rested on a 'one world' humanism: its colour-blind approach reinscribed racial categories and colonial hierarchies while claiming to enshrine 'universal' values (Bonilla-Silva, 2010; Sluga, 2010). For example, along with sanitation, health, and employment, education was an index of differentiation – producing, for instance, hierarchies of the educated/uneducated, literate/illiterate (Matasci, 2017). An 'arithmetic of standards', to borrow Nick Cullather's term, conjured into being people whose 'needs' must be calculated, interpreted, prescribed and 'certified to exist' before they could be confronted, tamed and overcome in the quest for societal improvement (Cullather, 2007). As historians of race have demonstrated, it is precisely through socio-historical processes of categorizing and differentiating human life that racial meanings and hierarchies are created and sustained (Anderson, 2003; Omi and Winant, 2015).

This was a period profoundly shaped by global fascism, military resistance against decolonization, the foundation of apartheid states, forced displacement, violent assertions of settler colonialism and anti-Blackness, as well as new forms of imperialism (Gilroy, 2004). The UN agencies, and UNESCO in particular, engaged in the intellectual and practical task of challenging the biological racism that sanctioned and legitimized these modalities of political domination (Brattain, 2007; Amrit and Sluga, 2008). However, their technocratic approaches to making the future disregarded the kinds of historical reflexivity that could be found, for example, in theories and practices of Indigenous self-recognition and anti-colonial radical humanism that offered, as they do today, resources to directly interrogate the futurity of racial oppression (Coulthard, 2014).

At UNESCO's founding in 1945, Mexican minister of education Jaime Torres Bodet remarked that the organization was trying to solve 'the problem of entering an era of human history distinct from that which has just closed' (UN, 1945, p 36). Bodet's phrase was, like so many in the foundational documents of the organization, richly allusive. It begs at least two sets of questions about the kinds of epistemic resources and practices that were debated, elevated and rendered legible to solve the problem of history that Bodet identified. The first pertains to how open UNESCO was to understanding the ongoing history of racial and colonial violence as part of imagining and creating a 'distinct' new era. The second, and related, is about what sorts of resources could become, in British prime minister Clement Atlee's address to the founding conference, the 'instruments of our co-operative international life in the future' (UN, 1945, p 21). Education sciences emerged as a key 'instrumentality' of international development, legitimizing the directives of elite 'experts' whose research, much like today, sought to shape educational systems, curricula and methods of teaching across the world (Sluga, 2013; Duedahl, 2016; Kulnazarova and Ydesen, 2016). Here, we draw attention to the racialized temporalities inscribed in this early work of UNESCO, particularly in the attempts of its Department of Social Sciences to find technical, disciplinary knowledge and methods for understanding and steering a new global future.

Our discussions in this section draw on an analysis by Kevin Myers and colleagues of UNESCO's Tensions Project, which ran between 1947 and 1953 (Myers et al, 2021). The Tensions Project was an ambitious programme of educational development that included 17 member states. With the expressed goal of identifying and overcoming 'tensions' that lead to national and international conflict, the project involved the design and conduct of research on a wide variety of topics, including 'national character', the socialization of children and the origins of prejudice and violence (Cantril, 1948). The project was particularly active in India, which also serves as a focus for discussions later in this chapter. The experts who sought to devise so-called 'instruments' of development through this research were disproportionately drawn from, and dominated by, scholars from North America and Western Europe. UNESCO staff on the Tensions Project for example, included successive directors; social psychologists Hadley Cantril and Otto Klineberg; sociologists Edward Shils, Robert Cooley Angell and Alva Myrdal; and the project consultant in India, psychologist Gardner Murphy. The course tutors, who designed and taught research methods training (including Erich Fromm, Claude Lévi-Strauss, Henry Dicks and the future peace educator Adam Curle), were all male, all white and all European. They were part of a community of social scientists promoting work that they understood to be scientifically progressive and which, they hoped, would usher in a new, and qualitatively different, internationalist era. The boundary-maintenance of this overwhelmingly white, male, epistemic community, however, meant their conceptual frameworks were far from open to the alterity of the historical experiences and interpretive resources of precisely those 'others' who would be the subjects of their work.

Acting politically 'envisages a desired future; [and] invokes a formative past' and it is thus steeped in normative notions of time (Maier, 1987). Post-war projects of international development understood 'progress' as a unilinear series of stages from 'primitive' to 'civilized' living – a view that sociologist Wolfgang Sachs (2010) terms 'chronopolitics'. We argue that the social scientists involved in the Tensions Project shared the same basic racialized temporality of development. Theirs was an intellectual world held together by the merger of history and chronology that achieved dominance in the wake of the industrial revolution and European imperialism (Hanchard, 1999; Chatterjee, 2001; Nanni, 2012). Time – linear, mechanical and absolute – became central to the scientific thought they championed, and influential in a range of intellectual theories drawn on to understand, and change, human behaviour. Chronological time provided a kind of abstract container into which discrete events and people could be gathered, synchronized and compared. So, while the 'universal' humanism of this period sought to 'include' every human phenomenon – personality, culture or society – historically and in the process of change, particular people, cultures or societies were allocated different positions or points in the process of empty and homogenous time (Weindling, 2012). Perhaps most influential of all was a universal developmental framework of phases and stages into which individuals, families, communities and nations could all be placed (Burman, 2008). In the Tensions Project, they were refugees who needed rehabilitating, children who needed developing, tribes in need of protection, villagers who needed to adapt, but underneath all was an imperialist and racialized teleology – an evolutionary account of change where the end point was modelled on European modernity.

Despite a declared interest in cultural difference, UNESCO activities, like the Tensions Project offered as an example here, tended to overlook or simplify the differing pasts that would become part of a collective future. Progress towards tolerance and peace, they seemed to imply, would be achieved without recognizing, far less addressing, the global inequalities produced by colonialism and other related forms of domination and exploitation. In practice, this meant that Tensions scholars were intolerant of any form or language of experience that could not be assimilated to a Euro-American model of historical development. Adam Curle, an Oxford University graduate in History and Anthropology, with fieldwork experience in the Middle East, and who took leave from his job at the Tavistock Institute rehabilitating war veterans to teach on the Tensions Project training course, was perhaps not an obvious proponent for a dogmatic Western social science. However, Curle appeared oblivious to the possibility that the many languages, belief systems and cosmologies that made up newly independent India could have competing ideas about, and experiences of, both past and present. Instead, the term 'fantastic' was used as an antonym for rationality, and societies experiencing conflict and tension were judged to be stuck in an

> emotional lag which prevents people from accepting the reality of new situations and retards the emergence of fresh and more appropriate structures ... Such escape mechanisms may become stereotyped and institutionalised in primitive society, where they have a long time to develop, but in modern society, in which a major trend of development is the freeing of the individual from the bonds of taboo and fantasy, they only cause an additional frustration and misery which very is apt to find an outlet in violence.[1]

It should be remembered that the strong conception of historical development at play here helped to shape UNESCO's educational outlook precisely as the moment the organization was assuming a global leadership role. Indeed Curle's emphasis on developmental deficiencies (lags, barriers, blockages, constraints and impediments) and racialized imagery (primitive emotions, taboo and fantasy) soon became a prominent feature not only of UNESCO's post-war world view, but of UN development policy in general.

The social scientists, administrators and planners who represented India at UNESCO, men like Sarvepalli Radhakrishnan, Ashfaque Husain and Tara Chand, both identified and criticized the dominance of Western knowledge and personnel in the fledging organization. However, opportunities for them to represent or explain the significance of diverse histories and cultures of the Indian subcontinent were highly circumscribed, not only by their social locations – having been part of the English-educated elite – but also by the dominance of Western social-scientific categories within the knowledge institutions in which they worked. Although they often invoked the anti-colonial sentiment of the period, their articulation of the legacies of colonialism and their discursive representations of the new citizen and nation were also conditioned by racial categories and temporalities of development. Biraja Shankar Guha, for example, was a Harvard-educated Indian anthropologist commissioned to lead research on refugees as part of the Tensions Project. Significantly, Guha also had a prominent role in the Anthropological Survey of India that informed the retention and renewal of upper-caste Aryanism in post-colonial India (Guha, 1959; on Guha's upper-caste Aryanism see Mukharji, 2017). Guha's 'absolute faith in the racial separation of upper and lower castes' was not challenged by, and may have reinforced, the evolutionary framework of UNESCO's research programmes (Mukharji, 2017, p 456).

Through this brief account of its early activities, we suggest that there was potential for UNESCO to be an intellectual arena in which a new humanism might have emerged, one based on a recognition of historical injustices and specifically of the dehumanizing premise of colonialism and racism. But there remain questions about how far UNESCO's organizational structures, epistemic frameworks and educational activities were committed to engage and reckon with different interpretive resources and multiple histories, and structural violences and racial injustices. It was not apparent within the available archival material that the Tensions Project, for example, cultivated a community of practice that was alive to questioning received historical narratives and supportive of forms of reparative remembering that could have led its participants to think critically about historical trajectories and envisage a wider range of futures (Dawson, 2008; Hall, 2018). Notably missing from Project discussions were the theories and educational visions of anti-colonial thinkers whose radical humanism offered a different future for the world (Wilder, 2015). Indeed, the example of UNESCO's Tensions Project helps us to identify a critical issue in the ongoing 'chronopolitics' of its Futures of Education. Try as we might, the future – or futures – can never be constructed by drawing a line in the sand with the past. Such ambitions remain stiflingly limited because they fail to recognize alternative histories that would themselves entail their own visions of the future or to imagine futures that reckon with reparative address for past injustices.

Learning with the past

This chapter has argued that an understanding of the past and its active formations today is crucial for futures-thinking. This section sets out, briefly, what we mean by historical knowledges and historical practices, to consider how critical approaches to history can be a generative process for imagining futures that are reparative rather than reproductive of injustices past and present. These approaches to history involve processes of dialogue and exchange; they are constituted through educational relationships and thus they point to the ways in which education is a necessary precondition of reparative address.

Historical knowledges

In our call to 'learn with the past', we are advocating for something more than, or different from, the 'common-sense' trope that 'history has something to teach us.' Such claims echo European enlightenment ideals of universal knowledge that, in practice, reduced the capacious category of the past to the disciplined procedures of scientific history. This science privileges apparently empirical knowledge that can only be established and verified through specific evidential standards and specialist hermeneutic techniques usually located within socially closed academic institutions. The resulting categories of this dominant European historiography have, for example, produced racialized temporalities of people and societies who are held to 'deviate' from, or lag behind, an assumed benchmark of European colonial-modernity (Chakrabarty, 2008; Gopal, 2019).

Thus, in emphasizing the importance of historical knowledge in futures-thinking, we argue that a reparative future requires an expansion of what counts as historical knowledge itself. This may involve what Ariella Aïsha Azoulay calls 'potential history': a rejection of the conceptual apparatus of colonial-modernity and its racialized chronopolitics. Potential history, Azoulay argues, is 'a commitment to attend to the potentialities that the institutional forms of imperial violence – borders, nation-states, museums, archives and laws – try to make obsolete or turn into precious ruins' (Azoulay, 2019, p 286; Stoler, 2016). For example, it would foreground and trace the experiences of and enduring questions of justice surrounding: slavery and genocide in empire building (Gueye and Michel, 2018); colonial projects of mass famine, poverty and dispossession (Nally, 2011; Pascoe, 2018); the emotional regimes and psychological consequences of different imperial formations (Hartman, 1997; Fanon, 2008; Nandy, 2009); programmes of forced removal, educational assimilation and state violence against Indigenous children (Nakata, 2008; Brown, 2019); and the different types, and impacts of, anti-colonial and anti-imperial movements and resistance (Choudry and Vally, 2018; Getachew, 2019).

Even in the scholarly disciplines where these histories are discussed and debated, there is still a tendency to dismiss them as polemical, excessively political or peripheral to the 'proper' subjects of study. Such judgements reflect the continued influence of narrow epistemological categories, and rules of method, that render themes of racism, violence, dispossession, slavery, famine and poverty forgotten, invisible or unspeakable. This is also despite growing acknowledgement in fields of practice and activism of the ways that histories shaped by violence, discrimination and poverty are traumas that are 'experienced over time and across generations' (Mohatt et al, 2014). Even though the concept of trauma should be treated with some care, it has considerable potential, along with concepts of memory, abolition and epistemic justice, to inspire educational practices that foster reparative futures (on epistemic justice and education, Bain, 2018; Borell et al, 2018; on abolitionist agendas in education, Love, 2019; for discussions on memory and education, see Paulson et al, 2020). The lived experiences of racism and colonialism – felt, in different formulations, over centuries – have been, by and large, excluded as an epistemic basis for the kind of futures-thinking occurring in state, corporate and transnational institutions. This, and the very narrow conception of historical knowledge that underpins such futures-oriented policy, needs to change.

Historical practices

What kind of historical practices, then, might support reparative futures? A first step in opening a space to listen to other pasts is to admit that the present, the contemporary, is not a unified, synchronic moment. Just as globalization does not mean that there is such a thing as a universal, single, global culture – however many points of contact and exchange there may be – nor is the present a simultaneous confluence of all pasts (Bevernage, 2016). And so, historical practices for a reparative future can begin by recognizing that, to the extent that they are constituted by myriad historical experiences, there are multiple presents and therefore multiple visions of the future that need to be heard in democratic deliberation (Sen, 2009). At a practical level, futures-oriented policy in education must give space to the experiences and knowledges of people whose histories have been silenced by or made marginal in educational systems and processes. The Tensions Project discussed earlier demonstrates the closing down of such space. It should not be a matter of paternalistic 'outreach' but an acknowledgement that such historical knowledges – as sources of expertise and learning for the future – exist beyond, and in spite of, institutional engagement (Rassool, 2010).

Recognizing this multiplicity requires opening up opportunities to have different pasts as well as different visions of the future understood. Educative cultures of listening, dialogue and reflection are thus key. Indeed, reparative futures can only be 'co-produced': they involve collective practices that are committed to learning about multiple pasts, to people seeking to tell their stories and make their histories, and to critically engaging with received histories (Lloyd and Moore, 2015; Pente et al, 2015). The usual building blocks of history – the actors and the periods and the concepts used to tell it – potentially become an object of discussion and debate. The framing of the story is no longer a matter of common sense or implied knowledge but a process open to dialogue and contestation. Such dialogue should be based on the recognition that the production and performance of histories is, in part, a creative act.

The historical practices we see as central to reparative futures are thus committed to expanding the identification, construction and use of sources in order to generate a new collective recognition of the injustices of multiple pasts. These are educational processes that can foster reparative remembering. The practices of oral history, the recording of life histories, the writing of autobiographies, public testimonies, performances of song and dance, and visual sources of all kinds offer salient examples of how histories are continually created at the 'margins' and 'from below'. Ideas about past-present relations are narrated and rehearsed through diverse and often mundane practices, circulating, for example, in families, communities and schools. The symbolic worlds they create are central to individual and collective claims for recognition and representation, for creating new solidarities, and for changing the way we think about the past and its legacies today.

Such a view understands historical 'archives' in open terms. Archival collections – from physical collations to databases and websites to walking tours and so on – are not repositories of inert data or historical facts but can be central to modes of representation for people and groups and are thus sites that can support collective engagement. The creation of digital archives, for example, has not only increased the number of people who can research the past, but also enabled new forms of collaborative interpretation that may have reparative potential. Take, for example, the creation of databases for tracking how universities have been funded through expropriated Indigenous land; mappings of housing injustice and narratives of displacement and resistance; data on the legacies of British slave ownership; publicly available records of colonial frontier massacres; and open-access immersive storytelling of present and erased localities under settler colonialism. Having such archives and sources to learn with can potentially open up new dialogues for reparative futures.

Education for reparative futures

UNESCO's International Commission on the Futures of Education proclaims the present moment as one of potentially transformative change whose immanent possibilities for addressing inequality and injustice can only be realized by a commitment to global solidarity (UNESCO, 2020). As we hope this chapter has demonstrated, this is not a new claim. UNESCO has been here before, expressing laudable hopes for the future, calling on scholars to help build a new world and, in doing so, posing a challenge that invites educators to move from positions of critique to projects of construction. We welcome that challenge, but, if our analysis is correct, it also clearly requires reformulation. A radical reshaping of the world cannot be achieved by leaving the past behind with exhortations for greater commitment to 'public education, common goods and global solidarity' (UNESCO, 2020). Instead, we need to encourage educative processes of reparative address because these are a necessary precondition for a politics of solidarity, justice and equality.

To be sure, important UNESCO's initiatives, such as its Slave Route Project and its ongoing work on truth, peace and reconciliation, position education as central to reparative justice. However, its work on global educational policy, under the rubrics of international development, continues to be captured by instrumental, technocratic and economically driven notions of education that remain actively silent about enduring histories of racism and colonialism (Sriprakash et al, 2020). The pledge to 'leave no one behind' encapsulates the unrelenting forward march of development (UNESCO, 2016). And so, the racialized chronopolitics of development continue, despite ongoing histories of dissent and different visions for the future. The Black Lives Matter movement refuses the continuation of what Tiffany Lethabo King (2019) has called 'conquistador humanism' – the seizing of the future to craft and sustain 'European human life and self-actualization through Black and Indigenous death.' Can UNESCO's programmes – from its coordination of Education Sustainable Development Goal 4 to its global initiative on Futures of Education – encourage learning with such histories of survivance and such visions of alternative futures?

Indeed, we suggest that it is imperative for UNESCO to imagine a future that is committed to reparative address and therefore to a different kind of education. Educational processes and practices for a reparative future would focus on the principles of a radical humanism that, as Aimé Césaire (2000, p 73) so clearly declared, is made to 'the measure of the world'. As anti-colonial thinkers have shown us, this is a humanism that is not established through a pre-defined, universal container for human life, as liberal humanism has sought. Nor is it oriented towards 'walled in' notions of difference and particularity that feed toxic nationalism and cultural chauvinism. Both have authorized systems of racial domination. Rather, as Gary Wilder summarizes, it is a humanism that works through histories of lived experience: it is situated, embodied and enriched by the coexistence of all particulars – an emancipatory world view 'that could indicate how to live a more fully human life' (Wilder, 2016, p 593). It is a humanism, therefore, that must be alive to past and present injustices. It calls for critical practices of history.

Our focus on historical knowledge and practices has not forfeited categories such as freedom, democracy and solidarity as important to futures-thinking, but rather underscores the need for dialogue across different lived experiences – indeed, for education as shared learning and unlearning – in order to fill hopeful categories, such as reparation, with meaning. Drawing on Edward Said's reflections, an education for reparative futures involves learning 'concretely and sympathetically, contrapuntally, about others' (Said, 1993, p 336). It is dedicated to what Satya Mohanty calls 'epistemic cooperation', a concatenation of ideas that recognizes that ideas of justice, democracy, freedom and so on, stem from, and thus have a debt to, subaltern lives and histories (Mohanty, 1997). Or, in Robin Wall Kimmerer's (2013) terms, it is a process of 'braiding' multiple knowledges and experiences for new forms of restorative reciprocity and responsibility. Education for reparative futures would seek to understand the entangled histories of people who have been differently positioned by systems of racial and colonial domination and would see this understanding as essential for building the kinds of solidarity that a future without racism requires.

Indeed, this is not a simple act of historical recovery, nor a historicist rescue of an oppositional identity in an imagined past. The radical humanism of Frantz Fanon, Aimé Césaire and, more recently, Paul Gilroy and Sylvia Wynter, warns against that particular seduction and argues, in Wynter's words, for a reimagination of the 'human in the terms of a new history whose narrative will enable us to co-identify ourselves each with the other' (see Wynter in Lawrence and Nettleford, 1996 and Scott, 2000). What we are calling for is an education that fosters processes of reparative remembering; questioning received narratives and supporting histories that 'revindicate' the life-ways of the oppressed (Pratt, 1992, p 2). An education for reparative futures takes seriously 'our knowledge of the past as a source of present and future action' and it accepts that humans have symbolic attachments to 'the past' that are located far from a register of historical events or empirical facts (Rothberg, 2017, p 515). In recognizing these attachments, and the psychic functions they serve, reparative education practices an ethics of humility, or a mode of thought that is cautious of not recentring dominant positions or recuperating an assimilative education. It creates spaces for listening to multiple, and often competing, knowledge traditions so that all have opportunities to be recognized, explored, debated and critiqued. These spaces, we argue, can offer possibilities for reparative remembering because they make available to individuals and groups new resources for interpreting individual life stories and group histories and the means to work through them.

Conclusion

We do not underestimate the practical, educational and emotional difficulties of these processes. Nor does our appeal to dialogue seek to evoke a liberalism of the kind that has become familiar in the statements and reports of institutions like UNESCO. As historians and political theorists alike have thoroughly demonstrated, liberalism has comfortably accommodated colonial relations of racial domination, particularly through assimilationist, colour-blind orientations to education (Lowe, 2015; Mills, 2017). Instead, we maintain that reparative futures cannot be based either on systemic silences or on oppositional models of remembering. Reparative futures require recognition that we are all differently marked by historical processes; that we all have capacities for affect and cognition and that dialogue – however challenging and difficult – is a starting point for all educational relationships that are self-consciously orientated toward material justice. We must not come to inhabit a future that carries with it uninterrogated injustices of the past and present. It is precisely through education that new forms of recognition of these injustices and a solidarity for creating something different can be fostered. Education is, therefore, necessary for reparative futures.

Note
[1] UAP, 327.5: 301.18 A 53 Tensions affecting Int. Understanding Community Studies Part I -up to 31/X/49. Adam Curle, 'Some Notes on Social Method and Theory in relation to Community Studies', p.2.

Disclaimer

References
Amrit, S. and Sluga, G. (2008) New histories of the United Nations, *Journal of World History*, 19(3): 251–274.

Anderson, W. (2003) *The Cultivation of Whiteness. Science, health, and racial destiny in Australia*, New York: Basic Books.

Andersson, J. (2018) *The Future of the World: Futurology, futurists, and the struggle for the post Cold War social imagination*, Oxford: Oxford University Press.

Azoulay, A.A. (2019) *Potential History: Unlearning imperialism*, London and New York: Verso.

Bain, Z. (2018) Is there such a thing as 'white ignorance' in British education?, *Ethics and Education*, 13(1): 4–21.

Bevernage, B. (2016) Tales of pastness and contemporaneity: On the politics of time in history and anthropology, *Rethinking History*, 20(3): 352–374.

Bonilla-Silva, E. (2010) *Racism Without Racists: Color-blind racism and racial inequality in contemporary America*, 3rd edn, Washington, DC: Rowman & Littlefield.

Borell, B., Barnes, H.M. and McCreanor, T. (2018) Conceptualising Historical Privilege: The flip side of historical trauma, a brief examination, *AlterNative*, 14(1): 25–34.

Brattain, M. (2007) Race, racism, and antiracism: UNESCO and the politics of presenting science to the postwar public, *American Historical Review*, 112(5): 1386–1413.

Brown, L. (2019) Indigenous young people, disadvantage and the violence of settler colonial education policy and curriculum, *Journal of Sociology*, 55(1): 54–71.

Burman, E. (2008) *Developments: Child, Image, Nation*, Abingdon: Routledge.

Cantril, H. (1948) The Human Sciences and World Peace: A report on the UNESCO Project: 'Tensions affecting International Understanding', available at: unesdoc.unesco.org/images/0015/001581/158131eb.pdf [accessed 30 January 2023].

Césaire, A (2000) *Discourse on Colonialism*, New York: Monthly Review Press.

Chakrabarty, D. (2008) *Provincialising Europe: Postcolonial thought and historical difference*, Princeton: Princeton University Press.

Chatterjee, P. (2001) The nation in heterogeneous time, *Indian Economic and Social History Review*, 38(4): 399–418.

Choudry, A. and Vally, S. (2018) *Reflections on Knowledge, Learning and Social Movements: History's Schools*, Abingdon: Routledge.

Coulthard, G.S. (2014) *Red Skin, White Masks: Rejecting the colonial politics of recognition*, Minneapolis, University of Minnesota Press.

Cullather, N. (2007) The foreign policy of the calorie, *American Historical Review*, 112(2): 337–364.

Dawson, G. (2008) *Making peace with the past? Memory, trauma and the Irish Troubles*, Manchester: Manchester University Press.

Duedahl, P. (2016) *A History of UNESCO: Global actions and impacts*, London: Palgrave Macmillan.

Fabian, J. (1983) *Time and the Other: How anthropology makes it object*, New York: Columbia University Press.

Fanon, F. (2008) *Black Skin, White Masks*, New York: Grove Atlantic.

Getachew, A. (2019) *Worldmaking After Empire: The rise and fall of self-determination*, Princeton: Princeton University Press.

Gilroy, P. (2004) *After Empire: Melancholia or convivial culture?* Abingdon: Routledge.

Gopal, P. (2019) *Insurgent Empires: Anticolonial resistance and British dissent*, London and New York: Verso.

Gueye, A. and Michel, J. (2018) *A Stain on our Past: Slavery and memory*, Trenton: Africa World Press.

Guha, B.S. (1959) Studies in Social Tension Among the Refugees from Eastern Pakistan, Department of Anthropology, Government of India.

Hall, C. (2018) Doing reparatory history: bringing 'race' and slavery home, *Race & Class*, 60(1): 3–21.

Hanchard, M. (1999) Afro-modernity: Temporality, politics, and the African diaspora, *Public Culture*, 11(1): 245–268.

Hartman, S. (1997) *Scenes of Subjection: Terror, slavery and self-making in nineteenth-century America*, New York and Oxford: Oxford University Press.

Kimmerer, R.W. (2013) *Braiding Sweetgrass: Indigenous wisdom, scientific knowledge and the teachings of plants*, Minneapolis: Milkweed Editions.

King, T.L. (2019) *The Black Shoals: Offshore formations of Black and Native studies*, Durham, NC: Duke University Press.

Kulnazarova, A. and Ydesen, C. (2016) *UNESCO Without Borders: Educational campaigns for international understanding*, Abingdon: Routledge.

Lawrence, V. and Nettleford, R. (1996) *Race, Discourse and the Origin of the Americas: A new world view*, Washington, DC: Smithsonian Institution Scholarly Press.

Li, T.M. (2007) *The Will to Improve: Governmentality, development and the practice of politics*, Durham, NC: Duke University Press.

Lloyd, S. and Moore, J. (2015) Sedimented histories: Connections, collaborations and co-production in regional history, *History Workshop Journal*, 80(1): 234–248.

Lorenzini, S. (2019) *Global Development: A Cold War history*, Princeton: Princeton University Press.

Love, B. (2019) *We Want to do More than Survive: Abolitionist teaching and the pursuit of educational freedom*, Boston, MA: Beacon Press.

Lowe, L. (2015) *The Intimacies of Four Continents*, Durham, NC: Duke University Press.

Maier, C.S. (1987) The politics of time: Changing paradigms of collective time and private time in the modern era, in C.S. Maier (ed) *Changing Boundaries of the Political: Essays on the evolving balance between the state and society, public and private in Europe,* Cambridge: Cambridge University Press, pp 151–152.

Matasci, D. (2017) Assessing needs, fostering development: UNESCO, illiteracy and the global politics of education (1945–1960), *Comparative Education*, 53(1): 35–53.

Mazower, M. (2012) *Governing the World: The history of an idea*, New York: Penguin.

Mills, C. (2017) *Black Rights / White Wrongs: The critique of racial liberalism*, Oxford: Oxford University Press.

Mohanty, S.P. (1997) *Literary Theory and the Claims of History: Postmodernism, objectivity and multicultural politics*, Ithaca, NY: Cornell University Press, p 241.

Mohatt, N.V. et al (2014) Historical trauma as public narrative: A conceptual review of how history impacts present-day health, *Social Science & Medicine*, 106: 128–136.

Mukharji, P.B. (2017) The Bengali Pharaoh: Upper-caste Aryanism, pan-Egyptianism, and the contested history of biometric nationalism in twentieth-century Bengal, *Comparative Studies in Society and History*, 59(2): 446–476.

Myers, K., Sriprakash, A. and Sutoris, P. (2021) Toward a 'New Humanism'? Time and emotion in UNESCO's science of world-making, 1947–1951, *Journal of World History*, 32(4): 685–715.

Nakata, M. (2008) *Disciplining the Savages, Savaging the Disciplines*, Canberra: Aboriginal Studies Press.

Nally, D. (2011) *Human Encumbrances: Political violence and the Great Irish Famine*, Notre Dame, IN: University of Notre Dame Press.

Nandy, A. (2009) *The Intimate Enemy: Loss and recovery of the self under colonialism*. 2nd edn, Oxford: Oxford University Press.

Nanni, G. (2012) *The Colonisation of Time: Ritual, routine and resistance in the British Empire*, Manchester: Manchester University Press.

Neizen, R. and Sapignoli, M. (eds) (2017) *Palaces of Hope: The anthropology of global organizations*, Cambridge: Cambridge University Press.

Olufemi, L. (2020) We can enact the future we want now: A black feminist history of abolition, The Guardian, available at: theguardian.com/books/2020/aug/03/we-can-enact-the-future-we-want-now-a-black-feminist-history-of-abolition [accessed 3 August 2022].

Omi, M. and Winant, H. (2015) *Racial Formation in the United States*, 3rd edn, New York: Routledge.

Pascoe, B. (2018) *Dark Emu: Aboriginal Australia and the birth of agriculture*, London and Brunswick: Scribe.

Paulson, J., Abiti, N., Bermeo Osorio, J., Charria Hernandez, C.A., Keo, D., Manning, P., Milligan, L.O., Moles, K., Pennell, C., Salih, S. and Shanks, K. et(2020) Education as site of memory: Developing a research agenda, *International Studies in Sociology of Education*, 29(4): 1–23.

Pente, E., Ward, P., Brown, M. and Sahota, H. (2015) The coproduction of historical knowledge: Implications for the history of identities, *Identity Papers*, 1(1): 32–53.

Pratt, M.L. (1992) *Imperial Eyes: Travel writing and transculturation*, London: Routledge.

Rassool, C. (2010) Power, knowledge and the politics of public pasts, *African Studies*, 69(1): 79–101.

Rothberg, M. (2017) Memory and Implication at the Limits of the Human: A response to Nathan Snaza, *Parallax*, 23(4): 512–516.

Sachs, W. (2010) Preface to the New Edition, in W. Sachs (ed) *The Development Dictionary: A guide to knowledge as power*, 2nd edn, pp x–xi.

Said, E. (1993) *Culture and Imperialism*, London: Vintage Books.

Scott, D. (2000) 'The re-enchantment of humanism: An interview with Sylvia Wynter', *Small Axe,* 120: 173–211.

Sen, A. (2009) *The Idea of Justice*, London: Allen Lane.

Simon, R.I. (2005) *The Touch of the Past: Remembrance, learning and ethic*, New York: Palgrave Macmillan.

Sluga, G. (2010) UNESCO and the (one) world of Julian Huxley, *Journal of World History*, 21(3): 396–397.

Sluga, G. (2013) *Internationalism in the Age of Nationalism*, Philadelphia: University of Pennsylvania Press.

Sriprakash, A., Tikly, L. and Walker, S. (2020) The erasures of racism in education and international development: Re-reading the 'global learning crisis', *Compare*, 50(5): 676–692.

Stoler, A.L. (2016) *Duress: Imperial durabilities in our times*, Durham, NC: Duke University Press.

UN (1945) Conference for the Establishment of an Educational and Cultural Organisation, London, ECO/Conf./29: 36.

UNESCO (2016) Education 2030: Incheon Declaration and Framework for Action for the implementation of Sustainable Development Goal 4, available at: unesdoc.unesco.org/ark:/48223/pf0000245656 [accessed 30 January 2023].

UNESCO (2020) Education in a post-COVID world: Nine ideas for public action, ICFE, available at: en.unesco.org/futuresofeducation/commission-meetings [accessed 30 January 2023].

Urry, J. (2016) *What is the Future?* Cambridge: Polity Press.

Weindling, P. (2012) Julian Huxley and the continuity of eugenics in twentieth-century Britain, *Journal of Modern European History*, 10(4): 480–499.

Wilder, G. (2015) *Freedom Time: Negritude, decolonization and the future of the world*, Durham, NC: Duke University Press.

Wilder, G. (2016) Here/Hear Now Aimé Césaire! *South Atlantic Quarterly*, 115(3): 585–604.

11

Decolonizing Citational and Quotational Practices as Reparative Politics

Esther Priyadharshini

Introduction

This chapter revisits practices of citation-quotation in academic writing within the context of an inequitable academia, operating amid a planetary crisis. After setting out how epistemological, material and ecological reparations are intimately entangled, the chapter attempts to draw together citational-quotational practices already in evidence and which may be usefully theorized to enhance diversity in the sources and types of knowledge we can valorize. It considers how such practices can help address the epistemic-material violence of knowledge-generating systems that are still inflected with colonial and patriarchal values. By focusing on the problematic of quoting Indigenous knowledges and ways of knowing-living that involve intimate, sometimes wordless, interactions with human-plant-animal-material elements the chapter considers the usefulness of experimental, multimodal means of communicating that go beyond our conventional reliance on human language and text. By paying critical attention to the politics and ethics of both citation and quotation, the chapter highlights the role of post-human practices that may help us to re-craft citational, quotational and publishing practices towards a more just world.

This chapter considers how key practices of knowledge generation in Western academic practice – citation/quotation – may be reimagined and freshly deployed. A central premise here is that the epistemological and the material are entangled and therefore citational-quotational practices can be crafted thoughtfully and inventively to invite alternative, more just and sustainable futures. The current epoch – the Anthropocene – and the debates around its naming serve as an entry point to reiterate the need for reparations that fix ongoing injustices and invite alternative futures that may serve more-than-human needs. Thus, the chapter first explores how conventional practices of citing create gendered, raced and myriad other inequalities in academia, and the sorts of reparative practices that are suggested by critical scholars. The later sections draw on moments in the works of scholars studying alongside Indigenous communities to argue for using post-human quotational practices that include human and non-human voices and interactions. This leads to considering multimodal presentations of academic work, grounded in an ethics of care, as a way of acting towards epistemic, material and ecological reparation.

Citation/quotation

In its most common use, the concept of citation in Anglophone academia is a way of attributing knowledge to correctly referenced research sources. It is also a way of avoiding plagiarism, a way of showing intellectual indebtedness or critiquing of existing work, and can function as a pivotal point in the building of novel or alternative works. These practices are an integral part of academic training and enculturation, with students being assessed on their adherence to the protocols of citation and referencing. In these varied uses, citations largely tend to be fragments of texts published by other academics. This practice has been identified as a key device that promotes the circulation of chosen texts, which in turn creates the topographies of academia, elevating or generating 'canons' and creating hierarchies of theories and bodies of knowledge (Ahmed, 2013; Hyland, 1999; Cronin, 1984). In French, the word 'citation' includes this meaning of citation as well as that of 'quotation'. Quotations, of 'raw data' or pre-published texts, are most visibly presented within quotation marks and form an important building block in argumentation and knowledge creation. This chapter considers both citation and quotation as foundational academic practices that constitute and reproduce research writing culture.

The idea that the practice of quoting/citing is far from neutral or objective, and that it is reproductive of norms, language and life, has been well-theorized and, in turn, heavily cited (Edmond, 2020). A range of influential scholars located in different disciplinary fields have made, modified and strengthened versions of this claim – Bhaktin, Derrida, Butler, Brathwaite, Tannen and many more. In particular, most often cited is the claim that the role of language and its iterability or quotability in different contexts allows for both the transmission/reproduction as well as the transformation of existing norms. For instance, the idea that gender norms can be repeated – performed/cited – in ways that allow them to be displaced is one of the most cited ideas from Butler. This itself is a re-situated citation–quotation of Derrida's idea of the iterability of language and possibility for the transformation of culture.

Citation has also been discussed for its role in the treatment of ideas 'as property', thus as capital produced in the dynamic of exchange (Kim, 2020). This idea of citation as academic currency (Fogarty, 2009) and capital reveals how the status and power of research accrues in uneven ways. Citational practices become complicit in 'academic plunder' (Edmonds, 2019) when particular kinds of scholarship either do not get credited appropriately or are erased from fields of study. Evidence that female scholars across disciplines are underrepresented in citation counts (Davenport and Snyder, 1995), that they are less likely to be named as the first author (West et al, 2013), and that, where they are increasingly cited, this tends to be in the work of other female scholars, with men tending to cite them at lower rates (Smith and Garrett-Scott, 2021, Lutz, 1990; McElhinny et al, 2003), all reveal how conventional citational practices create gendered hierarchies.

Sara Ahmed (2008) notes the erasure of earlier feminist thought in the theorization of new materialisms. When such histories or lineages of thought become invisible, citations become 'ways of making certain bodies and thematics core to the discipline and others not even part' (Ahmed, 2013). Such inequalities of course, extend beyond gender. Pailey (2016) writes of stark trends in publishing in the field of African studies that erase African scholarship on Africa, protecting the status of some non-Africans who have been positioned as the authoritative voices. Briggs and Weathers (2016) found that Africa-based scholars (though not women) who tended to generate detailed, country-specific knowledge were systematically cited far less compared with those outside Africa who tended to generalize and used the words 'Africa' or 'African' in their titles. Other studies show that publications arising out of international partnerships were seen to reproduce gender inequalities, and, where equitable relations between country partners are described as such, they were the result of intentional strategies for participative design (Asare et al, 2020).

Inequities also emerge in how researchers are cited. Edmond (2020) reveals how Black scholars – even influential names – are often cited for their knowledge of context, or for cultural value (for example as poets/ novelists), rather than as intellectuals or theorists in their own right. McKittrick (2020, p 21) writes movingly of how, even when Black women may be cited, their 'words and ideas become something else', they can be 'worn down', 'stepped over' and 'swept aside'. Todd (2016) similarly objects to the appropriation and erasure of Indigenous scholarship in the recent ontological turn to post-humanist approaches that call for the inclusion of more-than-human actors (such as land, animals, materials, ecosystems) as ontologically significant – something that has long been integral and visible in most Indigenous knowledge systems. All of these discriminatory practices combine to contribute to the presence of the Matthew effect (Merton, 1968),[1] reflecting the capitalist logic of citations, by which a small percentage of authors or works are repeatedly cited, accruing academic prestige and status, and thus reproducing academic structures of knowledge production.

In Western academies, citational counts have become an important, if controversial, way of signalling the influence or impact of research, with new and more sophisticated means of analysing bibliographic metrics routinely emerging (see Rüdiger et al, 2021). This is turn has a bearing (along with other data assemblages) on how research institutions are ranked and how performance-based funding can be allocated (Hicks, 2012), leading to the further embedding of neo-liberal market sensibilities within academia (Burrows, 2012). While citational metrics are not seen as a major factor in determining research awards, the trend of Black, minority ethnic or disabled academics receiving lower award rates and award values in the UK (UKRI, 2021) reveals a disturbing parallel to many other disparities within wider academic culture, from gender and ethnic pay gaps to uneven career progression in a sector characterized increasingly by the precarious employment status of new scholars. It is within this wider context of injustice – epistemic and material – that we are called to examine how the decision of whom to cite (or not cite), and how, leads us to a discussion of reparation.

Reparation

Reparation is a compensating for, a mending or repairing of, matters that we recognize need to be rectified. It is worth exploring how notions of reparation, usually framed in material and historical terms, can be expanded to cover current and future epistemic injustice, and how this move can also reframe how we may need to think of quotational-citational practices.

Traditionally, the notion of reparation has tended to be discussed as one of making amends through the compensation of money and materials, and a declaration of apology, demanded of governments and crowns that benefited from colonial and slave-owning practices. Pro-reparation communities around the world tend to hold views on reparation, based on the tort/ confrontational model or the atonement/conversational one (Obuah, 2015).[2] The argument being made here is that addressing material reparations alone (to the extent that it would even be adequate or possible) would leave the fundamental project of European modernity, and the academic practices that sustain it, intact.

Post-colonial criticism has revealed how the project of colonization was jointly predicated on territorial, economic, cultural and epistemic fronts. A key justification for colonial rule was the notion of progress; a historical progress that was seen to be manifested in and through European institutions and in knowledge that marked them as distinct from the 'premodern' and 'nonmodern' societies outside Europe (Bhambra, 2021). Central to European modernity and its case for progress was the organization of life through rational modes of knowing and governance – measuring, describing and classifying peoples, cultures, bodies, lifestyles and so on (Foucault, 1980; Said, 1978). As has been noticed, 'virtually all branches of European knowledge and science have grown with the confident conviction that the world is knowable only through those categories of knowledge that have been developed in Europe – indeed that the world may even exist only in and through such categories of European modernity' (Chakrabarthy, 1992, p 94). In turn, through colonial governance structures, these modes of knowing became ways through which colonial subjects were persuaded to know themselves – as inferior to European thought, literature, art and so on. In other words, the ontological and epistemological effects were intimately linked to everyday material, cultural and physical violence.

Hence, it is not sufficient for epistemological reparation to be treated as an isolated project that can proceed with the belated inclusion or recognition of previously denigrated knowledges. Many institutions in the UK have set up initiatives for decolonizing the curriculum or university that begin with compiling or expanding subject reading lists to include the works of women and scholars of colour. While this is a vital move in addressing the non-visibility of such scholars and knowledge, there is no guarantee that students and staff will become more inclusive in their citational (and other academic) practices by having access to more inclusive reading lists. As discussed in the following sections, knowledge erasures or appropriations are deeply embedded in structures and systems that are inflected with colonial and discriminatory values. A numbers or volume approach, based on the tort/confrontational model of citational reparation may not be able to produce long-term, sustainable effects. The task of addressing the systemic, academic and disciplinary work needed 'to effect both material and epistemological change' (Bhambra, 2021, p 75) is much grander.

The Anthropocene

Alongside the context of the inequitable academy, we could also locate this notion of reparation within the concerns of the Anthropocene. The naming of the current geological epoch as the Anthropocene has itself generated vigorous debate in recent years. The term is usually attributed to atmospheric chemist Paul Crutzen and is commonly understood as describing an entire geological period (similar to the Holocene, Pleistocene, Jurassic and so on) in which human action is identified as the primary driving force shaping conditions of life for the planet. In other words, we can trace the effects of human activity in geological records, most obviously in the rise in global temperatures and its attendant destructive effects. While the term rightly identifies 'anthropos' – humans – as largely responsible for the epoch, it does so indiscriminately, as the anthropos responsible for the state of the planet does not stand for or act on behalf of all humans. Most often, acts of dispossession, extraction, denigration, enslavement and colonization of swathes of 'othered' human populations were integral to establishing what we now call the Anthropocene. The idea that the status of 'human' that was denied to othered populations in earlier times but is now belatedly conferred on them at the precise point when culpability is being distributed is also a way of perpetuating injustice. Critical scholars have argued that, when the centrality of racist and capitalist exploitation of life forms and places in the formation of the Anthropocene is erased, or perhaps considered only as a supplementary analytical perspective (Yusoff, 2018), then it becomes a tool to consolidate Whiteness (Mirzoeff, 2016). Chwałczyk (2020) and Bould (2021) list and discuss the plethora of alternatives that have been suggested – the Accumulocene, Capitalocene, Misanthropocene, Plantationocene, White Supremacy Scene, and many others. These quarrels over terminology are not 'just' matters of academic discourse. The debates around vocabulary choice and labelling reveal how, in the current juncture, as in periods of colonial governance, issues of material, racial, ecological and epistemological justice are intertwined. While the idea of the Anthropocene and its implications are deeply unsettling, even overwhelming, as a global challenge, it is perfectly primed to confound taken-for-granted humanist norms, and its disruptive force can support the reframing of academic citational and quotational practices in ways that both look back critically and look forward aspirationally, to better futures.

Practices of citational reparation

Collective acts of reparation can feel just when they are part of a transformation of understandings instigated by a recognition of 'epistemological injustice'. Bhambra (2021) notes that this kind of reparation requires those who may benefit from structures of domination to acknowledge this and to engage with how the injustice of that domination structures the present. The call for a revolution in citational practices that attempts to redress both the epistemological injustice and the ways in which it perpetuates inequalities in institutions and knowledge production processes has echoed across disciplinary boundaries. Wendy Belcher calls for citational values that have a minimum bar to meet. Named the Gray Test[3] (after Kishonna Gray – #citeherwork), Belcher (2019, p 184) recommends that:

> a journal article must not only cite the scholarship of at least two women and two non-white authors but also mention it meaningfully

in the body of the text. ... If your article fails this bare-minimum test, it's biased and should be improved. If you can't find such scholars to cite, it's time for you to do something about the pipeline of scholars entering your field.

Sara Ahmed's blog (feministkilljoys.com) and her more conventional forms of publication offer ways of remaking citational practices. She explains the reasoning behind activist practices of citation, including her own self-imposed 'citation policy' (2014) while writing *Living a Feminist Life* (2017), when she decided to no longer follow the citational chains favouring male theorists. This remains a key strategy for many scholars who seek new ways of ushering in epistemological equity in the face of opposition (Ennser-Kananen, 2019). Katherine McKittrick (2020, p 22), while valuing such strategies for making us think about our epistemological grounds for theorizing, also problematizes such an approach:

> What does it mean to read Jacques Derrida and abandon Derrida and retain Derrida's spirit (or specter!)? Do we unlearn whom we do not cite? And what of our teaching practice? Do we teach refusal? Can we not teach our students to engage with various authors and narratives, critically, while also asking to raise up the work of black women and other scholars, writers, artists, interviewees, teachers, who go unrecognized? How do we teach each other to read (disapprove, evaluate, critique, use, forget, abandon, remember) 'white men' or other powerful scholars? Or is the critique (uncitation) to enact erasure?

These scholars ask us to think hard about who, why, how we cite, and also to question who we chose to exclude, why, and what futures this might create. A special edition of *Diacritics* (48:3, 2020) offers a rich resource on a range of alternative citational practices from diverse scholars – from deliberately moving away from the preoccupation with Eurocentric citational genealogies to seeking and generating alternative citational chains drawing on works from Caribbean, Asian diasporic and queer studies that expand the current narrow 'optics' of citationality. Articles in this issue pay attention to how the affordances of newer media offer alternatives to textual citations (to which I return later) and how examining citationality's affective dimension (anxiety or defensiveness, for instance) can turn citation into a site of stewardship or policing, and propose in its place, a model of 'capacious' affiliation (rather than a constrictive inheritance), a mutual aid (collective ownership of ideas) model of citations and a greater consciousness about the power we attribute to things we cite.

These inventive and justice-seeking ways of looking at citational practices also beg the question about what citational practices inevitably exclude by their very design and protocol. Citing published work, even by underrepresented communities, still preserves knowledge hierarchies, ways of knowing that are assigned greater status because they have been 'verified' and 'peer-reviewed'. As McKittrick (2020, p 22) asks, how can we include the contributions of everyday 'writers, artists, interviewees, teachers, who go unrecognized'? Their largely unpublished ideas are often available to us as quotational fragments, making their way into academic publishing as evidentiary building blocks, primarily as data to be analysed and much less as ideas offering an intellectual contribution. This awareness raises questions over the boundaries of knowledge ownership, something particularly relevant in the Anthropocene, when planetary challenges require us to engage more critically with the ethical relationships involved in knowledge building, not just between humans but also between human and non-human.

An awareness of the 'fragility of existence' that is common to all life and the environment that sustains it (including land, atmosphere and ocean-scapes; biological and mineral elements), opens up the possibility of paying attention to the relationships between these elements as constitutive of life, learning and knowledge (Common Worlds Research Collective, 2020). Such ontological understandings of how all life is constituted and reconstituted in a fragile and intimate web of relations have long been a notable, visible feature of many forms of Indigenous knowledge across the globe (Todd, 2016; Harris and Wasilewski, 2004; Rose, 2022). The challenge lies in how academic practice can now acknowledge and use this perspective without appropriating, misusing, or flattening it within existing ontological frameworks. Perhaps a small part of the solution lies in an ethics of care that acknowledges and respectfully cites-quotes the many ways in which the human and non-human contribute to knowledge production.

Uncitable knowledges

The following extract from an interview with Gayatri Spivak (1996) discusses the British in Bengal during the 18th century. It is offered as a thought-tool to aid our recognition of how epistemological injustice is tied to matters of material and ecological reparation, and to prompt a more critical relationship with academic knowledge production practices.

'[W]hen the British came into the area of Bengal that is now Bangladesh, they encountered fully developed 'ancient waterworks.' They were in fact very complicated irrigation canals so that the flood area could be managed. What they encountered was a feudal system there. The feudal chiefs actually made their serfs, their subordinates – I am using the European words – manage the canals and keep them up. When the British came in those feudal heads became tax collectors for the British, and they did not then do anything to keep up the canals; the feudal chiefs turned tax collectors did not provide their own subordinates, and no kind of servant of the East India Company was employed to keep up those irrigation canals. The British did not understand that they were irrigation canals for flood-management. What they thought they were I don't know, maybe waterways for transport or whatever. The canals soon became stagnant, infested with mosquitoes, and so they started to destroy these canals. Now the people, that is to say the former serfs of the feudal landlords, in fact fought with the British police constantly and they constantly failed.

It was in the thirties that a waterworks inspector of the imperial government, and therefore no friend of the subaltern, but simply a smart guy, worked out that these waterways had in fact been an irrigation and flood management system. It is from his report, a text from the other side, that we realize that the best thing that the British could do was to restore these completely destroyed ancient waterworks, because the affluence of the place had been destroyed, since the place had been left open to incredible floods. Now let me tell you that in that same area today, landless peasants and fisherfolk are breaking the enormous levees constructed by the World Bank. Two hundred years of continuity, always failing: subaltern insurgency. So that to an extent, and in fact, what the ecological workers now suggest is that those ancient waterworks destroyed two hundred years ago be restored, but, and I am paraphrasing Fred Pierce, they cannot be rebuilt because the way that they had been built was slowly, respecting the rhythm of those very young rivers, whereas the way things would be built today would be capital-intensive, cost-efficient, and fast. Now what we have here is the story of continuous subaltern insurgency, always failing, but continuous to this day.'

We cannot help but note that this scene is set in Bangladesh, a MAPA – one of the 'Most Affected Peoples and Areas' – in the Anthropocene, facing chronic floods and sea-level rises. It thus links past injustices to present and future lives. It shines a spotlight on the relation between the epistemic and the material: the affluence of the place was destroyed because those in authority did not have (or refused) the capacity to understand the waterworks systems built on local, long-standing knowledge of the rhythm and course of the river. Subsequent World-Bank-aided levees repeated a similar ecological violence on people and landscape with hardly any alleviation of the poverty in the region.

It also becomes painfully evident that it is no longer a matter of simply returning to unearth buried knowledge because colonial modernity and global capital have played their part in destroying a certain know-how that we are left mourning. Can this kind of ecological and epistemic injustice ever be compensated with material or epistemic, especially citational, reparation?

What is instructive, however, is that the extract also highlights how this form of epistemic extinction cannot even be recognized as such until the 'text from the other side' makes visible that which was erased. It seems that, if academic practice in the global North can make any useful reparations, it is precisely to create or facilitate similar texts, from its thoroughly compromised position.

Such texts can do more than 'just' bear witness to injustice. By noting how the human and more-than-human (land, river, rainfall in this case) constitute each other, they can help to question the dichotomy of nature and culture, self and world, embedded in modernist knowledge production. As we search for ways to stay within the planetary capacity to sustain life, such alternative knowledges also become a crucial resource. This awareness ought to provoke a remaking of the relationship between academic knowledge practices and the more-than-human elements (land, water, soil, climate, animals, microbes) that sustain life (Common Worlds Research Collective, 2020). When knowledge production recognizes the contribution of more-than-human agents, then citational practices that can only accredit published human records feel somewhat inadequate. In the final sections, this chapter moves to focus on quotational practices and their ethics and modalities as alternative practices that may aid reparations – epistemic, material and ecological.

Quotational reparation with more-than-human elements?

Extracts from the works of two scholars are offered here as a starting point to deepen our engagement with practices of citation-quotation and to help envisage alternative practices. These practices will need to include citations (already published and academically visible) but also rethink quoting practices, relating to culturally specific, historically evolved knowledges that involve encounters and conversations between human-land-animal elements.

Robin Wall Kimmerer: Braiding Sweetgrass

Robin Wall Kimmerer's (2013) *Braiding Sweetgrass: Indigenous Wisdom, Scientific* Knowledge *and the Teachings of Plants* offers a different way in which a citational revolution could occur. The book seems to be written for a popular audience and thus appears un-stymied by academic citational conventions. It contains a list of 19 works under the title 'Sources' (not the more academically conventional 'References' or 'Bibliography') at the end of the book. Neither are any works internally referenced as in a peer-reviewed journal article. It claims to braid together three strands – Indigenous ways of knowing, scientific knowledge and 'the story of an Anishinabekwe scientist bringing them together' and seems to enact this composition of braiding through this popular, bridging genre.

It is still worth pausing to consider the different ways in which the citational practices of this book could have been handled. As Zoe Todd (2021) has suggested, Kimmerer could have incorporated the long lineage of academic, Indigenous scholarship in the book and thus in its reference list. The importance of such visibility cannot be overstated – to a predominantly non-Indigenous readership, it could be easier to uproot, homogenize and co-opt such knowledges in reproductive, even repressive, rather than transformative, ways. Perhaps not citing the links to Indigenous scholarship does allow for a too-easy appropriation, and cherry-picking, of such work. What is notable though, is that in the book, Kimmerer persistently 'quotes' (even names) Indigenous scholars but does not 'cite' them in the conventional academic style. Indeed, Kimmerer does not 'cite' any academic works at all – either by white or Indigenous authors.

McKittrick (2020) notes how citation points to method – how we come to know what we know. When a scholar references an influential theorist, this is also often a 'reverential scaffolding' of what we know through who we know. She observes how, in the works of Black thinkers such as Wynter, Glissant and Fanon, there is an attention to how we know and how we come to know rather than *who* we know. In a world where the accumulative Matthew effect is rampant, it seems that Kimmerer's lack of citations (albeit in the 'popular' genre) could be read as one way of refusing to enter this citational economy that operates on the individual ownership of ideas.

What is also worth considering in Kimmerer's practice is the use of quotation, that is, the ways in which local, non-published knowledge and experience are included. In the academic genre, quotations tend to be typically positioned lower than citations of published, peer-reviewed academic work, even though it is well known that such quotations are a vital building block in the construction of research-based knowledge. In a particularly poignant chapter, '*Mishkos Kenomagwen*: The Teachings of Grass', Kimmerer charts how Indigenous knowledges – in this case about harvesting sweetgrass – can draw on material practices, inherited lessons, personal experience and spiritual beliefs about the relationship between land, plant and human communities. Her labour consists of documenting, translating and quoting/citing Indigenous knowledge on sweetgrass (botanical name: hierochloe odorata; in Potawatami: wiingaashk). Kimmerer's view that, 'To be heard, you must speak the language of the one you want to listen' (p 158) leads her to translate between academic/scientific and Potawatami, braiding them together with her translations and reflections aimed at a general reading public outside both camps. In closely reading this chapter, a generous quotational practice becomes visible. Greater attention to and valorization of such practices could engender new quotational sensibilities and be part of a new quotational-citational politics.

The chapter starts with Indigenous basket makers who found that sweetgrass, the raw material for their baskets, was disappearing from certain locales. Their questions about this initiated a research project: What might be the right way to harvest sweetgrass? Does a yanking/pulling method perhaps deplete it faster compared with a gentler pinching one? An experimental design was then drawn up to measure the different effects of harvesting methods, and the whole proposal presented as a graduate student's thesis to a faculty panel. One dismissive response was that 'There's not even a theoretical framework.' As Kimmerer insists, there most certainly was a theory, grounded in the ecological knowledge of Indigenous people, in particular of basket weavers and herbalists working closely with sweetgrass. But women scientists, she claims, are not unused to condescension and verbal smackdowns from white male authoritative voices, particularly directed at those who relied on traditional theories: 'I'm afraid I don't find this whole traditional knowledge thing very convincing,' and 'the committee could only struggle not to roll their eyes' (p 159) as the proposal was not seen as promising for the generation of new scientific knowledge. Members of the scientific community in this instance seemed to be flummoxed by the language of spirituality and affect – a language that speaks of love, reciprocity and responsibility to all life forms – and one that is not usually published in scientific journals of plant science.

Kimmerer observes that it is possibly the inheritance of Cartesian dualism that insists on the measurement of the visible/'real' as uncontaminated 'data', propagating the idea that researchers/humans are independent of the world around them, whereas plant science can be demonstrably much more than that which objective measures are able to yield. Scholars arguing for a broadening and a deepening of knowledge and educational governance systems (Orr, 1991; Odora Hoppers, 2020) note that Western evaluations of scientific 'quality' tend to neglect matters of values, consciousness or conscience in favour of theories, concepts, abstractions or efficiency (Wiesel, 1990). In contrast, Indigenous knowledges are often rooted in 'biophilia', an instinct or assumption that all life forms share an affiliation with each other (Cajete, 2000). Under the Western scientific paradigm, to claim that, if one tended to and looked after the land and its vegetation, the land would give back, indeed 'love you back', feels like unscientific, unverifiable, sentimentalism. But such views of science and reality exclude the affective, editing out 'the sacredness, the livingness, the soul of the world' (Odora Hoppers, 2020, p 5) and instead assert, without impunity, that these elements do not really exist (Little Bear, 2000) or that they exist as less consequential 'cultural or spiritual beliefs' (world views) rather than a part of the material life-world.

Perhaps it is the seemingly unbridgeable gulf between scientific and Indigenous worlds that leads Robin Wall Kimmerer (2013) to structure the chapter under subheadings most familiar to researchers in academia: Introduction, Literature Review, Hypothesis, Methods, Results, Discussion, Conclusions, Acknowledgements and References cited. It seems that this is a conscious strategy to braid the different worlds, to get them to a point where they may be able to speak to each other. Another example of such braiding is her description of 'the experiment' (p 158):

> To me, an experiment is a kind of conversation with plants: I have a question for them, but since we don't speak the same language, I can't ask them directly and they won't answer verbally. But plants can be eloquent in their physical responses and behaviours. Plants answer questions by the way they live, by their responses to change; you just need to learn how to ask. ... Experiments are not about discovery but about listening and translating the knowledge of other beings.

What Kimmerer is also demonstrating here is how practices of citing/quoting can and do go far beyond human language and interaction. This returns us to the subtitle of her chapter – the teachings of grass. Grass is positioned unequivocally as a pedagogical agent, offering teachings and lessons to those that will attune themselves to listen. What the experiment was able to prove was that sweetgrass flourished when the relationship between harvester and plant was balanced and reciprocal. In other words, the method of harvesting did not make a difference, as long as there was some kind of harvesting. In science-speak, this is about how absence of disturbance results in loss of stimulus, vigour and increased mortality for the plant. In the words of Indigenous knowers, this translates as 'never take more than half', but also 'do not take too little', as that too causes traditions to die, relationships to fade and the land to suffer. The experiment's findings meant that all parties learned something that had not been explicitly understood previously.

At the end of the chapter, the 'References' are stated simply as: Wiingaashk, Buffalo, Lena, the Ancestors. This signals a decision to valorize the inherited theories, dialogic, conversational knowledge and debates among Indigenous harvesters that are quoted extensively throughout the chapter. This works for the popular genre and, at the same time, as a strategy. It operates in a new, perhaps 'mutual aid' mode (Tierney, 2020), one that cuts across the more accumulative citational practices that circulate in the knowledge economy. In choosing to quote-cite those that have little recourse to established modes of knowledge production (textual publication), it enacts an alternative politics and practice of citation.

Eduardo Kohn: How Forests Think

A second case for experimenting with a new citational ethos can be argued from Eduardo Kohn's anthropological research with the Runa people in Avila in the Ecuadorian Amazon. Indigenous communities across the globe can be seen to be listening, conversing with and quoting/re-citing material, animal, plant and spiritual elements in everyday life. Kohn's (2013) *How Forests Think: Toward an anthropology beyond the human* allows a closer exploration of some such practices. Working with the Runa people, he attempts to offer a theory for how forests think (not how natives think about forests). In essence, this work puts forward an explanation that thought is not unique to humans and that the forest itself, through its inhabitants and the 'ecology of selves' is made up of living thoughts. Such thought in turn constitutes the multiple selves in and of the forest. Kohn documents and analyses how the Runa are routinely guessing what their fellow forest-dwellers – their dogs, the jaguars, parakeets, ants or monkeys – are thinking. Through a series of examples, he proposes that all forms of life make guesses, or arrive at speculative understandings about the world around them, 'however mediated, provisional, fallible and tenuous these understandings may be' (p 89). Kohn uses many examples in his book and a couple that stand out can help to explore the quotation/citational practices of both Kohn and the forest itself.

In the chapter 'The Living Thought', Kohn observes the Runa animatedly discussing the death of their dogs. The dogs had been heard by the women of the family, barking at first excitedly, *'hua' hua' hua' hua''*, as they would when following game. This then changed to *'ya ya ya ya'*, as when poised to attack. Then, disturbingly, changed again to a yelping as in great pain, *'aya-i aya-i aya-i'*, after which they fell silent. The women began to speculate on these changes, recalling barks and past situations in which they produced similar sounds. The barks are thus part of 'an exhaustive lexicon of canine vocalizations' (p 72). After some discussion, they concluded that the only explanation was that the dogs had confused a mountain lion with a red brocket deer as both are similar in size and colour. Their vexation with this confusion centred their conversations around imagining how their dogs must have thought: *'It looks like a deer, let's bite it!'* And then in sad frustration at this confusion, *'So so stupid!'* How dogs interpreted the world around them, how they thought, became confused and ended up losing their lives, was at the heart of the conversation.

Most people who live with domestic pets will be able to relate to this experience of frequently guessing or speculating about what they think. This is usually framed as the bad practice of anthropomorphism, an arrogant imposition of human-centred feelings or agendas onto non-human life forms. While the trap of anthropomorphism is real, Freccero (2017) warns us that a greater danger lies in relinquishing 'responsibility for (in the sense of responding, responding to) the coarticulations of lives, histories and cultures called human and animal.' It is this responsibility for co-articulation that we see enacted in the quotations interspersed through Kohn's book.

Later in the same chapter, Kohn describes how the Runa make scarecrows, or rather 'scare-parakeets', to discourage parakeets from the cornfields. These devices are made of flattened pieces of balsa wood tied together in the shape of a cross. Red and black strikes are painted across the wood. The top part is cut to resemble a head. Big eyes are painted on it and a real predator's tail feathers are tied to the end pieces of the wood so that they resemble a raptor's wings and tail. The detailed and specific decorations are an attempt to represent the raptor from a parakeet's point of view. Few would agree that the scaring device looked anything like a raptor to human eyes, but these scare-parakeets are so effective at keeping the parakeets away from the corn that they are made each year by the Runa. This successful guessing of how parakeets see, interpret and think (differently to humans) allows Kohn to argue that the Runa know something of what it is like to be a parakeet. An attentiveness, or an attunement, to the perspectives of other life forms signals their belief in the presence of selves with distinct points of view that may be guessed at by other life forms, however imperfectly. This leads Kohn to articulate his theory: 'Selves relate the way that thoughts relate: we are all living, growing thoughts' (p 89). This is one way in which he demonstrates how forests think.

Kohn's knowledge-generation practices follow the anthropological mode of living with and participating in the everyday life of the Runa, but his work recognizes how knowledge takes shape not just in learning about the Runa, but in learning with them and from them, and their forest. What is intrinsic to these examples from Kohn is the revelation that thinking is not specific to humans, and that thinking is therefore not solely limited by human comprehension of language (which tends to be heavily symbolic). The reading and interpretation of signs and symbols by all life forms in the forest include indexical and iconic representations[4] that are shared by non-human and human life forms. This is carefully documented and analysed by Kohn, sometimes with the aid of audio recordings and photographs (some reproduced in the book), but largely communicated to readers through the form of a standard academic text. Rather like Kimmerer, Kohn relies on quoting and translating between the different worlds to create and disseminate new insights and understandings.

For both authors, their quoting and translating involves thinking about, thinking with, learning from and often guessing for, or on behalf of, other life forms – sweetgrass, dogs, parakeets, humans – that make up the worlds they research. The scholarship that emerges is therefore indebted to the ideas and nascent or fully formed theorizations that emerge in the (sometimes wordless) interactions of human and non-human. Thus the act of quoting also requires an ethics of care in re-presentation, similar to citational practices, with the added technical challenge of how these interactions are scripted onto the page and acknowledged appropriately. The question that arises is: What does this awareness mean for how citational-quotational practices ought to be included in publications, to ensure that relationships, interdependencies and interactions are presented in non-extractive, hard-to-appropriate modes?

Multimodal formats for a reparative practice

Quotations have always posed challenges for the practice of research. Even quoting human speech to each other involves vocal and bodily demonstration. Quotations are therefore rarely verbatim (Blackwell and Fox Tree, 2012; Fox Tree and Tomlinson, 2008), especially when used to create imagined experiences, such as those recreated for the listener with a sense of drama and sensorimotor imagery (Pascual, 2014; Wade and Clarke, 1993). Even detailed linguistic analysis methods of 'verbatim' transcribing have limits to how much and how well they convey these interactions and the affective feel of the event being recreated. Quotations are thus already multimodal (Blackwell et al, 2015) and demand that we consider suitable multimodal forms of presentation that extend beyond the written page, indebted as it is to human symbolic communication.

Given the heavy reliance on quotation for knowledge generation in the social sciences, it feels as if multimodal formats that can include photos, sketches, texture (collage/craft), video, audio, or other ways of virtual enhancement that incorporate language beyond text, ought to be much more prevalent. The case for better multimodal publishing including enhanced e-books that integrate research text alongside audio/audiovisual clips in the document has been made (Hammond, 2013), particularly as a way of increasing transparency and engagement (whether in appreciation or critique) by readers. However, greater transparency or accountability is not always the most desired goal of multimodal publishing. In many cases, there may be a greater reliance on visuals, sound and image than detailed word-reliant explanation, for the explicit purpose of allowing readers/listeners/experiencers to engage in new, affective experiences that could be harder to fully access through purely traditional modes. Soundscapes uploaded on SoundCloud, for example, alongside images, mappings and conventional text can allow people to engage with, and reflect on, how moving across these modalities allows for new stories to be told and new insights to emerge (see Shillitoe et al, 2022). The new modalities themselves then become part of the knowledge generation and reception experience, underscoring the role of technology (old or new) in the knowledge cycle.

The call for better, innovative modes of presentation is not a technological panacea to the ethical and complex issues raised by the use of quotations. Kamau Brathwaite for instance, specifically demonstrated the use of new technology – in the form of tape recorders in the early 60s – as part of a decolonizing citing/repairing practice. By playing recorded words of other African and Caribbean artists and intellectuals during his talks, and then recording these talks, he drew attention to the acts of repetition, recontextualization and remediation, and developed a theory of decolonial citation (Edmond, 2020). This was an experiment in citing/quoting those who remained outside the bounds of European bibliographic traditions, and to privilege oral archival records. The recordings also encompassed music, poetry and drum rhythms as a way of showing continuities and discontinuities between African and Caribbean cultural lives, in ways that bypassed European resources that were tied to the written page. Brathwaite also experimented with computer-generated, graphically varied script as a way of trying to make the spoken 'visible' and as a way of attending to the different tones and multiplicity of voices.

Each of these experiments were a way of drawing attention to what we now call the 'affective' dimension – passion, feelings, performances that invoke deeper engagement; matters that go beyond the written page and conventional quotational-citational practice. They also feel relevant at a time when the more-than-human demands a visible and prominent place in the constitution of our lives (and knowledges) within the Anthropocene.

Brathwaite's experiments feel futuristic perhaps because most academic journal articles and books continue to be conventionally presented, even with the much greater technological resources at our disposal today. However, the dilemmas and benefits of editing and publishing such multimodal productions are beginning to be discussed (Hand and Gray, 2022 – an audio recording itself) and suggest that there may be more to be hoped for.

Conclusion

This chapter has drawn on contemporary scholarship that highlights how citation begets citation in ways that create inequalities and hierarchies of bodies, theories and knowledges. Citational practices traffic in a capitalist logic centred on ownership of ideas as property, leading to not just epistemic injustice but also material injustices that call for reparation. When citational and quotational practices are recrafted for reparative purposes, they can become a tool for dismantling, or at least challenging, European modernity, the traces of which still inflect knowledge production today. New approaches to citational practices embedded in an ethics of care have been proposed to help highlight the works of scholars of colour and other underrepresented groups within an academia that remains stubbornly unequal. These approaches show that this ethos goes well beyond the starting point of adding names to diversify and decolonize reading lists. Decisions about who to include or exclude, how to cite and how to teach and learn to cite are invariably complex and influenced by many factors, but they all recognize (and hope for) the epistemic and material benefits that radical citational practices can bring.

By also considering the concerns of the epoch of the Anthropocene, we can see afresh the ways in which material and epistemological injustices are linked to ecological matters. This awareness brings with it a disruption to established humanist norms of crediting knowledge. By closely examining the writings of Robin Wall Kimmerer and Eduardo Kohn, this chapter has tried to draw attention to better quotational practices, particularly those that involve plant-animal-human-material conversations. These interactions themselves draw on traditional beliefs and knowledges that operate within very different ontological frameworks that reveal more sustainable, less extractive worlds. The reliance of human knowledge creation to the non-human elements and to non-academic populations is revealed through such quotational practices. A key intention of this chapter has been to raise our awareness of this reliance, and thus to bring into more frequent practice post-human practices of citation and quotation that can be cognizant of these interdependencies. This more capacious ethos leads us to the limits of conventional formats – word-based, page-reliant – through which we tend to produce and disseminate knowledge.

Creating new kinds of texts through conscious, scrupulous citational-quotational practices will be demanding. It requires an ethics of care, a decolonizing desire, as well as the courage to take risks with multimodal formats that allow an acknowledgement of multi-species elements that contribute to new academic cultures. These new kinds of texts will need to fulfil many purposes: bear witness; repair and (at least) impede future knowledge losses; create new, non-canonical, rhizomatic gatherings of knowledges; and thus enact a reparative politics.

Notes

[1] Matthew 13:12, 'For whosoever hath, to him shall be given, and he shall have more abundance: but whosoever hath not, from him shall be taken away even that he hath' (KJV).

[2] Put simply, the tort/confrontational model can be characterized by the demand for monetary and judicial compensations as a form of economic and social redistribution. The atonement/conversational model focuses on re-characterizing situations or acts to spotlight the moral and political significance through 'believable' apologies, commemorations or memorializations to empower minority groups and work towards social transformation for all.

[3] It echoes the Bechdel-Wallace test for female presence in movies. dykestowatchoutfor. com/wp-content/uploads/2014/05/The-Rule-cleaned-up.jpg.

[4] Iconic modalities involve signs that share likenesses with the things they represent. Indexical modalities involve signs that are in some way affected by or correlated to the things they represent. Symbolic modalities are most evident in codified, text-based human language. Kohn's point, following Charles Pierce's semiotics, is that academic analysis tends to traffic in the symbolic, ignoring other modalities that we share with non-human life forms.

References

Ahmed, S. (2008) Open forum imaginary prohibitions: Some preliminary remarks on the founding gestures of the 'new materialism', *European Journal of Women's Studies*, 15(1): 23–39.

Ahmed, S. (2013) Making Feminist Points, Feminist Killjoys blog, feministkilljoys.com/2013/09/11/making-feminist-points [accessed 31 January 2023].

Ahmed, S. (2014) White Men, Feminist Killjoys blog, feministkilljoys.com/2014/11/04/white-men/ [accessed 20 March 2023].

Ahmed, S. (2017) *Living a Feminist Life*, Durham, NC: Duke University Press.

Asare, S., Mitchell, R. and Rose, P. (2020) How equitable are South–North partnerships in education research? Evidence from sub-Saharan Africa, *Compare*, 52(4): 654– 673.

Belcher, W. (2019) *Writing Your Academic Journal Article in Twelve Weeks: A guide to academic publishing success*, Chicago: University of Chicago Press.

Bhambra, G.K. (2021) Decolonizing critical theory? Epistemological justice, progress, reparations, *Critical Times*, 4(1): 73–89.

Blackwell, N. and Fox Tree, J. (2012) Social factors affect quotative choice, *Journal of Pragmatics*, 44(10): 1150–1162.

Blackwell, N., Perlman, M. and Fox Tree, J. (2015) Quotation as a multimodal construction, *Journal of Pragmatics*, 81: 1–7.

Bould, M. (2021) *The Anthropocene Unconscious: Climate catastrophe culture*, London and New York: Verso.

Briggs, R. and Weathers, S. (2016) Gender and location in African politics scholarship: The other white man's burden?, *African Affairs*, 115(460): 466–489.

Burrows, R. (2012) Living with the H-Index? Metric assemblages in the contemporary academy, *Sociological review*, 60(2): 355–372.

Cajete, G. (2000) *Native Science: Natural laws of interdependence*, Santa Fe: Clear Light.

Chakrabarthy, D. (1992), Postcoloniality and the artifice of history: Who speaks for 'Indian' pasts?, *Representations*, 37 (winter): 1–26.

Chwałczyk, F. (2020) Around the Anthropocene in eighty names – Considering the Urbanocene proposition, *Sustainability*, 12(4458).

Common Worlds Research Collective (2020) Learning to become with the world: Education for future survival, Background paper for the UNESCO Futures of Education initiative, available at: unesdoc.unesco.org/ark:/48223/pf0000374032 [accessed 31 January 2023].

Cronin, B. (1984) *The Citation Process: The role and significance of citations in scientific communication*, London: Taylor Graham.

Davenport, E. and Snyder, H. (1995). Who cites women? Whom do women cite?: An exploration of gender and scholarly citation in sociology, *Journal of Documentation*, 51(4): 404–410.

Edmond, J. (2020) Points of reference: Citing Kamau Brathwaite Decolonizing Citation, *Diacritics* 48(3): 10–39.

Edmonds, B. (2019) The professional is political: On citational practice and the persistent problem of academic plunder, *Journal of Feminist Scholarship*, 16(16): 74–77.

Ennser-Kananen, J. (2019) Are we who we cite? On epistemological injustices, citing practices, and# metoo in academia, *Apples – Journal of Applied Language Studies*, 13(2): 65–69.

Fogarty, J. (2009) Show me the money: Academic research as currency, *Accounting Education*, 18(1): 3–6.

Foucault, M. (1980) Governmentality, *Ideology and Consciousness*, 7: 5–21.

Fox Tree, J. and Tomlinson J. (2008) The rise of 'like' in spontaneous quotations, *Discourse Processes*, 45(1): 85–102.

Freccero, C. (2017) Wolf, or Homo Homini Lupus, in A. Tsing et al (eds) *Arts of Living on a Damaged Planet*, Minneapolis: University of Minnesota Press, pp 91–105.

Hammond, S. (2013) Enhanced eBooks and multimodal publishing: Spitting games and making claims with multimodal data, Qualitative Research, 14(4): 442–458.

Hand, H. and Gray, N. (2022) Coda: Reflections on multimodal editing podcast, available at: digitalcultureandeducation.com/volume-14-2 [accessed 31 January 2023].

Harris, L.D. and Wasilewski, J. (2004) Indigeneity, an alternative worldview: Four R's (relationship, responsibility, reciprocity, redistribution) vs. two P's (power and profit). Sharing the journey towards conscious evolution, *Systems Research and Behavioral Science*, 21(5): 489–503.

Hicks, D. (2012) Performance-based university research funding systems, *Research Policy*, 41(2): 251–261.

Hyland, K. (1999) Academic attribution: Citation and the construction of disciplinary knowledge, *Applied Linguistics*, 20(3): 341–367.

Kim, A. (2020) The politics of citation, *Diacritics*, 48(3): 4–9.

Kimmerer, R.W. (2013) *Braiding Sweetgrass: Indigenous wisdom, scientific knowledge and the teachings of plants*, Minneapolis: Milkweed Editions.

Kohn, E. (2013) *How Forests Think: Toward an anthropology beyond the human*, Oakland: University of California Press.

Little Bear, L.R. (2000) Foreword, in G. Cajete, *Native Science: Natural laws of interdependence*, Santa Fe: Clear Light.

Lutz, C. (1990) The erasure of women's writing in sociocultural anthropology, *American Ethnologist*, 17(4): 611–627.

McElhinny, B., Hols, M., Holtzkener, J. et al (2003) Gender, publication and citation in sociolinguistics and linguistic anthropology: The construction of a scholarly canon, *Language in Society*, 32(3): 299–328.

McKittrick, K. (2020) *Dear Science and Other Stories*, Durham, NC: Duke University Press.

Merton, R. (1968) The Matthew effect in science, Science, 159(3810): 56–63.

Mirzoeff, N. (2016). It's not the Anthropocene, it's the white supremacy scene; or, the geological color line, in R. Grusin (ed) *After Extinction*, Minneapolis: University of Minnesota Press, pp. 123–149.

Obuah, E.E. (2015) The politics of reparations: The academic epistemic communities and the implications of reparation debate on African-American and Africa's quest for reparations, *Open Journal of Political Science*, 6(1): 44–52.

Odora Hoppers, C.A. (2020) Knowledge production, access and governance: A song from the South, Background paper for the UNESCO Futures of Education initiative, available at: unesdoc.unesco.org/ark:/48223/pf0000374033 [accessed 31 January 2023].

Orr, D. (1991) What is education for?, In *Context*, 27: 52.

Pailey, R. (2016) Where is the 'African' in African Studies?, African Arguments, available at: africanarguments.org/2016/06/where-is-the-african-in-african-studies [accessed 31 January 2023].

Pascual, E. (2014) *Fictive Interaction: The conversation frame in thought, language, and discourse*, Amsterdam: John Benjamins Publishing Company.

Rose, D. (2022) *Shimmer: Flying fox exuberance in worlds of peril*, Edinburgh: Edinburgh University Press.

Rüdiger, M.S., Antons, D. and Salge, T. (2021) The explanatory power of citations: A new approach to unpacking impact in science, *Scientometrics* 126: 9779–9809.

Said, E. (1978) *Orientalism*, New York: Vintage Books.

Shillitoe, M., Hand, H. and Rowsell, J. (2022) Alone-together: Shelves as intergenerational maps of sense-laden, relational, multimodal pedagogies, Digital Culture & Education, 14(2): 5–17.

Smith, C. and Garrett-Scott, D. (2021) 'We are not named': Black women and the politics of citation in anthropology, *Feminist Anthropology*, 2: 18–37.

Spivak, G.C. (1996). Subaltern talk: Interview with the editors (1993–94), in D. Landry and G. MacLean (eds) *The Spivak Reader: Selected works of Gayati Chakravorty Spivak*, New York: Routledge.

Tierney, M (2020) Dispossessed citation and mutual aid, *Diacritics,* 48(3): 94–115.

Todd, Z. (2016) An Indigenous feminist's take on the ontological turn: 'Ontology' is just another word for colonialism, *Journal of Historical Sociology*, 29(1): 4–22.

Todd, Z.S. (2021) Twitter thread: twitter.com/ZoeSTodd/status/1356658436872626176.

UKRI (2021) Diversity Data, available at: ukri.org/what-we-offer/supporting-healthy-research-and-innovation-culture/equality-diversity-and-inclusion/diversity-data [accessed 31 January 2023].

Wade, E. and Clark, H. (1993) Reproduction and demonstration in quotations, *Journal of Memory and Language,* 32(6): 805–819.

West, J.D. et al (2013) The role of gender in scholarly authorship, *PloS one*, 8(7): e66212.

Wiesel E. (1990) Global education: An address at the Global Forum, Moscow.

Yusoff, K. (2018) *A Billion Black Anthropocenes or None*, Minneapolis: University of Minnesota Press.

12

Reparative Pedagogies

Julia Paulson

Introduction

This chapter explores reparative possibilities in and through education, with
a specific focus on reparative pedagogy. It does so by sharing examples I've
encountered and by documenting many ongoing conversations around the
possibilities and challenges of describing, designing and imagining pedagogy
as reparative. These include conversations with friends, researchers, educators
and activists, many (but not all) of which take place within the Education,
Justice and Memory network (EdJAM). EdJAM exists to support and learn
more about creative approaches to teaching and learning about past violence
and injustice and currently works in 18 countries. Some of the people with
whom I've been in conversation describe their work using the term 'reparative
pedagogy'. Others do not, but, as this chapter argues, there are features of
their pedagogical approaches that align with and enable repair and reparation
and therefore allow for the possibility of describing them as reparative.

As discussed in more detail later in the chapter, reparation generally, and
in its application to education specifically, is often described as encompassing
material, symbolic, epistemic and affective measures to right wrongs of the
past. There is growing attention to what Arathi Sriprakash and colleagues
(Chapter 10 in this volume, and 2022) call 'reparative futures in education'
and to education's roles in enabling reparative measures across the domains
listed here (see, for example, Ramírez-Barat and Duthie, 2016; Bellino et al,
2017). The material, symbolic, epistemic and affective are all present within
pedagogy, and pedagogy could therefore contribute towards these types of
reparative measures. This chapter, however, explores the possibilities for
understanding reparative pedagogies in their own right, as another form of
reparation. One motivation for this is to recognize the ongoing work by
educators, artists, activists and students in this area. Reparative pedagogies

can, and do, proceed without waiting for formalized programmes of reparation, transitional justice or systemic reforms to the structural injustices that permeate the education systems that they might complement. In not recognizing, describing and seeking to support reparative pedagogies, we risk missing spaces where futures of education are reimagined through pedagogical approaches to acknowledge and reckon with past injustices and their afterlives in the present.

For the purposes of this chapter, I adopt a broad understanding of pedagogy. In the vast literature on pedagogy, multiple meanings and debates circulate, with definitions ranging from 'the act of teaching together with its attendant discourse of educational theories, values, evidence and justifications' (Alexander, 2009, p 928) to 'a practice for freedom' (Freire as cited in Giroux, 2010, p 715; hooks, 1994). Rather than reviewing in depth these and other definitions and the differences between them, I think it suffices to say that the idea of reparative pedagogies can speak to and be pursued within several understandings of and ways of practising the pedagogical, including those that focus on teaching and learning relationships in schools and other formal education spaces and those that define pedagogical sites much more widely (Paulson et al, 2021; Gomez-Suarez, 2017; Burnyeat, 2022; Sriprakash et al, 2022). Schools and classroom practices are, of course, important sites for transmitting knowledge of the past and making sense of the present, but they are far from the only (or even the most important) spaces where young people learn about and the approach the past (Sriprakash et al, 2022; Sanchez Meertens, 2018; Bekerman and Zemblyas, 2011).

Though this chapter works with an expansive understanding of pedagogy, it is important to note that pedagogy is often understood very narrowly and instrumentally, with its focus purely on the delivery of information in the service of the acquisition of a narrow range of learning outcomes. This view of pedagogy, though widely critiqued, is predominant in global policy discourses around education, particularly within the framing of the 'global learning crisis' (Tikly, 2020). Within these narrow understandings of pedagogical processes and functions, I think the opportunities for reparative approaches are limited.

From the outset, it is important to acknowledge a few things. The first is authorship – positionality, the style of this piece and its many debts. I am a white woman, born in Canada, fortunate to spend a lot of time in South and Central America, and now having lived more than 15 years in the UK, ten of those in Bristol. I grew up and went to school in a suburb just outside Edmonton in Alberta, Canada: a prairie province, a small city with a river winding through it; Treaty 6 land; Amiskwacîwâskahikan – Meeting place of Cree, Saulteaux, Sioux, Blackfoot and Métis peoples. St Albert (Payhonin), the suburb where I grew up, was the site of two residential schools, which removed Indigenous children from their families to 'educate' them. Bishop

Vital Grandin, after whom the neighbourhood that I grew up in was named and a key architect of Canada's system of residential schooling, described their purpose: 'we instil in them a pronounced distaste for native life so that they will be humiliated when reminded of their origins. When they graduate from our institutions the children will have lost everything Native except their blood' (as cited in Thomas, 2020). The residential schools in St Albert closed before I was born (though others elsewhere remained open into the late 1990s), but their names (Poundmaker and D'Youville) are still firmly part of the city; I played sport on Poundmaker field and friends attended Marguerite D'Youville secondary school.

Not that I knew the history behind the names that marked my daily comings and goings or ever heard the name Payhonin. My family of settlers with roots in Iceland, Ireland, France and England didn't talk about residential schooling or settler colonialism. And, I didn't learn about it at school. I do remember learning about 'aboriginal Canadians' in the language of my 1980s and 1990s textbooks, in social studies lessons and at visits to heritage sites around Alberta. But the textbooks and the sites treated Indigenous people as history; worthy of noting, but from the past. I absorbed that their customs were interesting to explore and their art worth preserving through what Papaschase Cree scholar Dwayne Trevor Donald (2009) calls the 'tipis and costumes' approach. But, at school, I never grasped a sense of Indigenous cultures, languages and peoples as present, living next to me, resisting this totalizing absence and the settler colonialism that has sought to erase them physically, materially, linguistically, culturally and symbolically for over a century. I wasn't taught to recognize or reckon with what Alexis Shotwell (2016) calls 'the ghosts in my bones', or to see my own implication in the histories of dispossession that were silenced as I paged through textbooks of teepees and furs. I wasn't part of an education system or classroom where repair was an intention.

My education was steeped in what Charles W. Mills (2007) called 'white ignorance', an active form of learned ignorance that enables blindness to and denial of 'the long history of structural discrimination that has left whites with the differential resources they have today, and all of its consequent advantages in negotiating opportunity structures' (p 20). These consequent advantages have no doubt helped with my education and career since my childhood in Payhonin. The consequent disadvantages maintained by white ignorance are clear in their material and epistemic consequences for those whose histories are denied and excluded in the maintenance of structural discrimination. However, not learning the histories of the Indigenous peoples on whose meeting place I grew up is also a disservice to settler Canadians like me and my predominantly white classmates – it has led to gaps in my knowledge and in my ways of knowing, including in my understandings of pedagogy. Understanding the reasons for these gaps in my own knowledge and the ways in which violence and injustice are learned and elided in other contexts has been a motivation for my research.

The questions around citation and quotation in Esther Priyadharshini's Chapter 11 in this volume are relevant here, as I draw upon and learn from and in dialogue with the practice of others, whose labour I have tried to name, cite and describe in elaborating the concept of reparative pedagogies. In this chapter, outlining the pedagogical innovation, resistance and beauty created in many of the examples shared here by colleagues materially and epistemically disadvantaged by the ignorance, exclusions and inequalities of the education systems they passed through, I hope to write in a spirit of accompaniment, with the intention – that also underpins the work of EdJAM – to connect ongoing work to teach and learn about violence and injustice in ways that enable repair and to play a part in amplifying this work and enabling conversation around it.

Repair in pedagogy

Reparative pedagogies are necessarily not one thing. Repair is, in part, about imagining and glimpsing more just futures, working towards them without certainty in their shape while attending to past and present injustices such that they are not (and will no longer be) inevitabilities in these futures (Sriprakash et al, 2022). This imagining, working and creating, therefore, of course, happens in multiple ways. Describing even the characteristics, much less the definitive features of reparative pedagogies, might be a fool's errand. Yet, as so much pedagogy continues to do harm, it seems vital to describe the alternatives that educators, activists and artists are developing. A key part of much of the scholarship on reparative approaches is the idea that they enable something new, or at least enable the imagining, the glimpsing of something new. Ali Aslam (2022) argues that repair can be seen as glimmers of more just futures thanks to the mending work that is done in the present to redress the harms of the past. This means that a discussion of reparative pedagogies must be descriptive (rather than prescriptive), open (rather than bounded) and messy and unfinished (rather than tidy and complete).

The image I have held in my head to aid this description is of a flower – each petal, an entity on its own, complete and beautiful, but also creating something more when viewed next to its companion petals. This chapter describes and offers examples of some petals that, on their own, might be described as reparative pedagogical approaches and that, when and if combined, might create something more. The petals (or characteristics) of reparative pedagogical approaches that I describe here are: dignity, truth-telling, multiplicity, responsibility and creativity. Though, of course, these are not the only or the exclusive characteristics of reparative pedagogy.

Describing the reparative

This section briefly explores literature around reparations and the reparative turn, advancing a theoretical case for the idea of reparative pedagogies. The idea and practice of reparation has been developed in different ways, including through international human rights and humanitarian law, philosophically and theoretically, as a goal and demand of activist movements for liberation. In reviewing these different ways of defining and working towards reparation, this section seeks to connect the existing literature with each of the petals of reparative pedagogy described in the following section.

Legally, victims of gross violations of international human rights law and serious violations of international humanitarian law have the right to reparations that are 'adequate, effective, prompt, and should be proportional to the gravity of the violations and the harm suffered' (OHCHR, 2022). The United Nations Office of the High Commissioner for Human Rights (OHCHR, 2022) defines reparations measures as including restitution (which should restore the victim to their original situation prior to the violation), compensation (which should be provided for economic and moral damages), rehabilitation (which includes care and services), and satisfaction (which includes the cessation of continuing violations, truth-seeking and symbolic actions).

While financial compensation may be the first form of reparation to spring to mind, as these definitions make clear, reparations can take the form of material, restitutive, symbolic, epistemic and collective measures, and indeed these measures can be combined to mutually reinforce one another (ICTJ, 2022; de Grieff, 2006). Reparations are part of the United Nations definition of and approach to transitional justice, which it defines as 'the full range of mechanisms and processes associated with a society's attempt to come to terms with a legacy of large-scale past abuses, in order to ensure accountability, serve justice and achieve reconciliation' (UN, 2010). International human rights law establishes the obligation that states have to victims of human rights violations, and these responsibilities can extend to others that are responsible for violating human rights (such as armed groups – see Zegveld, 2002). These legal definitions establish the foundations for discussion around two of our petals; first, responsibility, since legal definitions are clear that reparations are something for which certain actors have responsibility due to their involvement in committing, or their failure to prevent, human rights violations; and second, truth-telling, since acknowledgement of harm, which requires unearthing silenced or denied histories and events, is a fundamental first step in opening the possibilities for repair.

The implementation of transitional justice processes broadly, and reparations programmes specifically, have been part of post-conflict and post-authoritarian transitions, often with a focus on economic compensation when pursued programmatically (de Grieff, 2006; Barkan, 2001). As the focus of transitional justice expands beyond its traditional attention to civil and political rights to encompass and respond to violations of economic, social and cultural rights, so too does the call for and practice of reparations under transitional justice (Roth-Arriaza, 2014). This expansion includes three elements important for the purposes of this chapter. First are the increasing possibility and practices of educational reparations as part of transitional justice (Roth-Arriaza, 2014; Bellino et al, 2017), through which scholarships or bursaries are provided as reparations to victims and family members, or collective and/or symbolic reparations are offered via, for example, renaming schools to honour victims. Second is the broadening of the conceptualization of cases in need of transitional justice to include calls for transitional justice to address crimes of colonialism (Löytömäki, 2013; Yusuf, 2018; Beckles, 2013), enslavement (Táíwò, 2022; Coates, 2015), genocide against Indigenous peoples (CARICOM, 2013; Cunneen, 2005) and ongoing settler colonialism (Park, 2020; Balint et al, 2014). And finally, these developments widen the idea of responsibility for reparations. These arguments to expand the remits of transitional justice also, arguably, extend discussions of responsibility to encompass structural injustices and intergenerational harm (Miller, 2021; Balint et al, 2014). These questions are being explored in the context of reparative pedagogy, as developed here, in the discussion of the responsibility petal.

Theoretically, scholars in law, philosophy and other disciplines have long accompanied and challenged the development of international human rights and humanitarian law around reparations and the programmatic development of reparations programmes (for example, de Grieff, 2006; Torpey, 2006). This work establishes both the moral case for reparations and the political challenges to their implementation, and also critically documents the implementation of reparations programmes around the world (de Grieff, 2006). More recently, what might be a called a 'reparative turn' is visible in the social sciences and humanities. Here the lens widens to examine silences and epistemic injustices in the development of academic disciplines and knowledge production more broadly, for example, in Gurminder K. Bhambra's (2022) powerful critique of how theorization of the nation state and the global elides 'the colonial histories that were constitutive of their formation' (p 11), and in Kevin Myers et al's (2021) attention to the racialized and racist discourses that underpinned UNESCO's early work.

The failure to understand empires as historically constitutive of contemporary nation states, Bhambra argues, 'mitigates against us being able to understand the past in connected terms' (2022, p 12). Connected understandings in the social sciences, she argues, would acknowledge that the inequalities (globally and in specific constituencies) that are the subject of much academic enquiry are connected to the generation of wealth and poverty through colonialism. This would also expand understandings of citizenship, belonging and entitlements beyond the confines of the nation state. This work is concerned with the opening of creative possibilities for generating knowledges otherwise, recovering silenced histories, and learning and unlearning the past and present in new ways. For reparative pedagogies, this highlights the importance of multiplicity (another of our petals) in the narration of the past, as Arathi Sriprakash and colleagues describe in their account of radical humanist historical thinking in education, which creates 'spaces for listening to multiple, often competing, knowledge traditions so that all have opportunities to be recognized, explored, debated and critiqued,' enabling what they call 'reparative remembering' (Chapter 10).

Olúfẹ́mi O. Táíwò (2022) outlines a proposal for reparation that is both backward looking, in terms of the necessity to identify those to whom reparation is owed, and forward looking in its ultimate goal and ability, which Táíwò argues is to enable present and future self-determination for those who have been denied it due to past and ongoing systems of oppression. Keston K. Perry's (2021) work also contributes to proposals for future-oriented, freedom-generating reparations and repair. Both Perry and Táíwò connect their proposals for reparations for past injustices with the contemporary realities of climate change and climate emergency, with Perry calling for climate reparations that challenge the 'colonial-climate ontology' whereby current global configurations remain silent on historical responsibility for uneven and extreme climate-induced consequences. Perry calls instead for a programme of reparations for historical and ongoing loss and damage related to the uneven effects of climate change, and sees these proposals as created " 'anew based on political acknowledgement of and mobilizing around differentiated responsibilities and impacts.' These reparative proposals share as fundamental the idea that reparation is a path towards freedom, self-determination and human dignity – goals shared by reparative pedagogical approaches as developed in the following sections.

Finally, and perhaps most importantly, reparation is, and has been, a key idea for many activist movements for liberation and in challenge to present-day systems of oppression. Reparation is learned through praxis (Aslam, 2022), connecting with theoretical traditions in critical pedagogies (Giroux, 2010; Freire, 2005; hooks, 1994) and pointing to the importance of the creative in bringing it to life. Much of the literature summarized here, and more, appears in the publications of social movements demanding reparations (see, for example, Movement for Black Lives' Reparations Now Toolkit, 2019; Reparations Bristol, 2022). However, they tend to add in their efforts towards understandings of reparation, a deeper attention to healing, care and protection from the daily lived experience of harm as both an outcome of and crucial part of the processes of repair and, therefore, a greater appreciation of the labour, creativity and improvisation involved in bringing reparative relationships and glimpses of more just futures into being. Ali Aslam (2022), writing on social movements for police and prison abolition in the United States, identifies what he calls 'repair praxis', which 'makes ready' people, norms and institutions in need of transformation. Aslam describes this praxis as made up of creative and interconnected approaches that are improvisational, multifaceted, flexible and expansive. (These ideas are explored in greater depth within the creativity petal.) Importantly, Aslam argues, repair praxis is also able, after careful investigation, to declare something 'beyond repair' (pp 2–3). This is a question that many of the colleagues whose approaches are highlighted in the following sections hold open in their engagements, or lack thereof, with formal education.

Describing reparative pedagogies

Reparative pedagogies can, and do, represent various ways of defining, imagining and working towards repair and reparations. This section of the chapter describes dignity, truth-telling, multiplicity, responsibility and creativity as some petals of a reparative approach. While we might imagine these as petals of a flower together producing something beautiful, educators, artists, activists and students may develop approaches that centre one, or some combination of several, but not all of these ideas, depending on the priorities and needs of the groups and communities with whom they are working. To illustrate each of these petals, the following descriptive examples draw on the practices of colleagues in and beyond the EdJAM network.

Dignifying

At an online presentation in 2020, I asked Lawrence Hoo, Bristol poet and founder of CARGO Movement, whether he thought the CARGO classroom resources were reparative. CARGO Classroom is a beautifully designed and powerful collection of educational materials that centre historical figures from Africa and of African descent and their stories of leadership, resistance and resilience. They begin with Imothep and move through history, including materials on Queen Nzinga, Mary Seacole, Marcus Garvey and many others. Hoo (2019) responded that:

> This is about *self* reparation first – we need to put ourselves together first. We need to see and teach our value to our communities and then we won't ask permission from others for reparations, once we are strong enough, we can make demands from others. Yes, reparations is a part of it, but first comes our own self repair.

Here, Hoo's arguments echo with writing on 'taking up space' (Dunn and Love, 2020, p 190) being developed by scholars arguing for Black Joy and pro-Black pedagogies in education (Parks et al, 2022; Dunn and Love, 2020). The CARGO resources celebrate historical figures of African descent who are, as Hoo describes in his poetry, remembering his own education (Hoo, 2019), otherwise largely absent from UK classrooms (for which the resources were designed, though they are being used more widely). Hoo argues that, in pulling these resources into a discussion of reparations, the necessary space for celebration and self-repair and healing may be prematurely closed down. When Arathi Sriprakash and I reflected on Hoo's responses later, Arathi was interested in how connecting this work with the idea of reparation returns the celebratory resources, and power they may have for Black students encountering them, to a conversation that includes or even centres (white) institutions and analyses of the reasons for these historic exclusions from curricula.

The importance of self-healing is also addressed by Tarcila Rivera Zea (Chapter 9). Quechua Indigenous leader and founder of CHIRAPAQ, Rivera Zea centres dignity in her discussion of reparative pedagogy, as do EdJAM projects working from and celebrating Indigenous knowledges and lifeways, like 'U kúuchil kaambal kuxtal: school for life', which is developing an alternative curricula for Maya young people in Yucatan, Mexico. Drawing from social justice theories prominent in educational research, these examples can be described as enabling representation and as working towards recognition (for example, Fraser, 2005; Novelli et al, 2017). But it is important to note that these are not the terms with which Hoo, Rivera Zea and Chan (who leads Ukúuchil kaambal kuxtal) use to describe their work. They use words like dignity, freedom, celebration, pride, healing, recovery and self-repair, resonating with Siettah Parks and colleagues' descriptions of pro-Black pedagogy as co-constructed, intentional, caring and loving. A claiming of healing and celebratory space on its own terms and without any necessary obligation to engage with institutions and groups who have upheld exclusions and injustice (Parks et al, 2022; Paris and Alim, 2017). In many cases, this engagement does follow – CARGO have been holding teacher trainings and are developing an online course to support teachers to use their resources, and Rivera Zea outlines the state responsibilities to respond to the educational proposals of CHIRAPAQ – but the reparative work starts with healing and celebration, dignifying pasts and presents that have been disrespected and denied.

Truth-telling

One part (or petal) of reparative pedagogies is to work against the denial of truth about oppression and its consequences; to clarify the ways in which histories of violence, dispossession and exploitation have produced structural injustices that endure in the present; to acknowledge, understand and work against the powerful ways in which ignorance and silence shape the history that is passed on in school and beyond it. The right to truth about gross violations of human rights and serious violations of international humanitarian law is enshrined in international human rights law alongside the protocols that establish basic principles for a right to remedy and reparations (OHCHR, 2014 and 2022). Truth and truth-telling are key principles of repair.

Research exploring education and transitional justice has tended to focus on this element of reparative pedagogy (though not always using this language), examining, for example, the ways that truth-commission reports enter into curricula, textbooks and classrooms (Paulson and Bellino, 2017) and the broader implications of societal truth-telling processes on education (Keynes et al, 2021). This work highlights the complexities in truth-telling in education given education's long-standing complicity in the silencing of some historical truths and the privileging of others. It also points to the limits imposed by the reliance on a collective memory approach to teach historical narratives in schools which, in transmitting a single narrative of the past that is necessarily partial and exclusionary, erases and excludes a multitude of historical experiences and truths (Paulson, 2015; Keynes et al, 2021, Psaltis et al, 2017). Finally, history teaching can naturalize violence, relying as it does on a linear movement that is often marked by and moves between one violent episode and the next, with truths about the alternatives to and resistances of violence that coexist alongside violent events usually remaining untold (Bermudez, 2021).

In this section, I explore examples of truth-telling that do otherwise. The section is inspired by this definition of truth by Juana Yunis in reference to the Colombian context as part of the Educapaz project discussed later[1]:

When we speak about truth in this methodological guide, we are *not* referring to a philosophical position in which there is one unique and absolute truth, nor to a political intention to impose one totalizing account of history and to repress alternatives. On the contrary, from a human rights perspective, we refer to the idea that ... it is necessary to guarantee the right to truth of victims and of society more generally as one of the preconditions to build a stable and sustainable peace ... We adopt the ethical position that, the testimonies of victims, perpetrators and other actors, combined with verification through reliable sources, establish facts that cannot be denied or relativized; in other words irrefutable facts. (Educapaz, 2020, p 18, emphasis in original)

This definition is important in capturing the necessity of truth for the repair of injustices, but also appreciates the ways in which a singular or absolute truth is also violent. The manual that it is drawn from goes on to develop a mosaic of methodologies for truth-telling in education based on this definition.

In 2018, I visited a courtyard of the Universidad del Norte's campus in Baranquilla, Colombia, where the results of years of work with this mosaic of methodologies were on display. The students and teachers present were from regions severely affected by Colombia's many decades of armed conflict. For several years, they had been working with *Escuelas de Palabra*, a programme designed by the civil society organization Educapaz to support the Colombian truth commission's call to make 'truth a public good' (Educapaz, 2020). The truth commission saw schools and the education sector more widely as key allies in its mandate for clarification of the truth, coexistence and non-repetition. Educapaz's project aimed to materialize this commitment and working relationship. The methodological mosaic that underpins the project offers five routes to support schools to work as sites of truth-telling. These range from a pathway that explores truth as a value and possibility to orient daily life and policies at school, through to active memory work that explores the ways in which the school is and was an active subject in armed conflict and in the construction of peace. In the courtyard, there was dancing, photography exhibitions, research projects, collectively designed school value statements and behaviour policies, plays, documentaries, small curated museums and art exhibits.

On each pathway, schools undertake their own truth-telling exercise around a conflict affecting their school, but they are not confined to 'cataloguing wrongs' (Táíwò, 2022), engaging with pasts that are actively traumatizing or potentially retraumatizing (Godobo-Madikizela and Van Der Merwe, 2009), or opening discussions that can make learners or teachers unsafe (Horner et al, 2015). Some schools did choose approaches inspired by what Javier Corredor and colleagues (2018) call 'historical memory education', combining personal and intergenerational memories of conflict, localized histories and the 'irrefutable facts' that transitional justice processes seek to establish beyond the possibility of denial (Educapaz, 2020). In one case, a school in a community with a strong paramilitary presence explored the ways in which this affected the school in a careful process that included children and families involved in paramilitarism and those who were directly and indirectly victimized by its presence. Another dug more deeply into the causes behind the forced displacement that had created the locality in which the school now operates. Others chose to explore everyday conflicts that they identified within their schools, for example why there were problems listening meaningfully to one another within the school community, or what factors explained the rising levels of drug consumption in their community.

This is an approach to truth that is far from totalizing, but that, equally, does not relativize away the irrefutable facts of injustice that reparative justice processes generally and reparative pedagogies specifically must confront. Escuelas de Palabra accepts not just multiple truths but multiple ways of engaging with truth and varying positions of readiness to confront the harms and wrongs of the past. Perhaps multiplicity and truth-telling should be one and the same petal, given the ways in which reparative truth-telling pedagogy eschews the idea of a single truth. I have kept them separate because of the degree of opposition that often exists to the introduction of previously silenced truths into educational spaces. Examples abound: the demonization of critical race theory in the US, UK and elsewhere and its equation with all teaching of race and racism; the resistance to teaching about Peru's armed conflict and the political framing of any discussion of the conflict as an 'apology for terrorism' and therefore inappropriate for children to discuss; the growth of residential school apologetics and denialism in Canada – the list goes on. Given how active, aggressive, defensive and harmful this denial can be – as Charles W. Mills (2007) anticipated when he described white ignorance and as Sriprakash et al, (2022) discuss when theorizing the affective states of whiteness – it is important to maintain truth as a key feature of repair. Despite the harms, exclusions and silences caused by teaching a universalizing and singular truth, I think it is important to hold truth as a petal and foundation of reparative pedagogy, and to imagine how truths can be taught and learned differently, including by engaging with multiplicity.

Multiplicity

Bophana Audiovisual Resource Center in Cambodia was founded in 2006 by film-maker Rithy Pahn with the mission of preserving and sharing film, television, photography and sound archives of Cambodia as a way of of recovering memories and heritage. The centre is at once a curator of this rich collection and a creator of new content, training young people in film-making and broadcasting. For several years, the centre has been working with materials from Bophana's archive and testimonies it has gathered to create a multimedia app for teaching and learning about the Khmer Rouge genocide. The app has been approved by the Ministry of Education for use in Cambodian schools, and Bophana has run training with secondary school History teachers on its use. The first version of the app included testimonies of victims and survivors of the Khmer Rouge regime. Bophana is currently producing a second version, which will also incorporate testimonies collected from former low-level members of the Khmer Rouge, perpetrators of crimes and also complex victims (Bernath, 2016) whose involvement was often compelled (Cooke et al, 2022). As the work with teachers begins in supporting them to use of this revised version of the app, questions around multiple perspectives in teaching and learning about the past are raised: How are the testimonies of victims and perpetrators learned alongside one other? Ought one version be given primacy or afforded more legitimacy? Does one narrative align more smoothy with reconciliatory, peacebuilding or reparative goals? How to engage with multiple perspectives and historical narratives of the past without relativizing them? Or, to re-pose Zvi Bekerman and Michaelinos Zemblyas' (2011) question, is it possible for multiplicity in History teaching to reconceptualize different accounts and memories of the past as non-dividing constructs?

Approaching the teaching of the past via multiple narratives is probably the element of reparative pedgagogies most established in the literature, with agreement among authors about the importance of this approach (Sriprakash et al in Chapter 10 of this volume; Bermudez, 2021; Keynes et al, 2021). As Arathi Sriprakash and colleagues outline (in Chapter 10), reparative education must attend to 'the epistemic erasures and active silences, political interests and interpretive closures of the production and legitimization of knowledge through educational and historical practice itself.' The acknowledgment and visibility of histories and knowledges that have been systematically excluded from dominant historical narratives and classroom spaces are important acts of representation and recognition as alluded to earlier. However, while Sriprakash et al's call for 'reparative remembering' requires and includes the expansion of representations of the past and of the historical narratives being voiced, with an explicit attention to creating space for silenced and elided pasts, it also for calls for more. It demands ways of working with these more representative narratives of the past that 'generate a new collective recognition of the injustices of multiple pasts' (Chapter 10).

Clear pedagogical pathways for how to use multiplicity to generate this collective recognition are hard to come by, both in literature and practice, but both often emphasize the centrality of dialogue and relationality. 'Relationality,' writes Gamilaroi scholar Michelle Bishop (2022), 'is not about separation, instead the emphasis is on coming together to share knowledge from different places, communities, teachings' (p 140). Dwayne Trevor Donald (2009), Papaschase Cree scholar writing from my home province, is clear about the way in which the single perspective on Indigenous history taught to children of my generation delivers the 'enduring message that Aboriginal peoples and Canadians occupy separate realities' (p 4). Donald proposes Indigenous Métissage as an approach to mutually overcome what he calls colonial frontier logics transmitted through curricula. This approach 'involves the purposeful juxtaposition of mythic historical perspectives (often framed as commonsense) with Indigenous perspectives' with a central goal to 'promote ethical relationality as a curricular and pedagogical standpoint' (pp 5–6).

Canada's Truth and Reconciliation Commission (TRC) (2015), which investigated the legacy of residential schooling, made a number of calls to action, including towards education. These involved many measures that, if implemented, might go some way towards material reparation of the grave inequities in education between Indigenous and non-Indigenous people in Canada. The calls to action also include the recommendation of mandatory age-appropriate education on residential schools' and 'Aboriginal peoples' historical and contemporary contributions to Canada' developed 'in consultation and collaboration with survivors, Aboriginal people and educators' (p 7). However, a 2021 curriculum review in Alberta, my home province, proposed steps backwards in this regard – removing rather than adding content around Indigenous peoples in a process that lacked consultation, much less collaboration (Kanygin, 2021). Vociferous opposition to the changes mean that the social studies curriculum is under further review, but the direction of changes, despite the TRC's calls for action, indicate a failure in this example on the part of non-Indigenous Canadians and educational policy makers to recognize and take responsibility for their roles in making ready the conditions where by dialogue and ethical relationality might become possible (Beausoliel, 2021).

Responsibility

As mentioned in the introduction to this chapter, Alexis Shotwell (2016) uses the idea of 'ghosts in our bones' to evoke questions about how we acknowledge, atone for and (though this isn't her focus) teach and learn about responsibility for past injustices. As discussed earlier, responsibility is a key part of transitional justice, though establishing it, and agreeing appropriate sanctions or responses to it, becomes more complex as crimes and harms become more historically distant, even as their afterlives persist in material, epistemic and affective ways (Sriprakash et al, 2022; Mills, 2007). Writing on reckoning with settler colonialism in Canada, Shotwell (2016) quotes Gramsci's argument that historical processes deposit 'an infinity of traces, without leaving an inventory.' This inventory that does not exist is a personal one, tightly tied to intergeneration biographies situated within geopolitical events and social systems. In Shotwell's words, the past 'has harmed and benefitted us, differentially, pervasively' (p. 24) – these harms and benefits are rarely discussed, much less accounted for. Assigning responsibility for reparations to states and other organized actors who have caused harm and violated human rights is a necessary part of reparatory justice, but these infinite traces and their pervasive but differential harms and benefits also demand other forms of reckoning and atonement.

The classroom is a place where individuals with different family histories and positions within social systems meet (though perhaps not with the frequency we might assume given the ways in which formal education remains segregated across many dividing lines in de facto if not de jure ways). Yet these meetings often remain unmediated and unexplored; 'ghosts in bones' unacknowledged and left to haunt in unchecked ways, as curricular attention is focused elsewhere.

Pedagogical approaches in peace education, critical education and anti-racist education often call for dialogue as a way to cross divides, acknowledge others and appreciate alternative narratives (Bekerman and Zemblyas, 2011; Bajaj and Hantzopoulos, 2016). But, ways in which responsibility – intergenerational and otherwise – figures within this dialogue is often unclear, and the affective starting points of those in dialogue are often also uninterrogated. Sriprakash and colleagues' (2022) exploration of the affective processes by which whiteness is learned highlights the ways in which historical benefits become largely unacknowledged yet comfortable and homely expectations for the future for those who possess and are socialized into them such that even the acknowledgement of these benefits is felt as a threat. As Emily Beausoleil (2021, p 4) argues, 'structural injustice, by its very nature, does not require villains to exist ... all it requires to keep such machinations in motion is for the majority of us not to listen.' These affective states can make concepts like atonement, accountability and responsibility seem unattainable even in dialogue, and much less in terms of material repair. Considerable preparatory work, especially on behalf of advantaged groups – what Beausoleil (2021) calls 'gathering our people' and 'clearing the gorse' – is required in order for dialogue to broach responsibility.

Scholars and educators are exploring the pedagogical possibilities of working with the idea of complicity – the knowing or unknowing contribution to wrongdoing (Leopora and Goodwin, 2013; Zemblyas, 2020), which is social, rather than individual, and therefore is shared. Everyone is complicit in structural injustice, though not in the same manner or to the same degree (Applebaum, 2010). Michalinos Zemblyas (2020) explores the possibilities of an 'anti-complicity pedagogy' that does not stop at making learners aware of complicity, but works to enable 'actions that actively resist social harm in everyday life' (p 318). He highlights complicity as both a political and affective concern, naming guilt, shame and hope as emotions attached to the complex interrelationships between historical pasts and presents, and calls for pedagogical approaches that can and do work with the 'affective roots of complicity' (p 321).

Reflecting on this reading and its connections to pedagogical practices that I have encountered, I am reminded of the memory-based explorations within Educapaz's methodological mosaic for truth-telling in education discussed earlier. For example, in the school that has dedicated its memory work to explore how paramilitarism has affected and become interwoven with the school community, it is possible to identify complicities that were necessary for safety and daily survival and complicities that were more implicit, affective and possibly harder to acknowledge and repair (Bermeo et al, 2022). Some of this memory work is also ongoing in UK universities, seeking to better understand their direct and indirect entanglements with colonialism and slavery. The challenges to accept ongoing complicities are clear. The University of Bristol, from where I write, has still to make public the report it commissioned Professor Olivette Otele to research into these legacies despite lip-service celebrating itself for undertaking the task. Constructive suggestions around this impasse in responsibility taking include Shotwell's (2016) invocation to 'claim our bad kin', instructing members of dominant or advantaged groups to work quietly within that group to challenge those with whom they have close relationships whose affective responses are defensive or denying; and Beausoleil's (2021) focus on listening and becoming 'ready to meet' – learning to listen in order to respond more usefully and effectively to claims of structural injustice.

Creativity

The memory work of the Colombian school community exploring its connections with paramilitarism involved life-history interviews, intergenerational dialogues, community discussions and the creation of art. As Rithy Pahn, founder of Bophana Audiovisual Resource Center explains (2022) in describing the purposes and methodologies of the centre:

> The past tells us what may happen tomorrow; and images are here to make us think and feed us; it is a great strength to move forward. Education helps us analyse the images and master the techniques; creation enables us to speak up but also express what we see and how we feel.

A final petal, or perhaps the centre of the flower, which holds all the other petals described so far, and likely those that others will add, is that of creativity. Many of the approaches described above are grounded in the arts and rely on the artistry of the educators practising them. They are relational and build relationships. They attend to emotion and affect and are active in their caring, not just for the learners with whom they work, but also for the people, including those now long gone, harmed by the histories with which they work, whose dignity they seek to recover and celebrate.

Importantly, however, adjectives like creative, relational and emotional are central to the ways that many influential theorists – from Jerome Bruner to Lev Vygotsky, Maria Montessori and Paulo Freire – understand their area of study: pedagogy. Pedagogy itself, it seems, is also being repaired and recovered by reparative pedagogies, which do not centre learning outcomes, value test scores or fit into neatly timetabled blocks. The degree to which many of the initiatives described here operate outside the formal education system, or seek to intervene rather than work incrementally from within it, speaks to the limits of reparative pedagogy within education systems that might yet be declared to be 'beyond repair' (Aslam, 2022). Reparative pedagogies go some way towards imagining and practising something new, building it by carefully repairing the harms of the past in dignifying, truth-telling, multiple, responsible and creative ways.

Conclusion: flowerings

This chapter offers the image of a flower, with its petals of dignity, truth-telling, multiplicity, responsibility and creativity, suggesting some of the features of reparative pedagogy. It argues that pedagogy is another area where reparative practices are happening and can be imagined, which can build upon, accompany and expand reparations in material, symbolic, epistemic and affective spheres. It builds on a growing body of research that shows the degree to which education itself is in need of repair. It highlights how those working with and towards reparative pedagogies are reclaiming the hopeful, creative and freeing in the pedagogical.

It is one flower, described in one way, which I hope might open conversations and nurture further flowerings and blooms. There are certainly more reparative pedagogies to be celebrated and described and alternative ways of describing and understanding the overlapping and interrelated petals that have been described here.

Note
[1] Author's own translation from the original Spanish.

References
Alexander, R. (2009) Towards a comparative pedagogy, in R. Cowen and A. Kazamias (eds) *International Handbook of Comparative Education*, Dordretch: Springer: 923–941.

Applebaum, B. (2010) *Being White, Being Good: White complicity, white moral responsibility and social justice education*, New York: Lexington Books.

Aslam, A. (2022) The Politics of Repair, *Contemporary Political Theory*. Onlinefirst: DOI 10.1057.s41296-022-00547-8.

Bajaj, M. and Hantzopoulos, M. (2016) *Peace Education: International perspectives*, London: Bloomsbury.

Balint, J., Evans, J. and McMilan, N. (2014) Rethinking transitional justice, redressing indigenous harm: A new conceptual approach, *International Journal of Transitional Justice*, 8(2): 194–216.

Barkan, A. (2001) *The Guilt of Nations: Restitution and negotiating historical injustices*, Baltimore: Johns Hopkins University Press.

Beausoleil, E. (2021) Calling in to cut back: Settlers learning to listen for a decolonial futures, *Ethnicities*, online first: DOI: 10.1177/1468796821-0629-8.

Beckles, H. (2013) *Britain's Black Debt: Reparations for Caribbean slavery and native genocide*, Mona: University of the West Indies Press.

Bekerman, Z. and Zemblyas, M. (2011) *Teaching Contested Narratives: Identity, memory and reconciliation in peace education and beyond*, Cambridge: Cambridge University Press.

Bellino, M.J., Paulson, J. and Worden, E.A. (2017) Working through difficult pasts: Towards thick democracy and transitional justice in education, *Comparative Education*, 53(3): 313–332.

Bermeo, J.D., Paulson, J. and Charria, A. (2022) Schools as sites of memory: The musealization of the armed conflict by students and teachers in Colombia, in C. Cross and J. Giblin (eds) *Critical Perspectives on Heritage for Development,* London: Routledge.

Bermudez, A. (2021) Narrative justice? Ten tools to deconstruct about violent past, in M. Keynes, Å. Elmersjö, D. Lindmark and B. Norlin (eds) (2021) *Historical Justice and History Education*, Cham: Palgrave Macmillan, pp 269–289.

Bernath, J. (2016) 'Complex political victims' in the aftermath of mass atrocity: Reflections on the Khmer Rouge Tribunal in Cambodia, *International Journal of Transitional Justice,* 10(1): 46–66.

Bhambra, G.K. (2022) For a reparatory social science, *Global Social Challenges.* 1, 8–20.

Bishop, M. (2022) Indigenous education sovereignty: Another way of 'doing' education, *Critical Studies in Education,* 61(1): 131–146.

Bophana Audiovisual Resource Center (2022) About Bophana Center: bophana.org/about.

Burnyeat, G. (2022) *The Face of Peace: Government pedagogy among disinformation in Colombia*, Chicago: University of Chicago Press.

CARICOM (2013) *CARICOM Ten Point Plan for Reparatory Justice*, available at: caricom.org/caricom-ten-point-plan-for-reparatory-justice [accessed 1 February 2023].

Coates, T.-N. (2015) The Case for Reparations, in S. Holt (ed) *The Best American Magazine Writing*, New York: Columbia University Press, pp 1–50.

Cooke, P., Hodgkinson, K. and Manning, P. (2022) Changing the story: Intergenerational dialogue, participatory video and perpetrator memories in Cambodia, *Memory Studies*, online first: DOI 10.1177/17506980221108474.

Corredor, J., Wills-Obregon, M.E. and Asensio-Brouard, M. (2018) Historical memory education for peace and justice: Definition of a field, *Journal of Peace Education*, 15(2): 169–190.

Cunneen, C. (2005) Colonialism and historical injustice: Reparations for Indigenous peoples, *Social Semiotics*, 15(1): 59–80.

de Grieff, P. (2006) Justice and reparations, in P. de Grieff (ed) *The Handbook of Reparations*, Oxford: Oxford University Press.

Donald, D.T. (2009) Forts, curriculum, and indigenous métissage: Imagining decolonization in Indigenous-Canadian relations in education contexts, *First Nations Perspectives*, 2(1): 1–24.

Dunn, D. and Love, B.L. (2020) Antiracist language arts pedagogy is incomplete without Black joy, *Research in Teaching English*, 55(2): 190–192.

Educapaz (2020) Mosaico methodologico. Caminos diversos para reflexionar en las escuelas sobre el valor de la verdad como bien publico fundamental para la paz en Colombia, Guia para facilitadores / Escuelas de Palabra (educapaz.co).

Fraser, N. (2005) Reframing justice in a globalized world, *New Left Review*, 36: 79–88.

Freire, P. (2005) *Pedagogy of the Oppressed*, 30th anniversary edition, New York: Continuum.

Giroux, H.A. (2010) Rethinking education as the practice of freedom: Paulo Freire and the promise of critical pedagogy, *Policy Futures in Education*, 8(6): 715–721.

Godobo-Madikizela, P. and Van Der Merwe, C. (eds) (2009), *Memory, Narrative and Forgiveness: Perspectives on the unfinished journeys of the past*, Newcastle upon Tyne: Cambridge Scholars Publishing.

Gomez-Suarez, A. (2017) Peace process pedagogy: Lessons from the no-vote victory in the Colombian peace referendum, *Comparative Education*, 53(3): 462–482.

Hoo, L. (2019) *CARGO*, Bristol: Inner City Tales.

hooks, b. (1994) *Teaching to Transgress: Education as the practice of freedom*, New York: Routledge.

Horner, L., Kadiwal, L., Sayed, Y. et al (2015) Literature Review: The role of teachers in peacebuilding, Research Consortium on Education and Peacebuilding.

ICTJ (International Centre for Transitional Justice) (2022) Reparations (see ictj.org).

Kanygin, J. (2021) Alberta to rewrite controversial K-6 social studies curriculum, pause implementation of several subjects, CTV News Calgary, available at: calgary.ctvnews.ca/alberta-to-rewrite-controversial-k-6-social-studies-curriculum-pause-implementation-of-several-subjects-1.5705518 [accessed 2 February 2023].

Keynes, M., Elmersjö, Å., Lindmark, D. and Norlin, B. (eds) (2021) *Historical Justice and History Education*, Cham: Palgrave Macmillan.

Leopora, C. and Goodwin, R. (2013) *On Complicity and Compromise*, Oxford: Oxford University Press.

Löytömäki, S. (2013) The law and collective memory of colonialism: France and the case of 'belated' transitional justice, *International Journal of Transitional Justice*, 7(2): 205–223.

Miller, Z. (2021) Temporal governance: The times of transitional justice, *International Criminal Law Review*, 21: 848–877.

Mills, C.W. (2007) White Ignorance, in S. Sullivan and N. Tuana (eds) Race and Epistemologies of Ignorance, New York: SUNY University Press, pp 11–38.

Movement for Black Lives (2019) Reparations Now Toolkit, available at: m4bl.org/wp-content/uploads/2020/05/Reparations-Now-Toolkit-FINAL.pdf [accessed 1 February 2023].

Myers, K., Sriprakash, A. and Sutoris, P. (2021) Toward a 'New Humanism?' Time and emotion in UNESCO's science of world-making, 1947–1951, Journal of World History, 32(4): 685–715.

Novelli, M., Lopes Cardozo, M.T.A. and Smith, A. (2017) The 4RS framework: Analyzing education's contribution to sustainable peacebuilding with social justice in conflict-affected contexts, Journal on Education in Emergencies, 3(1): 14–43.

OHCHR (2014) *Transitional Justice and Economic, Social and Cultural Rights*, available at ohchr.org/en/publications/special-issue-publications/transitional-justice-and-economic-social-and-cultural [accessed 1 February 2023].

OHCHR (2022) About Transitional Justice and Human Rights, available at: ohchr.org/en/transitional-justice [accessed 1 February 2023].

Paris, D. and Alim, S.H. (eds) (2017) Culturally Sustaining Pedagogies: Teaching and learning for justice in a changing world, New York: Teachers College Press.

Park, A.S.J. (2020) Settler colonialism, decolonization and radicalizing transitional justice, *International Journal of Transitional Justice*, 14(2): 260–279.

Parks, S. et al (2022) Going beyond anti-racist pedagogical practices: Co-constructing a pro-Black classroom, Journal for Multicultural Education, 16(3): 259–271.

Paulson, J. (2015) "Whether and how?" history education about recent and ongoing conflict: A review of research, Journal on Education in Emergencies, 1(1): 7–39.

Paulson, J., Abiti, N., Bermeo Osorio, J. et al (2021) Education as a site of memory: Developing a research agenda, International Studies in Sociology of Education, 29(4): 429–451.

Paulson, J. and Bellino, M. J. (2017) Truth commissions, education and positive peace: An analysis of truth commission final reports (1980-2015), *Comparative Education*, 53(3): 351–378.

Perry, K.K. (2021) The new 'bond-age', climate crisis and the case for climate reparations: Unpicking old/new colonialities of finance for development within the SDGs, Geoforum, 126: 361–371.

Psaltis, C., Carretero, M. and Čehajić-Clancy, S. (eds) (2017) *History Education and Conflict Transformation: Social psychological theories, history teaching and reconciliation*, London: Palgrave Macmillan.

Ramírez-Barat, C. and Duthie, R. (eds) (2016) *Transitional Justice and Education: Learning peace*, New York: Social Science Research Centre.

Reparations Bristol (2022) Reparations Bristol Power, reparationsbristol. org [accessed 1 February 2023].

Roth-Arriaza, N. (2014) Reparations for economic, social and cultural rights, in D. Sharp (ed) Justice and Economic Violence in Transition, New York: Springer, pp 109–138.

Sanchez Meertens, A. (2018). Los Saberes de la Guerra. Memoria y conocimiento intergeneracional del conflicto en Colombia. Siglo del Hombre.

Shotwell, A. (2016) Against Purity: Living ethically in compromised times, Minneapolis: University of Minnesota Press.

Sriprakash, A., Rudolph, S. and Gerrard, J. (2022) Learning Whiteness: Education and the settler colonial state, London: Pluto Press.

Táíwò. O.O. (2022) *Reconsidering Reparations*, Oxford: Oxford University Press.

Thomas, G. (2020) We need to review our commemoration programs, *Prairie History,* 1: 81–83.

Tikly, L. (2020) *Education for Sustainable Development in the Postcolonial World: Towards a transformative agenda for Africa*, London: Routledge.

Torpey, J. (2006) *Making Whole What Has Been Smashed: On reparations politics*, Cambridge, MA: Harvard University Press.

Truth and Reconciliation Commission of Canada (2015) *Calls to Action,* Ottawa: Truth and Reconciliation Commission of Canada.

UN (2010) Guidance Note of the Secretary General: United Nations Approach to Transitional Justice, available at: digitallibrary.un.org/record/ 682111?ln=en [accessed 1 February 2023].

Yusuf, H.O. (2018) Colonialism and the dilemmas of Transitional Justice in Nigeria, *International Journal of Transitional Justice,* 12(2): 257–276.

Zegveld, L. (2002) *The Accountability of Armed Organised Groups in International Law*, Cambridge: Cambridge University Press.

Zemblyas, M. (2020) Reconceptualizing complicity in the social justice classroom: Affect, politics and anti-complicity pedagogy, *Pedagogy, Culture and Society*, 28(2): 317–331.

Conclusion

Yvette Hutchinson, Artemio Arturo Cortez Ochoa,
Julia Paulson and Leon Tikly

Decolonizing Education for Sustainable Futures has explored connections between the two necessary processes within its title. Its key argument is that for future-making projects to be sustainable and to address the enormous planetary challenges facing human beings and natural ecosystems, certain approaches need to be in place. Future-making projects must be oriented towards justice. Therefore, they must seek to undo and transform the systemic and structural injustices of the past whose afterlives shape the present and will endure into the future if not confronted and repaired. In other words, they must contribute towards what Swilling (2020) describes as 'just transitions' (Chapter 1). The book reflects upon the UNESCO Futures of Education report, with its call for a new social contract for education. It builds from three online seminars hosted by the Bristol Conversations in Education series in 2020, at which many of the chapters presented here were first shared. The questions that guided the seminar series and the report published afterwards (Cortez Ochoa et al, 2021) have also animated this volume.

To conclude the volume, we reflect back on these questions, offering some tentative responses that emerge from its chapters. We hope that these might encourage conversation and build on practice about the necessary relationships between sustainable futures, decolonization and repair.

What is the relationship between sustainable futures and demands to decolonize education?

How are agendas for decolonizing education and sustainable futures connected?

The connection between sustainable futures and demands to decolonize education is at the heart of this book's challenge. It argues that sustainable futures cannot be imagined or achieved without addressing the demands for decolonization. This core argument is developed in different ways across the book, including in Chapter 1, where Leon Tikly examines five narratives of sustainable futures and, crucially, considers the extent to which those narratives respond to the challenges of rights, social justice, environmental and decolonial priorities. Referring to the scholarship of de Sousa Santos (2017), Tikly outlines the need for a 'pluriversality' based on a recognition of multiple ways of 'knowing' the world that can contribute to social and environmental justice. The processes of validating knowledge systems and the ways in which those knowledge domains are used politically is further explored in Catherine A. Odora Hoppers' chapter on knowledge production. Odora Hoppers imagines a future in which conversations between different, respected and validated knowledge systems are part of an ethically grounded transdisciplinary educational approach.

Common World Collective's argument accepts that learning about the world must come from different perspectives and traditions and goes further to demand a complete paradigm shift: from learning about the world in order to act upon it, to learning to become *with* the world around us. To some extent, Common World Collective's 'seven visionary declarations' see the planet and the ecosystem as neglected voices that need to speak and be heard, and they offer an alternative vision for a transformed education that would enable dialogue with and learning alongside these voices of planet and ecosystem.

Tania Saeed's chapter on student movements demonstrates how student activism interrogates interrelated injustices and creates powerful counter-narratives for critical pedagogy and feminist praxis. Arathi Sriprakash and colleagues warn against the dangers of a future that has not interrogated past and present injustices. Linking this acknowledgement of the past with prospects for reparative futures, they see education as the place where recognition of different perspectives, justice and solidarity can be brought together. These and other chapters lay out the crucial connections between sustainable futures and demands for decolonization, showing their interdependence for imagining and building more just futures.

What are the tensions?

Framing the conceptual discussion in Chapter 1, Leon Tikly points to how education was and is a vehicle for colonial expansion and domination and that subsequent Western development discourses have led to the undermining of Indigenously determined growth paths. One of the most significant tensions is education's role in the projects of colonialism and modernization. As Tikly describes, human capital theory continues to promote neoliberal visions of education that exclude many learners from the prospects of meaningful and flourishing futures. At the core of the book, and within each chapter in Part II, the authors share and reflect on ongoing efforts to decolonize in practice. Within these efforts is the tension, the contradiction even, of working for transformation within an institution such as the school, the university and international agencies that have hindered this transformation thanks to their roles in producing and reproducing oppression; a tension described by Arathi Sriprakash et al (2022) in their recent book *Learning Whiteness* as 'the capacity of education to be hopeful *and* violent' (p 88).

As Tikly reminds us, the vision underpinning modernization theory in education – Rostow's stages of growth model – is thoroughly unsustainable, with its linear expectations of indefinite economic growth, epitomized in its end point of 'high mass consumption'. Catherine A. Odora Hoppers, Tarcila Rivera Zea and the Common Worlds Collective are all clear about the harms to the planet and people within such uninspiring visions for the purposes of education. They propose renewed educational processes that seek to break from the long-standing entanglements and complicity of education with projects of domination, exclusion and environmental exploitation.

There are many tensions within and between the different decolonization and sustainability narratives. As noted in many of the contributions, there is an increasing reference to Indigenous knowledges and systems in debates about decolonization and sustainability. However, there is a danger that Indigenous knowledge systems are co-opted, creating a static monolith; a romanticized view of Indigenous ways of knowing and being that is almost always in the past, that isn't understood as multiple and specific to Indigenous peoples and their territories and isn't seen as evolving, relational or open to change and challenge. There is a risk of fetishizing Indigenous knowledge while only superficially engaging with the work of Indigenous scholars, elders and teachers, which the chapters by Catherine A. Odora Hoppers and the Common World Collective caution against.

Another tension that the authors have examined is the issue of different voices and the extent to which they are muted, heard or amplified. From a learner perspective, in the chapter on Indigenous education and activism, Tarcila Rivera Zea writes about the experience of entering the classroom to find that one's existence and values are negated. The impact on the dignity and humanity of the learner is devastating. Such a learner has been subjected to education's attempts to 'civilize', and education becomes a conduit of oppression. Rivera Zea offers an alternative vision of a healing and reparative education that would enable the building of genuinely respectful relationships across differences.

From an institutional perspective, Yvette Hutchinson's chapter on the British Council's decolonization activities outlines how some employees from 'liminal' positions use grassroots activism to negotiate a space for their voices to be heard within their organization's hierarchy. Adopting what Givens (2021) refers to as 'fugitive pedagogy', British Council staff adopt creative solutions to make their voices heard. Hutchinson's chapter also explores the tensions between the grassroots efforts of these staff and the British

Council's centralized efforts to develop its anti-racism work in response to the Black Lives Matter movement. This tension between institutional and grassroots efforts to decolonize are also present in Alvin Birdi's chapter, which explores the university as an institution where tensions arise when decolonizing initiatives are uncoordinated. While this allows for agency and activity within disciplines, it can also create inconsistency and generate institutionally unrecognized work for those taking it forward. Birdi highlights how, if these initiatives become part of the university's structures, they can become prey to a culture of managerial performativity that goes against the spirit of decolonizing learning.

The book does not resolve these tensions, but does offer insights into how authors writing from different institutional positions, geographical locations and professional roles are bumping up against and navigating them. Importantly, Part II, on practice, shows how the risks associated with the 'decolonial bandwagon' that Leon Moosavi (2020) describes and that were flagged in the introduction to this volume, do appear in institutions implicated in coloniality. These chapters also explore how particular individuals and groups have acknowledged and strategized about how to avoid or try to overcome these risks.

What are the roles and responsibilities of educational organizations, individuals and society stakeholders in decolonizing education?

How should decolonization be conceived and enacted in different settings?

Given the range of contributions to this volume, there is a variety of perspectives from which to consider the roles and responsibilities of educational organizations, individuals and civil society stakeholders in decolonizing education.

One of the paradoxes in education is that the demand for leadership in decolonization is being made of institutions that are often reluctant to change and that have been established on the very colonial structures that need to be dismantled. Alvin Birdi comments on the university's culpability in establishing epistemic divides, while Arathi Sriprakash and colleagues refer to 'epistemic communities' of the privileged whose conceptual frameworks dominate our education systems. Yet the authors also acknowledge that, while education has helped to cause many of the problems, it has the power – and indeed the responsibility – to repair some of those injustices. Tania Saeed's chapter identifies the role of the educational institution in 'developing civic, human, ecological and environmental values among the younger generation, equipping them with the tools necessary for meaningful activism.'

Collectively, the chapters spotlight many different actors involved in decolonizing education. Across the book, examples are provided of the decolonizing efforts of students (from primary through to higher education), teachers (again, from primary through to higher education), school and university leaders, civil society organizations and their staff across all roles and responsibilities, activists, artists and social movements. Catherine A. Odora Hoppers' call for 'ethical warriors' also points to the decolonial demand for action that addresses everyone, as does Common World Collective's attentiveness to the calls from the planet and ecosystem. While responsibility is a collective obligation, Julia Paulson's attention to responsibility in her discussion of reparative pedagogies offers insights into how this responsibility might take different forms based on the 'ghosts in the bones' (Shotwell, 2016) that individuals carry thanks to their entanglements with past and present injustices. Paulson's discussions of different literatures and traditions on reparation show the established responsibility of states to acknowledge and seek to repair gross human rights violations for which they are responsible. However, given that states are so entangled in ongoing processes of environmental, (settler) colonial and racial injustices, justice-seeking and - making processes and projects necessarily also take place elsewhere and on their own terms (see, for example, Hartman, 1997).

Throughout the book, the authors argue that institutions need to accept responsibility for doing the work of decolonization. Education institutions must ensure that the work of challenging 'epistemicide' (de Sousa Santos, 2017), ecological damage and the injustices that arise from colonialism are not left to those whose very life-chances have been constrained by imperialist and colonial practice, or to future generations whose prospects for living well are compromised by our unsustainable presents.

What does decolonizing education for sustainable futures involve?

In order to understand what decolonizing education involves, Alvin Birdi begins his chapter by commenting on the fluidity of the term and the wide range of practice that falls under its changing definition. Referring to Bhambra et al's (2018) two elements of decolonization as the situating of knowledge within the context of colonialism and the offering of alternative ways of thinking of the world, Birdi argues for decolonizing education at the University of Bristol in three main ways: first, decolonization of the curriculum in partnership with students, subject and disciplinary systems and a plural approach to knowledges in learning; second, decolonization through partnership with local agencies; and finally, decolonization through institutional change. He further posits that the continuum to decolonize education looks to address the past through redressing the future. Tania Saeed writes about how students have begun the process to decolonize education through campaigns such as School Strikes for Climate and Fridays for Future, taking action to fight for a future that adults have failed to secure. On a practical level for teachers, Terra Glowach et al comment on teacher agency to decolonize education and illustrate how teachers in England can act intentionally within the constraints of the current National Curriculum. Applying this agency, Tanisha Hicks-Beresford presents her teacher self-reflection questions as a heuristic for teachers to decolonize their approaches to pedagogy and the curriculum.

Catherine A. Odora Hoppers argues that decolonizing education requires system reform, with governance of knowledge systems that are ethical and democratic. Arathi Sriprakash et al argue that it is through learning with the past and reimagining how we understand historical knowledge that decolonization of education can be progressed. Clearly, the responses to this question vary across the volume and according to the histories and needs of the contexts under exploration in each chapter. A core argument of the book, however, and one that is expanded upon here, is that decolonization of education for sustainable futures necessarily involves repair.

What are the possibilities for reparative justice in and through education, given education's enduring complicity with coloniality and environmental injustice?

Part III of the book develops the argument that reparative justice can connect sustainable futures and decolonization and is a requirement for both. This is illustrated in different ways across Part III and in the book more widely. The book explores various forms of repair, including by advancing the idea of reparative futures, and exploring reparative justice in education, reparative pedagogies and reparative citation. Several chapters make the case, implicitly or explicitly, for reparative justice in education. Leon Tikly tackles the dichotomy of an education system that has been complicit in supporting unsustainable practices while, on the other hand, having the potential to play a major role in providing solutions. However, he also recognizes that the contested space within which educational discourse is located means that the road for education from oppressor to liberator is insecure and largely untravelled. Arathi Sriprakash and colleagues open an invitation to call for 'reparative futures'. They recall how much of the global discourse around education 'continues to be captured by instrumental, technocratic and economically driven notions of education that remain actively silent about enduring histories of racism and colonialism' and begin to imagine how education might dismantle this active silence and enable dialogues that begin from a position of anti-racist humanism. Importantly, their work holds both the past and future as contingent; being shaped and struggled over in the present. In opening the idea of 'reparative futures', Sriprakash et al point to the possibilities for dialogue and collective responsibility inspired by a shared radical humanism that insists on reckoning with past injustices such that their future inevitableness is dismantled.

Tarcila Rivera Zea calls for a dignifying and healing education to repair the damages that education has bestowed on her Indigenous Quechua community. She also invokes redistributional reparative justice, arguing that the state has a responsibility to redress enduring educational inequalities and to open space to reimagine educational possibilities such that Indigenous knowledges and practices can shape and guide learning. Rivera Zea's work with CHIRAPAQ to develop dignifying and healing education together with her community demonstrates the truth of Gamilaroi scholar Michelle Bishop (2022), writing from Australia, that: 'Everyday Indigenous Peoples are practicing and theorizing Indigenous education sovereignty in ways which may not be observed, written about, peer-reviewed, published/publishable or able to be cited. But it is happening.' In publishing and translating Rivera Zea's words as she spoke them in our seminar series – opening with her Quechua greeting and delivering the rest of her talk in Spanish – this book makes a modest attempt at the repair work that Esther Priyadharshini imagines in her discussion of decolonized citational and quotation practices. Esther Priyadharshini's chapter offers guidance on how intentionally scrupulous creation of new texts can lead to repair of academic practice. This approach also invites an innovative rethinking of how we refer to texts and species and how we can reimagine the ways in which knowledges are authored, cited and referenced, generating a more caring, horizontal and transparent process of knowledge production that is aware of and actively seeks to challenge and repair epistemic injustices.

The book provides insights into what Julia Paulson's chapter calls 'reparative pedagogy', an area of reparative practice that has been relatively underexplored in the wider literature on reparation but, as this book shows, is vibrantly alive in formal and non-formal educational practices. According to Paulson's flower metaphor, reparative pedagogies have distinct but complementary 'petals' that enable responsibility, dignity, truth-telling, multiplicity and creativity. Reparative pedagogies acknowledge education's enduring complicities with coloniality, environmental injustice and other forms of oppression as a starting point and then develop possibilities for dialogue, action and glimpsing more just futures. The work of describing reparative pedagogies aligns with and highlights the importance of truth-telling and recovering silenced pasts as crucial to the reparative process, but it also points to the importance of practices that do not centre violence and oppression, that recover histories from before and enduring beyond colonialism, enslavement and white supremacy, as Tanisha Hicks-Beresford does in her own practice of centering Black joy in her teaching, described in Chapter 7.

An attention to reparative possibilities does not escape education's enduring complicities with colonialism and environmental injustice. Reparative approaches are 'possibility positioned' at the intersection, and trying to tip the balance of, violence and hope in education (Sriprakash et al, 2022). Indeed, repair and reparation insist on acknowledging and understanding these complicities. Some reparative responses seek to act consciously from within these compromised positions, working with the idea of 'constructive complicity' (Joseph-Salisbury and Connelly, 2021) and the challenges this entails. Others seek to work outside of institutionalized systems of injustice as much as possible, recrafting and reimagining histories and presents infused with dignity and joy. Both might make marks – footprints and handprints – that deserve further study and attention in educational research.

Handprints

In answering these questions, this book raises new ones about sustainable futures and the role of students, educators, policy makers, activists, artists, institutions, researchers and communities. Given Robin Shields' reminder of the handprint of our endeavours, we can ask the question: What might be the handprint of this book in relation to policy, practice and research?

One theme that emerged very strongly from the work of the children of May Park Primary School was, in its own way, almost a challenge to the title of this project. These chapters bring together the themes of decolonization and sustainability at the nexus of educational futures. As policy makers, practitioners and researchers, we demarcate those differences, perhaps in order to see how their unique features and properties can be brought together. The children made no such distinction. They see a decolonized curriculum where their thoughts, ambitions and cultural and ethnic traditions and realities are located as inextricably tied to the future of the planet, to climate and eco-pedagogy. As Audre Lorde said in her speech at Harvard University in 1982: 'There is no such thing as a single-issue struggle because we do not live single-issue lives' (Lorde, 2012). Thus, for real sustainable futures, policy makers may need to bring together their portfolios so that education and economics, equality and environment form the basis of futures planning. Practitioners must bring their 'whole selves' to the areas of learning, whether in the classroom, the community or with young and adult learners. Reconsidering whom we deem practitioners will enable us to look to Odora Hoppers' 'ethical warriors' in the community, in Indigenous spaces and on local, national and global platforms.

As researchers, we need to ask ourselves why we are asking certain questions and how we acknowledge our learning sources and recognize the areas where unlearning is critical. We need to challenge our assumptions about where the answers might be found, attune ourselves to listening as much (or more than?) answering, and ensure that the benefits of our work are experienced within the communities with whom we work and from whose mandate we should organize our analyses.

References

Bhambra, G.K., Gebrial, D. and Nişancıoğlu, K. (eds) (2018) *Decolonising the University*, London: Pluto Press.

Bishop, M. (2022) Indigenous education sovereignty: Another way of 'doing' education, *Critical Studies in Education*, 63(1): 131–146.

Cortez Ochoa, A.A., Tikly, L., Hutchinson, Y. et al (2021) Synthesis report on the Decolonising Education for Sustainable Futures, Bristol Conversations in Education and UNESCO Chair Seminar Series, University of Bristol, DOI: https://doi.org/10.5281/zenodo.50124.

de Sousa Santos, B. (2017) *Decolonising the University: The challenge of deep cognitive justice*, Newcastle Upon Tyne: Cambridge Scholars Publishing.

Givens, J. (2021) *Fugitive Pedagogy*, Cambridge, MA: Harvard University Press.

Hartman, S.A. (1997) *Scenes of Subjection: Terror, slavery and self-making in nineteenth-century America*, New York and Oxford: Oxford University Press.

Joseph-Salisbury, R. and Connelly, L. (2021) *Anti-Racist Scholar-Activism*, Manchester: Manchester University Press.

Lorde, A. (2012) *Sister Outsider: Essays and speeches*, Berkeley, CA: Clarkson Potter/Ten Speed.

Moosavi, L. (2020) The decolonial bandwagon and the dangers of intellectual decolonisation, *International Review of Sociology*, 30(2): 332–354.

Shotwell, A. (2016) *Against Purity: Living ethically in compromised times*, Minneapolis: University of Minnesota Press.

Sriprakash, A., Rudolph, S. and Gerrard, J. (2022) *Learning Whiteness: Education and the settler colonial state*, London: Pluto Press.

Swilling M (2020) *The Age of Sustainability*, Abingdon: Routledge.

Afterword

Robin Shields

Introduction

This volume has undertaken an original and highly ambitious examination of the link between sustainable futures and decolonization of education: drawing upon original studies in many contexts to show how dismantling the practices and structures of oppression is essential to a sustainable future. Furthermore, chapters in Part II of the book specifically investigate issues of praxis: ways in which students, teachers and communities can collectively apply concepts and theories of social justice to transform educational institutions. Finally, Part III touches upon the theme of reparation, of how past injustices must be addressed in order to create a sustainable future.

A fitting extension of this inquiry, then, is to consider this work itself as a form of praxis and identify how it might promote a sustainable future, but also reproduce unsustainable practices of the past. This consideration is particularly relevant in relation to climate change, the warming of the Earth's atmosphere as a result of greenhouse gasses (mainly carbon dioxide from fossil fuels), and the destruction of ecosystems that have regulated the Earth's atmosphere in the past. Climate change is a clear threat to the sustainable futures of our planet. It is often described as an existential risk to human societies as we know them, leading many to suggest 'climate emergency' as a more appropriate term. It is also part of a larger systemic ecological crisis, comprising the loss of biodiversity that scientists are suggesting constitutes Earth's sixth mass-extinction event (Barnosky et al, 2011).

Climate change is also an issue of social justice: it creates inequalities in the rights of present and future individuals to live healthy and prosperous lives. These inequalities disproportionately affect marginalized groups within and across countries: racialized minorities, Indigenous communities and formerly colonized societies (Perry, 2020). Finally, climate change is also a problem with deep historical roots: it results not just from the unsustainable practices of today but the accumulated emissions of several centuries. These historical emissions were concomitant to the projects of colonization and oppression that characterize industrial society and global capitalism. Therefore, a truly reparative approach to decolonization also requires addressing the climate emergency.

Counting our footprints

A common way to consider the climate impacts of a project, activity or production of a tangible good is by calculating a carbon footprint, which estimates the warming caused by the project, activity or good through the equivalent amount of carbon dioxide emitted in the atmosphere. *Equivalent* is a key term, as in many cases, the activity does not emit carbon dioxide directly, but rather indirectly. These indirect emissions may occur through the use of electricity generated by fossil fuels, other activities that contribute to climate change (such as deforestation), the release of other greenhouse gasses that contribute to climate change (methane, for example), and ozone depletion. The carbon equivalent measure puts these various sources of global warming onto a common scale based on the warming caused by the release of CO_2 into the atmosphere. For these reasons, carbon footprints are helpful metrics used across a wide range of sustainability initiatives. However, accurate estimation of a carbon footprint of an activity requires a significant amount of data, including but not limited to the energy consumption (both fossil-fuels and electrical, including the methods of generating the electrical energy). In addition, it needs to consider changes to land use that may have occurred and the carbon footprint of other items in the supply chain (for example, the carbon footprint of a book depends on the carbon footprint of paper).

Carbon footprints of the publishing industry are well established. Several studies have used data on paper production, manufacturing and shipping from a variety of sources to estimate the amount of CO_2 released for each book produced. These estimates of the carbon footprint of an individual book range from 2.71 kg for a paperback (Wells et al, 2012) to 10.2 kg for a large, hardcover textbook (Ritch, 2009), with an industry-commissioned study suggesting about 4 kg per book (Borealis Center, 2008). A carbon footprint of 5 kg, therefore, seems a reasonable estimate for a single copy of a book such as this.

Considered as part of the 34,041,046,000,000 kg (or 34 gigatonnes) of CO_2 emitted globally in 2018 – the most recent year for which data are available – (World Bank, 2018), 5 kg is a drop in the ocean, but it gains more meaning in relation to other activities. According to conversion factors from the UK's Department for Business, Energy and Industrial Society (DBEIS, 2021), one would have the same impact on the climate by driving a medium-sized passenger car approximately 30.3 km (18.8 miles), based on emissions of 0.165 kg per km. Similarly, when burned, a 1.73 kg lump of coal would also create about 5 kg of CO_2, using the DBEIS conversion factor of 2.88 kg of CO_2 per kg of coal. Based on a density of $2g/cm^3$ (Keshavarz et al, 2018), this lump of coal would have a volume of 867 cm^3, roughly the same as a book with dimensions of 22 by 15 by 2.7 cm. Thus, in some senses, we have traded fossil fuels to create a book on a one-for-one basis.

Nevertheless, it is important to recognize that not all readers of the book will need a physical copy: many will access it online through a library or on an e-book reader. The carbon footprint of downloading an e-book is likely to be very small. While reliable estimates are hard to come by, one industry study suggested 36 g per MB, or 0.36 kg for a 10 MB download (Climate Neutral Group, 2022). If a dedicated device is used (such as a Kindle or an iPad), the manufacture of the device has a substantial carbon footprint – an estimated 168 kg for a Kindle or 75 kg for an iPad (Ritch, 2009, Apple, 2021a). Because of different methods of power generation globally, and different assumptions about book sharing and reuse, estimates of the climate impacts of e-books and paper books vary (Enroth, 2009; Naicker and Cohen, 2016). In all cases, simple steps to encourage reuse, reading library copies and purchasing second-hand books and devices will decrease the impact on the climate.

In a similar vein, the editors of this book diligently recorded video meetings and emails as part of their efforts to fully consider its social impact. With an estimated carbon footprint of 4 g per email (Berners-Lee, 2011), the 116 emails recorded would generate 464 g (0.464 kg) – far less than even one printed volume. It is harder to calculate the carbon emissions from a video call. Still, one study estimates a server has emissions of 6360 kg over a four-year lifetime, including both manufacturing and power usage (Stutz et al, 2012). However, computed on an hourly basis, this works out to just 0.182 kg per hour, and a single server would be likely to handle dozens or even hundreds of calls simultaneously. Computer manufacturers have made significant progress in monitoring the lifetime emissions of the products the team would use to connect to the call. These range from 152 kg for a Microsoft Surface tablet to about 300 kg for an Apple MacBook and 543 kg for a Dell desktop (Manne, 2020, Apple, 2021b, Dell, 2020). However, these figures are calculated for a three-to-four-year period, which is likely to involve over a thousand hours of use. Thus, it is expected that each video call has a carbon footprint of less than 1 kg, totalling a maximum estimate of 11 kg for the 11 calls the authors recorded and 15 kg for all calls and emails undertaken to write the book.

The figures show that the climate impact of video conferencing and online working is negligible in relation to in-person travel. For example, a one-way long-haul flight (for one person) would likely generate over 900 kg of CO_2 emissions (Shields, 2019), many times the total of all online work associated with this project. Amid legitimate concerns about the rising energy consumption of data centres, it is important to keep in mind that online forms of international collaboration have far less climate impact than in-person alternatives. One study estimated that a five-hour meeting conducted by video conference would have approximately 7 per cent of the carbon footprint of an in-person meeting (Ong et al, 2014). Such calculation does not include additional carbon emissions that would occur in the manufacture of testing and personal protective equipment (PPE) during the Covid-19 pandemic.

On closer inspection, however, this method of analysis is both ambiguous and insufficient, as it assumes a neat separation between the work contained in the book and other social and economic conditions and activities that make possible its intellectual and material production. For example, most of the authors who contributed to this book are employed in higher education institutions, which have substantial physical infrastructure, energy usage and construction projects, all of which contribute to climate change to some extent. Should some portion of these impacts be considered as part of the book? Furthermore, the authors' insightful contributions are often made possible by access to opportunities such as international study and attendance at international conferences; thus, in some senses, the book is made possible through their air travel.

Carbon accounting becomes very difficult because it is hard to convincingly draw a boundary around any activity or project given the interconnected and interdependent nature of social life. This accounting problem is replicated on a global scale when we consider the emissions of nation states. In particular, national carbon emissions have raised questions over accounting for the emissions occurring within a country's borders (often called territorial or production-based accounting) versus 'consumption-based accounting', which includes emissions created in products and services that are imported to the country (Peters, 2008). This distinction is particularly important in a globalized economy, in which high-income countries with economies focusing on technology and finance primarily consume goods that are manufactured abroad. Territorial accounting attributes the emissions from these goods to the country of manufacture, while consumption-based accounting looks at where they are purchased.

The carbon accounting perspective implied in the notion of a 'footprint' also suggests the possibility of a remedy: the reversal of emissions through an offset. Offsetting schemes propose to create a kind of 'credit' in the ledger of carbon accounting through various mechanisms: paying for the conversion of fossil fuels to renewable energy, planting trees that capture CO_2 as they grow, or even capturing CO_2 directly from the air using new technology (Lovell and Liverman, 2010). Carbon offsets have drawn much criticism, however, including arguments that they continue unsustainable forms of consumption, that they are insufficiently regulated to be reliable, and that the effects of carbon-reducing projects in communities where they are implemented have significant downsides (Dhanda and Hartman, 2011; Jindal et al, 2012, Lovell et al, 2009). Furthermore, in conjuring and then forestalling an alternative reality with greater harm to the climate (one where the offset did *not* occur), offsetting schemes also neglect an even better alternative in which the harmful activity did not happen, but the offset did.

Conclusion: from footprints to handprints

Accounting is ultimately a reductionist strategy, and nihilistic if its logics are followed to their full extremes. Clearly, the lowest carbon 'footprint' would be to have no book at all, nor any researchers, university, or anything at all. The accounting perspective seems to suggest reducing or removing most human activities, leaving one to wonder about the point of such a low-carbon yet torpid world.

This reductionist perspective is ultimately rooted in the binary distinction between 'humans' and 'nature' – largely a by-product of the European Enlightenment that positions the non-human world primarily as 'natural resources' for human benefit (Common Worlds Research Collective, 2020; Nuwategeka et al, 2021). A better approach understands humans and their well-being as an integral of natural ecosystems. For the vast majority of their history, humans have lived, learned and laughed as an integral part of the biological processes that regulate the Earth's climate. A goal of climate justice should not, therefore, be concerned only with the reduction of emissions that cause climate change but also with restoring (or *repairing*) human societies' place within sustainable natural ecosystems.

An alternative method of considering climate impact takes account not only of the footprint but also the 'handprint' (Nikula and van Gaalen, 2021), the ways in which an activity might prevent future harm to the climate and promote socially just and sustainable futures more generally. As Nikula notes, there is a tendency to focus only on a footprint and ignore the positive changes that an activity can bring about.

The carbon handprint of this book cannot be calculated because it has not happened yet. The carbon handprint of the book does not depend on what the authors did while writing the book, nor how it was produced and 'consumed'. It is determined by what you, the reader, do after you read it. The changes you can make in your work with learners, your social interactions, your research and your daily life are innumerable, meaningful and beyond any form of accounting we can undertake here. A significant handprint is the best way to repair the costs of the journey, and it is something that is entirely in your control.

Thus, while the book ends here, the vision it sets out does not; in fact, it is only just beginning.

References

Apple (2021a) Product environmental report: iPad (9th generation), available at: apple.com/environment/pdf/products/ipad/iPad_PER_Sept2021.pdf [accessed 20 February 2022].

Apple (2021b) Product environmental report: 14-inch Macbook Pro, available at: apple.com/environment/pdf/products/notebooks/14-inch_MacBook_Pro_PER_Oct2021.pdf [accessed 20 February 2022].

Barnosky, A.D., Matzke, N., Tomiya, S. et al (2011) Has the Earth's sixth mass extinction already arrived?, *Nature*, 471(7336): 51–57.

Berners-Lee, M (2011) *How Bad are Bananas? The carbon footprint of everything* Vancouver: Greystone.

Borealis Center (2008) Environmental Trends and Climate Impacts: Findings from the US Book industry, report commissioned by the Book Industry Study Group and Green Press Initiative.

Climate Neutral Group (2022) Carbon usage of data usage increasing, but what is yours?, available at: climateneutralgroup.com/en/news/carbon-emissions-of-data-centers [accessed 20 February 2022].

Common Worlds Research Collective (2020) Learning to become with the world: Education for future survival, Background paper for the Futures of Education initiative, Paris: UNESCO.

DBEIS (2021) Greenhouse gas reporting: Conversion factors 2021, available at: gov.uk/government/publications/greenhouse-gas-reporting-conversion-factors-2021 [accessed 20 February 2022].

Dell (2020) Dell OptiPlex 7780 All-in-One Desktop, available at: dell.com/en-us/dt/corporate/social-impact/advancing-sustainability/sustainable-products-and-services/product-carbon-footprints.htm [accessed 20 February 2022].

Dhanda, K.K. and Hartman, L.P. (2011) The Ethics of Carbon Neutrality: A critical examination of voluntary carbon offset providers, *Journal of Business Ethics*, 100(1): 119–149.

Enroth, M. (2009) Environmental impact of printed and electronic teaching aids: A screening study focusing on fossil carbon dioxide emissions, *Advances in Printing and Media Technology*, 36: 2009.

Jindal, R., Kerr, J.M. and, Carter, S. (2012) Reducing poverty through carbon forestry? Impacts of the N'hambita community carbon project in Mozambique, *World Development*, 40(10): 2123–2135.

Keshavarz, A., Akhondzadeh, H., Sayyafzadeh, M. and Zagar, M. (2018) Enhanced gas recovery techniques from coalbed methane reservoirs, in A. Bahadoori (ed) *Fundamentals of Enhanced Oil and Gas Recovery from Conventional and Unconventional Reservoirs*, Cambridge, MA: Gulf Professional Publishing (Elsevier), pp 233–268.

Lovell, H. and Liverman, D. (2010) Understanding carbon offset technologies, *New Political Economy*, 15(2): 255–273.

Lovell, H., Bulkeley, H. and Liverman, D. (2009) Carbon offsetting: Sustaining consumption?, *Environment and Planning A*, 41(10): 2357–2379.

Manne, S. (2020) Examining the carbon footprint of devices, available at: devblogs.microsoft.com/sustainable-software/examining-the-carbon-footprint-of-devices [accessed 20 February 2022].

Naicker, V. and Cohen, B. (2016) A life cycle assessment of e-books and printed books in South Africa, *Journal of Energy in Southern Africa,* 27(2): 68–77.

Nikula, P. and van Gaalen, A. (2021) Practice and research of climate action in international education, Critical International Studies Network, available at: youtube.com/watch?v=6nDGk3Cu2nE.

Nuwategeka, E. et al (2021) Exploring environmental justice in educational research, *JustEd*: DOI: 10.5281/zenodo.5517300.

Ong, D., Moors, T. and Sivaraman, V. (2014) Comparison of the Energy, Carbon and Time Costs of Videoconferencing and In-Person Meetings, *Computer Communications*, 50: 86–94.

Perry, K.K. (2020) For politics, people, or the planet? The political economy of fossil fuel reform, energy dependence and climate policy in Haiti, *Energy Research & Social Science*, 63(101397).

Peters, G.P. (2008) From production-based to consumption-based national emission inventories, *Ecological economics*, 65(1): 13–23.

Ritch, E. (2009) The environmental impact of Amazon's Kindle: Executive brief, San Francisco: Cleantech Group, LLC.

Shields, R (2019) The sustainability of international higher education: Student mobility and global climate change, *Journal of Cleaner Production*, 217: 594–602.

Stutz, M., O'Connell, S. and Pflueger, J. (2012) Carbon footprint of a Dell Rack Server, *2012 Electronics Goes Green 2012+*, Institute of Electrical and Electronics Engineers (IEEE), pp 1–5.

Wells, J.R. et al (2012) Carbon footprint assessment of a paperback book: Can planned integration of deinked market pulp be detrimental to climate?, *Journal of Industrial Ecology*, 16(2): 212–222.

World Bank (2018) World development indicators: CO2 emissions (kt), available at: data.worldbank.org/indicator/EN.ATM.CO2E.KT [accessed 20 February 2022].

Index

References to endnotes show both the page number and the note number (231n3).